FRENCH LITERATURE
AND ITS BACKGROUND

4

The Early Nineteenth Century

FRENCH
LITERATURE
AND ITS
BACKGROUND

EDITED BY
JOHN CRUICKSHANK

4

The Early Nineteenth Century

OXFORD UNIVERSITY PRESS

Oxford University Press

LONDON OXFORD GLASGOW NEW YORK
TORONTO MELBOURNE WELLINGTON CAPE TOWN
IBADAN NAIROBI DAR ES SALAAM LUSAKA ADDIS ABABA
KUALA LUMPUR SINGAPORE JAKARTA HONG KONG TOKYO
DELHI BOMBAY CALCUTTA MADRAS KARACHI

ISBN 0 19 285029 6

First published by Oxford University Press, London,
as an Oxford University Press Paperback, 1969
Reprinted 1976

Printed in Great Britain
at the University Press, Oxford
by Vivian Ridler
Printer to the University

Contents

Introduction

THIS is the fourth of six volumes appearing under the collective title: *French Literature and its Background*. It has been written by a group of scholars working together in the University of Sussex. The period covered extends roughly from the beginning of the nineteenth century to the 1850s, and the aim is to discuss some of the leading literary figures and some of the main theoretical ideas associated with the Romantic movement in France. The second half of the nineteenth century is the subject of a separate volume, the fifth in the series.

In the course of exploring certain literary, philosophical, and social manifestations of Romanticism, our aim has been to raise questions and challenge interpretations as well as to convey historical information. Contributors were encouraged to follow up their own particular interests and enthusiasms, with the result that certain writers (for example Nerval and Senancour) receive a proportionately large amount of attention. Chateaubriand did not figure prominently in the various discussions which we had, but Hugo, Stendhal, Balzac, and Baudelaire are also treated in separate chapters. The volume begins with an attempt to look closely and critically at the concept of 'Romanticism' itself, and the consequences of the Romantic attitude for social theory and historical scholarship are separately examined at some length.

As with the other volumes in this series, the arrangement adopted here means that a major writer is not necessarily dealt with fully in a single chapter. In the case of Hugo, for example, his plays are only briefly referred to in the chapter entitled 'Hugo', whereas they are discussed much more fully in 'Violence and Identity in Romantic Drama'. Yet other comments on his reputation will be found in 'Social Romanticism'. This latter chapter also includes remarks on Balzac supplementing some of those made in the chapter bearing his name. Generally speaking, the Index is the quickest guide to cross-references.

Finally, attention should be drawn to the 'Chronology' which enables the reader to relate French Romantic literature to historical events (mainly French), to the literature of England and Germany, to the main European painters and composers of the period, and to major works of ideas, from *Le Génie du christianisme* to Kierkegaard's *Training in Christianity*.

JOHN CRUICKSHANK

University of Sussex
April 1968

1. The Concept of Romanticism

THE word 'Romantic' has proved to be one of the most bothersome in the vocabulary of literary history. To adapt a saying used about Lamartine in another context, 'it is impossible to get along without it, and it is impossible to get along with it'. The difficulty, quite simply, is to know what it means when it is applied, as it commonly is, to a wide variety of writers and works (including many in other arts besides literature) which made their appearance in France and other countries during the first thirty years or so of the nineteenth century. What is it about them that makes them all Romantic? To know exactly when and where to start and to stop applying the word is, of course, merely another aspect of the same difficulty.

Now this problem, which occurs generally wherever an attempt is made to define the character of a literary period, has a particular historical connection with some of the Romantic writers themselves. There are grounds for claiming that Mme de Staël was one of the first to conceive of writing literary history in the modern sense. Her *De la littérature considérée dans ses rapports avec les institutions sociales* (1800) suggests that, apart from the artistic qualities of individual works, a whole literature may be said to have a common spirit or character. Thus, Shakespeare's 'défauts', which she judges by the conventional criteria of neo-classical taste, appear to her after all understandable, and by implication positively interesting, 'dans leur rapport avec l'esprit national de l'Angleterre et le génie de la littérature du Nord'. The conception here is too vague to command much serious attention; but it is doubtful whether literary history, as distinct from biography or criticism, would ever have developed, let alone have established itself as a subject for scholarly study with all kinds of dependent forms of apparently critical but often largely historical understanding, if this idea had not persisted, that the literature of one country (and perhaps of larger regions as well) forms some kind of coherent whole with a meaning over and above that of any individual literary works.

There is, further, a close factual connection between Mme de Staël's notion of a northern spirit and that of a Romantic quality in literature. For this quality was first defined by A. W. Schlegel, whom Mme de Staël met in Berlin during the winter of 1803-4 and invited to her famous country house at Coppet. He then travelled with her to Italy, in the company also of another future writer of literary history, Sismondi, whose *De la littérature du Midi de l'Europe* (1813) was to start from similar broad assumptions about the spiritual character of a whole culture. Something of the Romantic atmosphere of this *voyage à trois* may be felt in the aesthetic romance which it inspired Mme de Staël to write; her *Corinne* (1807) plays on two contrasting moods, that of Rome on the one hand, symbol of imaginative perfection and fulfilment in art, and on the other hand of Scotland, homeland of the hero, of Ossian, of isolation and melancholy. Schlegel had evidently not yet suggested to her the appellation 'Romantic' for the latter mood, but it is not difficult to sense here the background of German aesthetic theory from which this concept was soon to emerge. The great mass of this speculative philosophy cannot be surveyed briefly, but three points may be singled out for their particular bearing on the concept of the Romantic. First, there was the need felt by Germans as cultural latecomers to oppose a new creative principle to the long authoritative rules of French neo-classicism. Second, there was a growing philosophical tendency to regard the mind's conceptions not as imprints or reflections of the world, but rather as creatively involved in making reality (in some ideal sense that was to prove capable of many different interpretations). Third, an interest in history, which sounds like a far more down-to-earth pursuit, readily took on metaphysical overtones in Germany, where the process of becoming, the dimension of time, the vital resources of the will, so often undervalued by philosophers in the past, were variously regarded as the foundation of all being.

Schlegel's distinction between classical and romantic art was reported by Mme de Staël, after another visit to Germany in 1808, in her *De l'Allemagne*, which she completed in 1810. The book was suppressed by Napoleon's police, then published in London in 1813, in Paris in 1814, translated into Italian (1815), and everywhere widely noticed. 'Le nom de romantique a été introduit nouvellement en Allemagne, pour désigner la poésie . . . qui est née de la chevalerie et du christianisme. . . . La littérature *romantique* ou *chevaleresque* est chez nous indigène, et c'est notre religion et nos institutions qui l'ont fait éclore.' It was her old theme under a new title; the northern disposition towards melancholy, fantasy, yearning, and the like, which she had described in *De la littérature*, is illumined with greater philosophical subtlety by Schlegel's new concept. Romantic art may be less perfect than classical art, he explained, but it is more profound. The superiority of its religious spirit, aspiring to infinitude, over the mere realism of antiquity may strike us as rather similar (perhaps suspiciously similar) to the superiority over the rationalist culture of enlightened France to which the renascent spirit of Germany was just then aspiring. Of course, neither Schlegel nor Mme de Staël meant to say that their own generation was Romantic; they were thinking of the literature of the Middle Ages and of Dante, Cervantes, and Shakespeare. But it was something more than mere journalistic convenience which made the word stick, when it came to be applied to contemporary writers who turned away from classical styles and themes for what seemed a more 'indigenous' way of writing. Schlegel's distinction, and the new way of looking at art which it implied, revealed more about the mind of his own generation than it did about the mind of the Middle Ages.

In making this last statement, however, it should be noted that we are leaving the sure ground of independent fact in order to speculate in the Romantic manner; we are assuming that a generation of writers has a 'mind'. We may postpone discussion of the problem of method, which this involves, until the end, and confine ourselves here to observation of some apparently corroborating facts of literary history. For instance, a revulsion from neo-classical poetic diction, an admiration for primitive or ballad poetry, a predilection for melancholy, metaphysical moods can be discovered in many European writers of the time, even though they may never have heard of Schlegel's theory. In France, moreover, a number of factors combined to give the Romantics the appearance of being a school with a programme: the centralization of culture in Paris, the long established habit of forming salons and *cénacles*, the atmosphere of party politics into which the press, and to some extent the theatre, tended to draw writers in the period after 1815. And there seem to be, besides, many other influences which flow in the same direction to produce, say, the spate of Romantic dramas in the 1830s. We may note, for instance, the recurrent enthusiasm for Shakespeare since Le Tourneur's French edition of 1776, in whose prefatory *Discours* the word 'romantique' is used, and about which Voltaire protested: 'J'ai vu la fin du règne de la raison et du bon goût.' Or again, there is the growing interest in Schiller after Constant's translation of *Wallenstein* in 1809; and the popular taste for melodrama after about 1800, which also might be said to be 'romantique', if only in the sense that plots and scenic effects were often imitated from rather poor novels. In the background, too, there are still further circumstances, whose effect cannot be measured, but whose very presence seems to favour Romantic taste: the disruption of the social order with which neo-classicism had been associated, the contact with more colourful cultures resulting from Napoleon's campaigns, the Napoleonic opportunity to prove what inspired individualism might achieve, the experience of history's dramatic power which nothing can withstand, neither the reign of reason nor of power—and surely no mere restoration. To the extent to which elements such as these are seen to be part of the total phenomenon of French Romanticism, it must become apparent that the ideas of Mme de Staël and Schlegel are not so much the inspiration for a new literary movement as rather themselves an expression of a far more general cultural change.

Since Schlegel's concept has come to be accepted as the proper name for this cultural change, we may appropriately ask what it can lead us to know about the period as a whole. Here we should bear in mind that, before acquiring its present use as a historical term, the word romantic had undergone two changes of meaning. One of these, the application of the word to the literature of Schlegel's own time rather than to the writings he meant to describe as Romantic, and which his contemporaries indeed imitated and admired, points towards an important insight: namely that the quality of being Romantic resides more in the mind of the beholder than in the thing beheld. Thus, folk-song and ballad cannot sensibly be considered as Romantic in themselves, but they may acquire this character in the experience of a Romantic mind. The same is true of Shakespeare and the Middle Ages and even of antiquity, which was still able to supply themes and images to Romantic imaginations. Probably no objective definition could be given of what constitutes a Romantic subject, or even a Romantic style, for in both cases their variety is immense, particularly when the whole range of European Romantic writing is considered.

In France, it is true, the long-established code of neo-classical taste seems to lend, by simple opposition, an appearance of unity to all forms of reaction against it. But this unity resides less in the Romantic accomplishment than in the attitude of resistance; the cause of liberty not infrequently derives clarity of meaning from the common experience of its opposite, tyranny.

> Je mis un bonnet rouge au vieux dictionnaire.
> Plus de mot sénateur! Plus de mot roturier!

declaims Hugo; and his rhetorical stance is characteristic of much Romantic determination to declare what the real state of affairs is, especially as regards human feeling and suffering, and not to sub-scribe to the polite pretences of the *ancien régime*. But again, the determination is often more clearly Romantic than the result. Something of a high style and a grand manner still clings in places to the Romantics' protestations of revolutionary frankness and plain feeling. The result can be an air of incongruity, even of affectation or slightly pathetic pretence, as though they had not realized the full implications of the break they were making. Did these poets find themselves in a similar dilemma to actual revolutionaries of the period, imagining to be 'natural' what was still a highly artificial code, and indeed borrowing from the code they sought to overthrow their own assurance of noble purpose and absolute principle?[1]

---

[1] Hugo's revolutionary declarations, for instance, must not be read in isolation, for they are often accompanied by affirmations of absolute principle. When in the *Préface d'Hernani* he speaks for 'la liberté dans l'art, la liberté dans la société', he in fact wishes to champion

Thus the Romantic poets give the impression of wanting to declare both that there should be no high art, and that life itself, the real anguish of their hearts and of all passionate human experience, is the stuff of the highest art. Or again: that there should be no royal sovereignty and that the people are 'sovereign'. (The altered character of the word, which applies now only in a transferred or mythological sense, might be taken as a blackboard example of Romantic rhetoric: an abstraction highly charged with emotive associations.) Or again, they seem to invoke a 'nature' more living and wild and organically real than the religiously civilized universe of the gods (or God), and yet they address it with grandiose appeals or complaints, as though it should hear them. Or, simply, they declaim their spiritual solitude in the accents of one standing before a large audience. No wonder, then, that neither nature, nor the people, and sometimes not even the movements of the heart, entirely convince us of their reality in much French Romantic poetry; what we hear is rather the rhetoric of the poet's self-consciously strong feelings about these things. Perhaps we should observe, finally, that the achievement of a truly distinctive post-classical style seems to have occurred where it was recognized that art and reality are, once the classical convention is broken, opposed. In France perhaps no poet attains this insight before Baudelaire (though Stendhal and Flaubert knew it too); but in Europe generally, it contributes that profound touch of self-understanding to the inspiration of Keats and Hölderlin and Leopardi, without which Romantic poetry never quite shakes off its aura of subjective fantasy.

The second change of meaning which the word Romantic had undergone in order to become a historical name is no less instructive. For the word had originally meant the same as 'romanesque'; it described scenes and situations such as might appropriately appear in romance, a distinct if somewhat lesser genre according to the neo-classical canon, which could be written in verse or, as had

'des lois'. And when in the *Préface de Cromwell* he proclaims: 'Il n'y a ni règles ni modèles', he at once continues: 'ou plutôt il n'y a d'autres règles que les lois générales de la nature, qui planent sur l'art tout entier, et les lois spéciales qui, pour chaque composition, résultent des conditions propres à chaque sujet.'

become more usual, in prose (it was thus that the neo-classical mind generally thought of the novel). The associations tended towards the fantastical and marvellous and were gradually extended from the scene to the situation and mood of the observer.[1] The extension of the word to other genres, however, indeed to a whole literature, clearly suggested that something much more was meant than could be comprehended by any conventional literary category. To speak of a 'romantic tragedy' or a 'romantic elegy' ought, strictly speaking, to be regarded as a contradiction in terms. But the contradiction may be meaningful for all that, if—and this was precisely what was dawning on the mind of the Romantic generation—life itself does not correspond to any single set of artistic terms, any single genre or style. The reason why Dante, Cervantes, and Shakespeare were so much admired was that they came closer to representing 'life' than any classical author. And by 'life' the Romantics meant precisely the thing which cannot be defined, which transcends categories, which embraces opposites, and which could, so it seemed, only be rendered by a mixture of genres. Hugo's criticism of neo-classical theatre is revealing: 'tout ce qui est trop caractéristique, trop intime, trop local, pour se passer dans l'antichambre ou dans le carrefour, *c'est à dire tout le drame*, se passe dans la coulisse'. What Hugo and Vigny wanted, and Stendhal savoured as the most perfect moments of theatrical enjoyment, and Coleridge was prepared to suspend all disbelief to have, and Schiller enviously admired Goethe's capacity to produce, was the thing itself, the illusion of life.

Our analysis of the two new shades of meaning acquired by the old genre word 'romantique' seems to have led to a paradoxical result. The meanings appear to be diametrically opposed, the one implying that Romantic literature is primarily subjective, the other that it is primarily objective. It must be remembered, however, that these terms are themselves relative. Moreover, in the absence of any transcendent idea of truth such as had traditionally regulated the relationship of mind to reality, objective and subjective may be imagined to relate only to one another. This confusing speculation, it may be recalled, was a source of continuing inspiration to German

[1] Instances are cited by F. Baldensperger in *Harvard Notes and Studies* (1937).

philosophers throughout the Romantic period. There may be grounds, therefore, for supposing that both the subjective and the objective tendencies of the Romantic mind are aspects of the same psychological situation. The Romantic imagination is indeed often fascinated by the vast presence of the outer world, with nature and history, with 'toute la vie — depuis l'Océan qui se soulève sous les pâles baisers de Diane jusqu'au scarabée qui s'endort jaloux dans sa fleur chérie', or in the two words which sum all this up for Musset's Valentin, with 'l'éternel amour'. But the mind which is so deeply fascinated by these things knows itself to be different from them; Valentin is the characteristic Musset hero, the self-conscious intellectual, amoral and sceptical, whose deepest passion is aroused precisely by *naïveté* and innocence. The Romantic fascination has the tension of an impossible love, as between irreconcilable opposites, longing forever to be reunited. René's impassioned invocation to the 'orages désirés', which echoes that of Werther (who was quoting Ossian), and which was to be re-echoed in many Romantic souls, implies not only a Romantic view of nature but a Romantic sense of the self. Only to spirits intensely aware of nothing but their own solitary state, who believed their true self to be discovered in such isolated *rêverie* and to be obscured by any social participation, could the body of nature reveal itself with such alluring totality. And the seduction exercised by nature, and by the whole organism of life of which landscape is only the most picturesque embodiment, could not allay but only intensify the mind's sense of otherness. For the thing itself was so beautiful just because it was a spectacle, an aesthetic illusion. To have it, to enter into it, to try and be it or live it was impossible. The penalty for indulging oneself in this illusion was that most frequent reversal in the Romantic mood, from ecstatic longing to *ennui*, disenchantment, and *Weltschmerz*.

Let us adopt, then, both of the new shades of meaning in the word Romantic, despite their apparent contradiction, and accept that the concept consequently denotes not only a Rousseauistic preoccupation with the self, nor any single attitude to nature alone, but rather both these things, a polarity of mind and world, and in particular a certain tension existing between them. This tension, barely more perceptible than a mood, can pervade many different genres of writing, even different styles and subjects and points of view, and gives rise to the sense that they are all Romantic. By adopting this approach we may even be able to suggest why the word, which in so many European languages (though not English) proclaims its kinship with the novel, should have been chosen as appropriate to describe this new quality in literature. The weakness of the conventional explanation, according to which Mme de Staël had pointed to rich new areas of subject-matter in 'romance' or Christian literature, is that the Romantics were generally not much interested in either romance writing or Christian belief. The genre which began most signally to develop in the Romantic period, to become the outstanding literary form of the century, was in fact the novel; initially its subjects were historical, but it was evolving new techniques that were soon to prove their suitability for contemporary themes. And the outlook which was beginning to be most typical of imaginative writers was only fitfully and uneasily religious; in fact, it was becoming ever more self-consciously aesthetic. The activity of the poetic imagination began to be virtually a religion in itself, founded upon an often acute sense of spiritual isolation.[1]

A word that looks back to romance and carries a hint already of the novel is certainly appropriate to mark a boundary between an older and a more modern type of literature. For modern fiction represents the furthest movement of literature away from the

[1] The truth of this may seem to be belied by the gestures of political and moral protest, of which some Romantics, for instance Hugo, were particularly fond. We have already noted the kind of stylistic difficulties in which they found themselves as a result. One further instance of the way Hugo confuses moral with aesthetic truths may be cited from the *Préface de Cromwell*. Drama he asserts to be the essentially Christian and modern genre, because it proclaims the duality of man, his higher spirit wrestling with his lower nature: 'le drame . . . est-ce autre chose, en effet, que ce contraste de tous les jours, que cette *lutte* de tous les instants entre deux principes opposés . . . ?' In the next paragraph, however, he defines the truth which art shows us as 'le réel', and reality as 'la combinaison toute naturelle de deux types, le sublime et le grotesque, qui se croisent dans le drame, comme ils se croisent dans la vie'. These are no longer moral opposites, of course, but aesthetic opposites: or rather, one suspects, there is always the same basic sense of polarity, however it is labelled, and the same Romantic expectation that art will somehow 'resolve' it. 'Car la poésie vraie, la poésie complète, est dans *l'harmonie* des contraires.' What this means in moral terms is extremely difficult to grasp, as is Hugo's other confusing equivalence: 'la liberté dans l'art, la liberté dans la société, voilà le double but auquel doivent tendre *d'un même pas* tous les esprits conséquents et logiques.'

conventions of a spoken art; it is addressed to no particular public, it speaks no particular language, indeed it pretends to be a record of life itself. The embarrassment which this pretentious lack of artistic pretence caused the neo-classical mind can be gauged from the convention, unnecessary as it now seems, but often introduced into eighteenth-century novels, that what is really being presented is a collection of letters or other documents. The embarrassment persists in another guise to confront any critic who asks what the form of the novel is, or on what formal grounds he is to judge it. The novel seems capable of assuming as many forms as Romanticism, and yet—like Romanticism also in this—of somehow remaining recognizably distinct. Is what distinguishes both of them a new kind of psychological relationship between imagination and experience? For the novel offers us a very strange form of art by traditional or classical standards: it treats the make-believe of romance with complete seriousness, as though it were history. And this simulated fabric of reality we then enjoy in utter inwardness, abstracted from the world, undisturbed by any conventional artistry of language or public performance. For a while we may have the illusion that life *is* art, only to see, with the novelist's familiar realistic disgust, that alas it is not. But is not this ambivalent state of mind, in fact, very 'romantique'? 'On est détrompé sans avoir joué; il reste encore des désirs, et l'on n'a plus d'illusions. L'imagination est riche, abondante et merveilleuse; l'existence pauvre, sèche et désenchantée.'

The condition which Chateaubriand is describing in this celebrated chapter (II. 3. ix) of *Le Génie du christianisme* (1802) he attributes to 'la multitude de livres qui traitent de l'homme et de ses sentiments, [et qui] rendent habile sans expérience'. Elsewhere he makes clear that he has in mind, particularly, sentimental romances of irreligious import, which have been so largely responsible for producing 'cette coupable mélancolie' that is like the Christian 'dégoût du monde', but with no monastery, or monastic impulse, to give it sanctuary. It was to show the evils of this condition that he wrote his own romances, *René* and *Atala*, for his apologetic work on Christianity. Again, there is in *Le Génie* an apparent discrepancy between intention and technique, which

Chateaubriand partly acknowledges in his *Défense* of the book, when he speaks of the difficulty of linking its two parts: on the one hand 'le christianisme proprement dit, à savoir ses dogmes, sa doctrine et son culte', and on the other 'la poétique du christianisme', by which he means the cultural history and influence of Christianity. It is this historical and cultural spectacle which he had intended to offer as new evidence in favour of the Church ('Qui est-ce qui lirait maintenant un ouvrage de théologie?'). Critics then and since have wondered whether *René* and *Atala* did not rather 'romanticize' the very condition Chateaubriand meant to condemn, just as they have criticized his apologetics for 'historicizing' and 'aestheticizing' the faith he wished to justify. Doubtless much depends on the beliefs of the critic; but many unbelievers must have reacted like Sainte-Beuve: 'C'est de la beauté et non pas de la vérité qu'on cherchera dans son ouvrage.' For what Chateaubriand had invoked in defence of Christianity, namely, the modern historical imagination, has obvious connections with the art of the novel and was capable during the early nineteenth century at least of producing distinctly aesthetic raptures. When Michelet read Chateaubriand's other historical apologia, *Les Martyrs* (1809), he was inspired to become not a Christian but a historian: his imagination was struck by the truth not of the ostensible religious lessons but of the poetry, in a famous descriptive passage, of a barbarian battle chant. Because of their love of facts, we tend to overlook the Romantic element in these historians' dreams; they too longed for 'the thing itself', or in Thierry's phrase 'la vue des choses elles-mêmes', or, in a still more striking one of Michelet, the 'résurrection de la vie intégrale'. The following passage from Barante is revealing both for what it says about history and for what it says about the novel: 'J'ai tenté de restituer à l'histoire elle-même l'attrait que le roman historique lui a emprunté . . . [et] de faire disparaître entièrement la trace de mon propre travail, de ne montrer en rien l'écrivain de notre temps. Je n'ai donc mêlé d'aucune réflexion, d'aucun jugement les événements que je raconte' (1826).

The instrument which Chateaubriand had chosen to drive out the devil of Romantic doubt and melancholy was, in fact, a largely Romantic invention. Or, if historicism itself was not invented by the Romantic mind, the vast imaginative potential of historicism which Renan declared to be the dominant 'philosophy' of the nineteenth century was certainly realized increasingly throughout the Romantic period. The point of connection between historicism and Romanticism which is most usually instanced is the new interest shown by the historical imagination in the diversity of phenomena: 'à moins d'être varié l'on n'est pas vrai', wrote Thierry, and added: 'les esprits médiocres ont le goût de l'uniformité.' Our inquiry has shown the importance, however, of considering not only the nature of the subject-matter but also the relationship of the mind to this subject-matter. In this case it looks too harmless to be important: 'aucune réflexion, aucun jugement'—let events speak for themselves. But therein lies precisely the attraction for Romantic minds. The progress of rationalism during the neo-classical period had forced the imagination into an ever more subordinate position: its conceptions were unclear, it pandered to the emotions, it could never be quite argued out of its love of adventure, nor out of its superstitious reverence for religion. History offered a way of evasion, an entirely reasonable, entirely factual inquiry into truth, which yet reconquered all the lost territory of colour, passion, intrigue, ages of chivalry, and ages of faith. It is tempting to say, reconquered life itself. But the historian really stood, of course, outside the spectacle in which he was so deeply immersed. Looking back, Michelet commented on this paradoxical situation: 'On s'oublie tout à fait. . . . Poussant toujours plus loin dans ma poursuite ardente, je me perdis de vue, je m'absentai de moi. J'ai passé à côté du monde, et j'ai pris l'histoire pour la vie.' It might be a Romantic poet speaking, or many a novelist of the century. Their connection with the historian, then, lies not so much in common subject-matter, though that too is found, as in psychological situation: a Romantic relationship between self and world, which is both one of intense participation and one of complete exclusion; perhaps the aesthetic relationship, *par excellence*.

What made the historical spectacle so fascinating, it seems, was not merely its variety and colourfulness, but rather the thought that it was alive. The imagined dimension of time linked past and present in a vital continuum. This conception owed much to the feeling for nature as a living organism (rather than as some kind of machine), which is sometimes held to be the distinguishing feature of Romanticism, though its origins lie far back in the eighteenth century. The great advantage of this organic analogy, which often influences the style of Romantic poets and thinkers alike, particularly in their choice of metaphor, lies in its application to the 'culture' of earlier periods. The difficult question of what attitude to take towards the products of less enlightened times could be answered by thinking of them as the 'roots' of the present, or as an earlier phase of growth. What mattered about these products was not their truth, or their beauty according to one immutable canon of art, but rather their historical character: the substance or flavour they contained like sap drawn from the soil of their time. The concept of Romanticism itself we observed to be a discovery made by this way of thinking. After Mme de Staël, the emphasis in literary criticism shifted more and more away from the judgement of excellence towards historical understanding, first with Villemain and then with Sainte-Beuve. The latter's fondness for organic metaphor suggests almost that he wanted to write a *natural* history of literature. 'Tel arbre, tel fruit' is his criterion, and this meant understanding not only a book as a whole, but a man's *œuvre* as a whole, and all aspects of his life and of the life going on around him. His celebrated concept of the literary group, which put the great figures of the neo-classical age itself into a new perspective, was designed, he said, 'à répandre enfin dans cette infinie variété de la biographie littéraire quelque chose de la vie lumineuse et de l'ordre qui préside à la distribution des familles naturelles en botanique et en zoographie'.

In the end it becomes difficult to know how widely we should extend our notion of the Romantic mind, and this difficulty could itself be said to be characteristic of the concept and the way of thinking it implies. An evolutionary theory is, after all, common to various thinkers of the period with otherwise no great claim to be considered Romantic: we find it, for instance, in the theocratic philosopher Ballanche, in the positivist Auguste Comte, and, in more strictly scientific terms, in Lamarck. Moreover, we should not overlook the diametrically opposed views which it was possible to take of history and the historical process. Reactionaries and revolutionaries alike could appeal to history, and it is this diversity of political attitude, together with the similar apparent division between those Romantics who felt nature to be sympathetic and those who felt her to be indifferent (which as often as not shows the same Romantic poet to be divided against himself on the matter), which has made later scholars doubt the meaningfulness of the term. For the Catholic Bonald, the course of history has seen men's minds move away from the first revelation of the spirit through God's gift of language. For the Protestant Constant, the process of revelation continues as mankind evolves. For de Maistre, the historical process appears to destroy everything it produces according to '*la grande loi de la destruction violente* des êtres vivants'. To Hugo's mind the process of mankind through time suggests an image of some imperishable frieze, 'de la chair vivante avec du granit brut'. The Romantic question seems to be this: does man's spiritual alliance with the temporal flow of life, the forces both of history and of natural history, immortalize him or crush him? The Romantic answer vacillates between extremes of optimism and pessimism, inspired now by *hubris*, now by despair. This is the situation which Lamennais described in 1828 as follows:

Il n'existe aujourd'hui . . . qu'une philosophie qui se produit sous deux formes diverses: sceptique, lorsqu'elle suit rigoureusement la méthode rationnelle, panthéiste, lorsque, lasse du doute, elle affirme ce qu'elle n'a logiquement aucun droit d'affirmer. Fondée sur le *moi* individuel, ou elle arrête l'homme en lui-même, ou elle le jette sans guide dans un vague infini, le forçant de conclure au milieu d'une solitude éternelle, qu'il est *tout*, ou qu'il n'est rien.

Can such extremes of thought properly be called 'une philosophie'? We have preferred to speak of Romantic here as describing rather a psychological 'situation', within which many different moods and attitudes are possible. This attempt to distinguish the character of 'a philosophy' from any of its particular contents is itself a Romantic enterprise. Using this method of historical generalization, we are likely to find our own inquiry hovering uncertainly between glimpses of what we hope is Romanticism as a whole and what we fear may be nothing but a mental abstraction. It would be convenient if we could recognize *this polarity* as constituting the essence of the Romantic situation. This would be sensible if it served to make us aware that part of what Romanticism 'is' resides in our own minds. Whether the thing is absolutely there in its own right we cannot know; we can only know it at all in terms of our subjectively entangled method. It is possible to realize the limitations of the method, but not possible entirely to transcend them. A temptation presents itself, however, to regard a critique of the concept and of the polarization of world and mind it involves as offering a transcendent insight into what Romanticism *really* is. But the insight, we repeat, is into the concept primarily, and into the thing only to the extent to which the shape of the concept lends convenient shape to certain aspects of the world, so that they take on the appearance of one definite thing.

Instead, therefore, of sticking 'Romantic' like a label on to every manifestation of the literature (and art? and music?) of the early nineteenth century, when its meaning becomes so vague that the word serves no useful purpose, we may choose to recognize as 'Romantic' certain situations in literature which correspond more closely to the way of thinking, or the intellectual situation, which the use of the concept involves. To use a historical universal to characterize the literature of an entire period produces a paradoxical type of understanding, at once more intimate and more remote. Every further step that is taken towards embracing the vast reality of the period more fully leads at the same time further away from the phenomenon, towards a still vaster generalization. Thus, it is with a sense of recognizing our own dilemma that we may describe certain scenes as particularly Romantic: for instance, moments of solitude and inner recollection by some water's edge, where a mind self-consciously confronts the immensity of its mysterious opposite; or Paris seen from high up on the towers of Notre-Dame, its people (in the ever-recurring image of Hugo's novel) merging into a flood, an organic flow of life, from whose totality has emerged this cathedral, 'œuvre colossale d'une époque'; or the more profoundly self-aware attitude of Stendhal to the mirage of the past and the disillusionment of the present: 'Être aimé, n'est-ce que ça?' 'Un duel, n'est-ce que ça?' Thus his hero exclaims, who longs for the romance of Napoleon's campaigns. But for such minds the romance could never really be experienced, not even at Waterloo. Perhaps nowhere in Romantic literature is the underlying tension between self-consciousness and spontaneity more clearly exhibited than in Stendhal's writing. The polarization of mind and world, of vitality and artificiality, of the real and the imagined was known to him intimately in the act of writing, and his heroes act it out. Is not this same Romantic situation to be sensed when Balzac's Rastignac looks out over Paris and realizes his relationship to the life before him: 'A nous deux maintenant'; and when Musset's Lorenzo, about to revenge himself on life for not being made of the stuff of dreams, exclaims: 'Il faut que le monde sache un peu qui je suis, et qui il est'? Such examples do not illustrate all that was felt in such situations or all that is intended by these books. But they may illustrate the kind of Romantic situation which it is possible to recognize in a literary work, and which is yet not to be identified entirely with any particular genre, or style, or subject-matter, or moral attitude, or philosophical theory—and certainly with no particular degree of artistic excellence. The recognition of these other attributes and qualities remains the task of a different kind of critical appreciation.

NOTE

Romanticism. A celebrated demonstration of the contradictory meanings attributed to the word was made by A. D. Lovejoy in 'On the discrimination of Romanticisms' (*PMLA*, xxix, 1924) and in the same author's *Essays in the History of Ideas* (1948). Rebuttals maintaining the unity of Romanticism include R. Wellek, *Concepts of Criticism* (1963), M. Peckham's 'Toward a theory of Romanticism' (*PMLA*, lxi, 1951), and the same author's essay, 'Toward a theory of Romanticism—reconsiderations', in *Studies in Romanticism* (1961). It is interesting that Peckham, in a larger work devoted partly to the Romantic period (*Beyond the Tragic Vision*, 1961), moves away from an organic theory of nature towards an idealist theory of mind as marking the distinctive character of the Romantic *Zeitgeist*. As we have seen in the above chapter, these are the twin poles of this period. The weakness of Lovejoy's suggestion—that we should think of Romanticism not as one thing but as several—is that it is semantically illogical. If there is no connection between the different things called 'Romantic', then the word should be dropped entirely; if the word is found to be suggestive of meaning when applied to different things (as Lovejoy seems to accept), then it must be possible to say what they have in common.

Other general studies. Literary considerations bulk large in C. M. Bowra, *The Romantic Imagination* (1949); N. Frye (ed.), *Romanticism Reconsidered* (1963); H. G. Schenk, *The Mind of the European Romantics* (1966); A. K. Thorlby, *The Romantic Movement* (1967); and H. Peyre, *Qu'est-ce que le romantisme?* (1971). Romantic music and painting are discussed by A. Einstein, *Music in the Romantic Era* (1947); M. Brion, *Romantic Art* (1950); W. Friedlander, *David to Delacroix* (1952); G. Pelles, *Art, Artists and Society: Origins of a Modern Dilemma* (1963). The intellectual and social background to Romanticism is studied in C. Bouglé, *Le Romantisme social* (1938), W. Jackson Bate, *From Classic to Romantic* (1946), J. J. Saunders, *The Age of Revolution* (1949), J. L. Talmon, *Political Messianism: the Romantic Phase* (1960), and the same author's *Romanticism and Revolt: Europe 1815–1848* (1967). It is also worth consulting the papers contributed to the 1966 Colloquium at the École Normale Supérieure de Saint-Cloud and published under the title: *Romantisme et politique, 1815–1851* (1969).

Romanticism in France. Among a vast number of books mention may be made of P. Moreau, *Le Romantisme* (1932), R. Bray, *Chronologie du romantisme: 1804–30* (1932), F. Brunot and C. Bruneau, *Histoire de la langue française*, vol. xii (1949), P. Van Tieghem, *Le Romantisme français* (1951), G. Michaud and P. Van Tieghem, *Le Romantisme* (1952), D. O. Evans, *Social Romanticism in France, 1830–1848* (1951), A. J. George, *The Development of French Romanticism: the Impact of the Industrial Revolution on Literature* (1956), J.-P. Richard, *Études sur le romantisme* (1970), and B. Juden, *Traditions orphiques et tendances mystiques dans le romantisme français, 1800–1855* (1971).

2. Rhetoric and Self-expression in Romantic Poetry

BEFORE trying to assess the contribution of the Romantics to French poetry, it will be useful to characterize separately the work of four individual poets who were first published between 1819 and 1830: Chénier, Lamartine, Vigny, and Musset. The giant Hugo is the subject of the next chapter.

Although Chénier belongs temperamentally as well as chronologically to the eighteenth century, his poetry was not published until 1819, and the Romantics hailed him as a predecessor whose work showed them how to break loose from the past. Indeed, Chénier's deepest concern, in his philosophical ideas and in his attitude to life, in politics and poetry, is the love of liberty:

> L'enfer de la Bastille, à tous les vents jeté,
> Vole, débris infâme, et cendre inanimée;
> Et de ces grands tombeaux, la belle Liberté,
>   Altière, étincelante, armée,
>
> Sort. Comme un triple foudre éclate au haut des cieux,
>   Trois couleurs dans sa main agile
> Flottent en long drapeau. Son cri victorieux
> Tonne.

('Le Jeu de paume')

In these triumphant *enjambements*, one of them spanning the division between two stanzas, the jubilant freedom of form reflects the theme of the poem, and the link between politics and poetry is made explicitly in the opening stanzas when Chénier hails 1789 as the inauguration of a new period of greatness in the arts. In this supple use of the alexandrine the rhythm can disappear almost

entirely as the sense overflows with controlled casualness from one
line to the next. Such liberties, together with the not infrequent
looseness of syntax, account for the failure of Chénier's contemporaries to recognize his achievement. His brother, for example,
considered his poetry talented but careless. But the post-Napoleonic
generation had broader views, and the young Victor Hugo, review-
ing Chénier's works in 1819, said timidly that 'chacun des défauts
du poète est peut-être le germe d'une perfection pour la poésie'.
Musset, as well as the later, bolder, Hugo, was to follow Chénier
in his free treatment of the alexandrine, and in reintroducing the
familiar tone of voice which Du Bellay's *Regrets* or La Fontaine's
Fables had achieved so happily, but which had almost disappeared
in the neo-classical verse of the eighteenth century.

   In the theory as well as the practice of poetry Chénier puts the
accent on freedom. The poet's imagination, lifted on the wings of
enthusiasm, is liberated for voyages through time, or absorbed in
the harmonious tumult of wind and sea (*Hermès*). Whereas for the
insipid versifier poetry is a matter of laborious compilation, the true
poet is possessed by an inner voice which makes his blood run hot
and his hair stand on end. Poetry pours from him in an involuntary,
incandescent flood. It comes from the heart, and cannot be counter-
feited even by the most accomplished jugglers with words, for it
is born in an instantaneous fusion of feeling and language. Whereas
for Boileau, the high priest of classicism, the poet must marshal his
thoughts into a state of perfect clarity before he begins to look for
the words which will fit them, for Chénier thought and expression
are simultaneous: 'un langage imprévu . . . naît avec sa pensée.'
These views look forward to Baudelaire's *Notes nouvelles sur Edgar
Poe* (1857) and the influential theories of Valéry.

   Chénier would say of poetry as he does of politics: 'il n'est point
de liberté sans loi.' Even the play of echoing repetition of sound and
word is discreetly restrained to produce the 'enchaînement de
syllabes sonores et harmonieuses' which he admired in Malherbe
and so admirably achieved himself:

> Pleurez, doux alcyons, ô vous, oiseaux sacrés,
> Oiseaux chers à Thétis, doux alcyons, pleurez.
>   ('La Jeune Tarentine')

What one might call the internal refrain has the immediate, almost primitive consolatory power of the lament from which it derives. The musical use of language (which we will find again in Lamartine) is an essential part of poetry's power to stimulate an emotional or even physical response in the reader, and its rediscovery by Chénier contributes more than any other single factor to the liberation of poetry from the status of versified prose to which, after Boileau, it had been increasingly relegated. At the same time the inversion of the opening phrase at the end of the second line is neat and elegant. So, too, the triumphant climaxes of Chénier's poems are orchestrated with superb control.

By his own special method of creative imitation, which he called 'imitation inventrice', Chénier managed to combine, at least on the technical level, the freedom of self-expression with the discipline of the conscious poetic apprenticeship constituted by the study of his great predecessors. In the following example one can see how, in expressing the bitter-sweet torment of jealousy and separation, he retained his own inimitable ease of style, while absorbing not only the imagery of *Phèdre*, but also the very rhythm and texture of some of Racine's finest lines:

> Ah! seul et loin d'une ingrate chérie,
> Mon cœur sait se tromper. L'espoir, la rêverie,
> La belle illusion la rendent à mes feux;
> Mais sensible, mais tendre, et comme je la veux:
>
> . . . .
>
> Je la feins quelquefois attachée à mes pas;
> Je l'égare et l'entraîne en des routes secrètes.
> Absente, je la tiens en des grottes muettes.
>
> ('Camille', in *Les Amours*)[1]

This is creative pastiche in which the borrowed and the invented elements, as Chénier himself claims, are so cunningly sewn together that the seam is invisible.

Chénier admired Racine so much that he could not bear to point out the master's weaknesses, but his deepest love and study were given to the poets of antiquity. Hence his ideal, inspired by the

---

[1] See Racine's *Phèdre*, Hippolyte's fifth speech in Act II, scene ii and the heroine's sixth speech in Act II, scene v.

example of David in painting, was to combine ancient and modern:
'Sur des pensers nouveaux faisons des vers antiques' ('L'Invention'). In the quarrel of the Ancients and the Moderns he adopts
the only sensible attitude, one of compromise. The apprenticeship
of tradition is to be used to express all that is new and exciting in
contemporary thought: the discoveries of Newtonian science in the
style of Virgil. He planned to apply this programme in two vast
epic poems, *Hermès* and *L'Amérique*, which were to cover the whole
progress of European civilization. But only fragments got written.
In this attempt to express a contemporary view of civilization,
Chénier failed to find a disciplined way of using the enormous store
of material to which his imaginative enthusiasm gave him free access.

But he was not, as one critic has put it, 'un poète du passé qui
chantait au milieu des ruines, le dos tourné à l'avenir'. It is true that
in his second *Élégie* he depicts himself as an 'inutile poète' seeking
'le doux oubli d'une vie inquiète', but this means only that he wants
to create in art a serene happiness which he has not found in life.
This ideal is fulfilled most perfectly in the *Bucoliques*, perhaps
Chénier's most characteristic achievement, which use the 'tender
fictions' of antiquity as the setting for an ideal pastoral, a recon-
structed Golden Age. But the *Bucoliques* are an idealization of life
rather than an escape into a gratuitous aestheticism. Francis Scarfe
notes that the excellent *Épigramme*, 'La Fille du vieux pasteur',
which looks like an imitation, is in fact based on Chénier's own
delighted observation of country life. Chénier's reconstruction of
the age of heroic simplicity is lovingly felt.

La Mort d'Hercule[1]

> Œta, mont ennobli par cette nuit ardente,
> Quand l'infidèle époux d'une épouse imprudente
> Reçut de son amour un présent trop jaloux,
> Victime du Centaure immolé par ses coups,
> Il brise tes forêts. Ta cime épaisse et sombre
> En un bûcher immense amoncelle sans nombre

---

[1] I have substituted a comma for the full stop which is given in most editions at the end
of line four and which does not make sense. Readers unfamiliar with classical mythology
will need to look the story up in, for example, Robert Graves, *The Greek Myths* (Pelican,
2 vols., 1955).

Les sapins résineux que son bras a ployés.
Il y porte la flamme. Il monte; sous ses pieds
Étend du vieux lion la dépouille héroïque,
Et l'œil au ciel, la main sur sa massue antique,
Attend sa récompense et l'heure d'être un Dieu.
Le vent souffle et mugit. Le bûcher tout en feu
Brille autour du héros; et la flamme rapide
Porte aux palais divins l'âme du grand Alcide.

If the rhyme-scheme were different, we might take this perfectly balanced fourteen-line poem for an exceptionally fine sonnet by the Parnassian poet Hérédia who was a great admirer of Chénier (see Volume 5, Chapter 2). Like Hérédia, Chénier has the art of breathing life into a scene from the heroic past whilst making it glitteringly definitive. After the opening invocation the poem, urged forward by the concentrated strength of the terse sentences which open lines 5, 8, and 12, moves on to the stately ascension of the finish, which at once completes the formal pattern and raises the imagination to a new dimension outside the poem.

It is likely that Chénier, after the failure of his attempt to influence the course of the Revolution in the direction of moderation, planned to devote himself to a life of study. But events intervened to produce the harshly new (though not entirely unprecedented) tones of his last work, the *Iambes*, written after he had been imprisoned on suspicion and was daily expecting the call to the guillotine:

Mourir sans vider mon carquois!
Sans percer, sans fouler, sans pétrir dans leur fange
        Ces bourreaux barbouilleurs de lois!
Ces vers cadavéreux de la France asservie,
        Égorgée! O mon cher trésor,
O ma plume! fiel, bile, horreur, Dieux de ma vie!
        Par vous seuls je respire encor:
Comme la poix brûlante agitée en ses veines
        Ressuscite un flambeau mourant,
Je souffre; mais je vis. Par vous, loin de mes peines,
        D'espérance un vaste torrent
Me transporte. Sans vous, comme un poison livide,
        L'invisible dent du chagrin,

Mes amis opprimés, du menteur homicide
      Les succès, le sceptre d'airain;
Des bons proscrits par lui la mort ou la ruine,
      L'opprobre de subir sa loi,
Tout eût tari ma vie; ou contre ma poitrine
      Dirigé mon poignard. Mais quoi!
Nul ne resterait donc pour attendrir l'histoire
      Sur tant de justes massacrés?
Pour consoler leurs fils, leurs veuves, leur mémoire,
      Pour que des brigands abhorrés
Frémissent aux portraits noirs de leur ressemblance,
      Pour descendre jusqu'aux enfers
Nouer le triple fouet, le fouet de la vengeance
      Déjà levé sur ces pervers?
Pour cracher sur leurs noms, pour chanter leur supplice?
      Allons, étouffe tes clameurs;
Souffre, ô cœur gros de haine, affamé de justice.
      Toi, Vertu, pleure si je meurs.

The alternating lines are perfectly adapted to the ebb and flow of concentrated passion, though from time to time the stuttering voice of anger chops them into its own abrupter rhythms. Chénier shifts with marvellous ease from the almost decorously conventional image of the opening line in the fragment quoted to the private and intensely felt metaphor of the torch in whose veins, as in his own, hatred stirs as scalding and sticky as tar. The choking poison of hate becomes a nourishment which his body welcomes avidly. The force of the lines is enough to make us accept their uncompromising self-righteousness, quite apart from our reaction to the fact that Chénier was virtually under sentence of death when they were written.

It is sad perhaps to see him reaching this high pitch of poetry under the influence of venomous hatred, using the weapons of his enemies. Violence squeezed from him a power to stir our feelings which he never quite achieved in the quest for a pastoral happiness. Yet Chénier is as true to himself in the *Iambes* as he was in the *Bucoliques*. Both stem from the same love of life and liberty. In the *Bucoliques* it flows with ease and grace. In the *Iambes* it erupts with compressed force, poisoned with the hate which always threatens us.

B

'Le Lac', by Alphonse de Lamartine, is too long to quote here, but it can be found in most anthologies, and I wish to comment on it at some length. This beautiful poem is a miracle of insubstantiality. Reality seems to have been volatilized. There is no detail to arrest the attention, no thought to awaken the intellect. The epithets are unoriginal ('beau lac', 'rocs sauvages'), the images are familiar and therefore make no demands on our powers of visualization ('l'homme n'a point de port'). This is the limpid expression of the commonplace. The reader is lulled into a state of almost mindless receptivity.

But these are negative qualities which might be found in any bad poem. How does Lamartine infuse beauty into the commonplace? First, by steering with great accuracy just this side of banality. If Lamartine was only the poet of the mindless cliché, we might have been given 'un rivage charmant' in stanza five. Instead, he has created a particular impression with 'rivage charmé': the woman's voice casts a spell over things. Second, by the rhythm, which, especially in the alternating six- and twelve-syllable lines of the middle section, seems to come and go with the quiet, interior naturalness of breathing. (Comparison with Chénier's *Iambes* shows how similar rhythms can be adapted to quite different tones of voice.) Third, by basing the whole poem on a single image which, though perfectly obvious, is perfectly appropriate, and perfectly realized. The poem is about the struggle between the transience of happiness and the human desire to make it permanent; and Lamartine, having set the scene beside a lake, conveys the passage of time by the traditional image of water, whose elusive gliding movement fills the poem. Subsidiary metaphors such as casting anchor, representing the attempt to arrest time, derive from the great central image.

But the real secret is that the unifying effect of the image of water extends into the language itself. Lamartine's vocabulary in this poem is as limited as Racine's, so that we have an almost monotonous recurrence of the same great, simple words ('jour', 'nuit', 'temps', 'onde', 'flots', 'beau'), as well as the more concentrated repetition, in the space of a few lines, of less fundamental words: 's'asseoir' (stanza 2), 'ainsi' (3), 'laisser' (5-6), 'suspendre' (6), 'n'a point' (9), which is reminiscent of Chénier, though Lamartine's use of the device is less elegant and perhaps less self-conscious. Thus the eternal repetitions of time murmur on in the recurrent vocabulary as much as in the explicit reminders of its irresistible momentum. And the principle of repetition applies also to sounds and syllables. In the lines 'Coulez, coulez pour eux . . . Oubliez les heureux', the twelve syllables are made up of only three basic sounds: *ou, lé, eu*. The result is that the poem has an extraordinary evenness as a system of sounds which seems the exact embodiment of its theme.

Opposed to this is the anxious human need for permanence. The restless turmoil of the water described in stanza three is forced for a moment, in stanza five, into a stillness which holds the promise that the ensuing plea may be listened to: 'le flot fut attentif', the rapid alliteration in 't' and 'f' forming a contrast to the surrounding evenness of sound which is perfectly appropriate to the state of alertness. But—and here again one sees how perfectly the poem's message permeates the manner in which it is expressed—the appeal to time is couched in language whose smooth repetitiveness is itself an image of time:

> O temps, suspends ton vol! et vous, heures propices,
>   Suspendez votre cours!

Over and over again the prayer to time is absorbed in the flux of time.

In stanza fifteen the image of the echo which was introduced in stanza five returns even more strongly, again offering a system of rhythmic alliteration which is a precise verbal image of the idea: 'Dans le bruit de tes bords par tes bords répétés'. But whereas before, the echo had occurred in a context of recurrence and was therefore a potentially tragic feature of irresistible flux, now it occurs in a context of reflection: nature, by absorbing the lovers' experience, is to become its image, thus rendering it permanent and redeeming it from the seemingly inevitable descent into the maelstrom of night. The unobtrusive and elusive echoing of single words and sounds gives way to a more positive series of repetitions of grammatical constructions. Only one example had occurred previously; now examples appear prominently in each of the last four stanzas.

Lamartine is the poet of reassurance. Despair is soothed into a musicalized melancholy which becomes delectable and shades off into a deeply conservative faith in the rightness and the continuity of things. The success of the *Méditations* was due in the first place to their appeal to stock responses. Lamartine's readers were offered a comforting familiar world, a world of commonplaces in which children are unfailingly compared to birds in their little nests. This is the sense in which we can accept his own romantic image of himself as a natural poet, as Aeolian harp vibrating in response to the harmonies of nature: the poet's voice is not that of nature, but of perennial *human* nature, the voice of reassuring cliché. When Flaubert, that connoisseur of cliché, wanted to characterize the influence of Romanticism on a provincial girl thirty years after the publication of the *Méditations*, the example of Lamartine came readily to hand: 'Emma se laissait glisser dans les méandres lamartiniens' (*Madame Bovary*, Part I, chapter vi).

Lamartine's language was correspondingly undemanding: his readers were given the limited, abstract vocabulary, the imagery of lutes and swansongs, the dignified periphrases ('le char vaporeux de la reine des ombres'='la lune') to which they were accustomed from their experience of eighteenth-century poetry. 'Le Lac' has not become hackneyed through subsequent over-familiarity; it is intrinsically hackneyed, and ought to be impervious to the changes of fashion. But if the manner was old, the matter was new, at least in poetry. Readers of Rousseau and Chateaubriand had been offered a prose literature of intimate personal feeling in which the friendly presence of nature was called upon to witness the outpouring of the soul. To be given this in a poetry whose suavely discreet harmonies were equal to Racine's produced an authentic *frisson nouveau* like that which Hugo was to recognize in Baudelaire. The *Méditations* contained the combination of novelty and familiarity which is a condition of any profound response.

Vigny sums up his aims as a poet in his *Journal d'un poète* for 1829: 'Concevoir et méditer une pensée philosophique; trouver dans les actions humaines celle qui en est la plus évidente *preuve*; la réduire en une action simple qui se puisse graver en la mémoire. . . .' For him, thinking was an operation not of the rational faculty but of the imagination, and his ideas are expressed, in both prose and poetry, as dramatic metaphors. Early poems like 'Eloa' and 'Le Déluge' are too diffusely epic in their scope and treatment to concentrate the reader's mind in the manner prescribed by the *Journal*, and the aim is more consciously pursued in *Les Destinées*, the poems of his maturity. But, apart from a reduction of the inversions, periphrases, and epic similes which gave poems like 'Eloa' a rather old-fashioned air, there is no obvious poetic development in the later work, and the ideal of the *poème philosophique* is perhaps most completely realized in 'Moïse', written when Vigny was twenty-five. Here the episode of Moses' death dramatically embodies Vigny's idea of the genius as outcast. The richly coloured *tableau* describing the hero's ascension of the mountain is a visual statement of his relation to the crowd (both dominating and excluded), and his proud prayer for release is conveyed with cumulative force by the poetic device of the refrain:

> O Seigneur! j'ai vécu puissant et solitaire,
> Laissez-moi m'endormir du sommeil de la terre!

Occasionally Vigny achieves the expression of an idea as an integral part of living experience, the fusion of thought and feeling in poetic language, which T. S. Eliot saw as 'the direct current of English poetry' ('The Metaphysical Poets', in *Selected Prose*, Penguin, 1953). He does it superbly in the last stanza of 'La Maison du berger', combining thought and image in a harmonious verbal system to make us see and feel the fragile beauty of human love:

> Nous marcherons ainsi, ne laissant que notre ombre
> Sur cette terre ingrate où les morts ont passé;
> Nous nous parlerons d'eux à l'heure où tout est sombre,
> Où tu te plais à suivre un chemin effacé,
> A rêver, appuyée aux branches incertaines,
> Pleurant, comme Diane au bord de ses fontaines,
> Ton amour taciturne et toujours menacé.

But this peak of poetry is surrounded by flat, featureless expanses of versified prose. It is as though Vigny's imagination was stirred rather by seeing the loose, immediate connection between idea and metaphor than in working out their detailed poetic interrelation. His *Journal* is full of short prose sketches for *poèmes philosophiques* which were never written. Clearly, he found composition difficult. Apart from his successful handling of the seven-line stanza used in 'La Maison du berger' (which he tends to overwork), his command of poetic form and language is uncertain. His reputation for density of expression seems to me to be unwarranted. His lines are often depressingly laborious. Even in the best poems there are disastrous lapses of tension and of taste: Vigny is a master of bathos. But the real trouble is his failure to weld metaphor and idea into a continuous unity of form. In poems like 'La Mort du loup', 'La Femme adultère', and 'La Colère de Samson', the moral message is detachable from the dramatic metaphor in which it is framed rather than embedded. The description of the wolf-hunt is a fine set-piece, full of atmosphere and suspense, but it does not, as La Fontaine's fables do, illuminate the moral nature of the protagonists, so that it has no organic poetic relation to the flatly stated moral exhortation that follows. The voluptuous images which open 'La Femme adultère' and 'La Colère de Samson' are striking enough, but these poems too fail to realize a coherent total statement of their theme: the tragic dichotomy between man's propensity for pleasure and his vulnerability to the defamation and betrayal which may be the consequences of pleasure. One reason for this is that Vigny's philosophy (like anyone else's) is a product of his own temperament and circumstances rather than of an objective process of reasoning, so that the metaphorical framework is twisted in different directions by the pressure of self-expression and the strain of providing a rhetorical structure for the ideas. In 'La Colère de Samson' the dramatic episode is used to convey not only the general insight that man needs woman for the maternal understanding which her sexual nature prevents her from giving him, but also Vigny's seething indignation at having been personally let down by a woman he loved, and consequent exaggeration of his own suffering nobility. It is indignation rather than insight which leads to the hysterical fantasy of the two sexes retiring into the camps of Sodom and Gomorrah to glare at one another for ever after. There is no intrinsic reason, of course, why the metaphor should not be braced and sustained by the conflicting tensions of personal feeling and general moral insight. In fact, the second ought normally to follow from the first. But in Vigny's poem it does not. Samson's speech consists of explicit condemnations by an interested party, and adds no depth or complexity to the visual images of the strong man enslaved by insidious, lascivious woman. Moral insight is incompatible with the poem's heavily one-sided judgement, which arises not from what we have been shown about Samson and Delilah, but from particular feelings which remain half-submerged. We feel that a poem of straightforward sexual vituperation would have been more honest and more satisfying.

On the level of language, too, Vigny fails to bring about the unity of idea and metaphor. In 'Les Oracles' he refers to the revolutionary doctrines of the 1840s in the following line: 'Des dogmes révoltés j'entendais les abois.' This seems incomprehensible. Why should dogmas bark? On reflection, we see that they have been made to do so from contamination with the near-homonym 'dogues': mastiffs do, indeed, bark. Now, it is true that this punning, allusive use of words is germane to poetic language. In a poem like Rimbaud's 'Le Bateau ivre' it becomes a principle of composition: instead of the words being determined by a pre-existing meaning, a strange, fresh meaning arises out of combinations of words which have been drawn together by analogies of sound or syllabic shape:

> Sans songer que les pieds lumineux des Maries
> Pussent forcer le mufle aux Océans poussifs.

The sea becomes a wheezing, recalcitrant animal, untamed by religious faith, as a result of the sound-logic which groups the consonantal patterns 'p-ss-f'. And the meaning of this language-born image fits into Rimbaud's over-all vision of the sea as a boundless area of restless liberty. The trouble with Vigny's line is that his poem is not, as Rimbaud's is, a tightly interdependent system of sound, image, and sense. The latent image 'dogues–abois' is not part of a coherent context of language and thus remains concealed.

The reader's sensibilities have not been alerted to receive the suggestive overtones of words. The line lies uneasily *between* the prose statement of a pre-existing idea and its realization through the language of poetry. It does not sound 'right', as the words in good poetry immediately do.

The unity of Vigny's work lies not in but between individual poems, in the myth which can be extracted from them. It is no doubt the appeal of this myth that has maintained him, of recent years, in his consecrated place in the literary canon as one of the 'four great Romantic poets'. The anguished defiance of man in the face of a gratuitously cruel universe has direct relevance for an age which has recognized Camus as one of its chief moral spokesmen. But a reputation resting on a moral attitude that never really engages with the difficulties and complexities of living is surely undeserved.

Musset habitually referred to himself as a child, and irresponsibility is a key to his work. This can be an asset: when Musset is not taking himself seriously, the reader can. Musset as a clever minor poet reviving the Marot-Voiture tradition of elegant *badinage* is still enjoyable if one is in the right mood. Like a naughtier Chénier, he employs the alexandrine with adroit casualness, dropping the fixed caesura:

> Il en est de l'amour comme des litanies
> De la Vierge. — Jamais on ne les a finies;
> Mais une fois qu'on les commence, on ne peut plus
> S'arrêter.

('Mardoche')

This is Voiture in the manner of Byron, the form making fun of poetic respectability, the content rather self-consciously wicked about religion. Much of Musset's later work places him as a brilliant album poet, as in 'A Sainte-Beuve' (*Poésies nouvelles*), in which he takes a quotation in prose to the effect that poetry is a young man's game and neatly makes it contradict itself by writing it out as verse. Like Gautier, Musset is a virtuoso, treating poetry as an elaborate game, choosing the cheeky rhyme in the short line for the pleasure of exhibiting his own skill, though his occasional lapses into doggerel make him a highly gifted amateur rather than a true professional like Gautier.

Musset's playfulness is already evident in the self-consciously Romantic poems of his early manner. Dashing heroes in whom he only half believes move against a colourful but cardboard décor taken invariably from a guide-book dream of Italy or Spain. There is a set-piece on almost every page: the hero swarms up a silken ladder to embrace the Andalusian or Venetian beauty who waits voluptuously in her boudoir. These poems hover amusingly on the edge of self-parody and, whereas Lamartine would probably have been annoyed if he had read Flaubert's devastating analysis of the faded appeal of the *Méditations*, Musset would more likely have been amused by the parody, which occurs in the same chapter, of the cardboard exoticism of poems such as 'Don Paez'.

But when Musset tries to reach our deeper responses, we tend to balk. 'Souvenir', written in the same rhythm as 'Le Lac' and invoking the same pathetic fallacy, seems deliberately to invite comparison. Despite some beautiful images, Musset's poem only occasionally matches the effortless musicality of Lamartine, and in trying to force a tone of pathos he achieves only a stiff peroration on the theme of love and time. Intimate self-revelation turns too easily into the vulgar dramatization of the poet's experience—a temptation to which Lamartine certainly succumbs in some of the poems of the *Nouvelles Méditations* and the commentaries which he appended to his poems later, but which in poems like 'Le Lac' he so effortlessly avoids. The spell cast by the words of 'Le Lac' is such that even the modern reader conditioned by the idea of nature's neutrality can suspend his scepticism and respond sympathetically to the final words: 'Que tout dise: ils ont aimé.' But to Musset's 'O nature! ô ma mère' we are tempted to retort with the derisive parody of Rimbaud: 'O nature! ô ma tante.'

The pelican in that famous passage from 'La Nuit de mai', which provides an archetypal image of the Romantic artist feeding the public on his own palpitating entrails, is a theatrical exhibitionist, and we notice that he waddles carefully to the top of a hill before beginning his act of self-sacrifice. The image tells us nothing about what it is like to suffer. It is designed, not to define experience, but to incite an easy reaction. This is the rhetoric of self-pity, and in the poems it is not leavened, as it is in the autobiographical novel, *La Confession d'un enfant du siècle*, by lucid self-analysis.

There is of course good rhetoric as well as bad. 'La Nuit de décembre', for example, has an extended sentence spanning seven stanzas, leading us in the hopeless pursuit of hope towards the predictable but splendidly withheld climax: the poet's confrontation with the personified loneliness which is his other self. The poem called 'Stances à la Malibran' is a fine amplification of the Romantic theme that the great artist must experience the feelings he depicts; the famous singer is consumed by the flame of genius which burns within her and to which her life is given in willing sacrifice. But the fact that Musset could express a theme so much a part of the intellectual climate of the Romantic era, in a poem for whose careful construction any neo-classical poet would have been proud to be responsible, marks the degree to which his literary 'Romanticism' was incidental. Rolla fails to convince us because, just as much as Mardoche, he is a *persona* assumed in order to impress, which can be discarded when the poet finds another part to play. For at heart Musset, like Lamartine, is a conservative, a classic instance of the man whose advanced ideas are a product of youthful exuberance rather than conviction, so that they give way to a staid and, in the case of the dissolute Musset, a premature old age.

It might be concluded that the lighter Musset is, the better he is, that irresponsibility makes the flippant, minor work as it mars the serious work. But this does not quite do him justice. The best of Musset, after all, is in that peculiarly appealing blend of flippancy and melancholy which we find in some of his *Comédies et proverbes* and the little songs they contain:

Chanson de Barberine

Beau chevalier qui partez pour la guerre,
        Qu'allez-vous faire
        Si loin d'ici?
Voyez-vous pas que la nuit est profonde,
        Et que le monde
        N'est que souci?

Vous qui croyez qu'une amour délaissée
De la pensée
S'enfuit ainsi,
Hélas! hélas! chercheurs de renommée,
Votre fumée
S'envole aussi.

Beau chevalier qui partez pour la guerre,
Qu'allez-vous faire
Si loin de nous?
J'en vais pleurer, moi qui me laissais dire
Que mon sourire
Était si doux.

The virtuoso rhythm is superbly handled, giving the poem a lilt which lifts it effortlessly from one simple utterance to the next, and the rhyme-scheme, in which the sixth and final line answers the third, gives each stanza a poignant finality. This little poem conveys much more effectively the sadness of love's betrayal, introduced so discreetly in the last three lines which suddenly crystalize the melancholy of the rest, than the lengthy perorations of the *Nuits* or the 'Lettre à Lamartine'. Musset surely deserves to be remembered as the supreme exponent of what Baudelaire called 'l'École mélancolico-farceuse'.

We are now in a better position to assess the contribution of the Romantic poets. Musset's early verse follows the example of Chénier in the freer and more familiar use of the alexandrine, though it is Hugo who consolidates the new freedom, and even his work now looks very traditional by comparison with the *vers libres* introduced in the 1880s, or even with the *vers libérés* of Verlaine. Lamartine and Chénier are after all surprisingly close to Racine, though they extend his use of internal assonance and verbal harmonies, while Vigny's work remained, and Musset's later work increasingly became, formally conventional. The Romantics renewed, but did not disrupt, traditional prosody. Their work should be seen, not as a sudden reversal of classical standards (even if, characteristically, that was how they saw it themselves), but as part of a continuous tradition.

Looking forward, the inspirational theory of art proclaimed in Chénier's 'L'Invention', in Lamartine's 'L'Enthousiasme', and in Musset's 'Stances à la Malibran', with the complementary notion that true poetry is by definition sincere, opens the way to the modern concept of poetry as self-expression. Chénier in his *Élégies*, Lamartine in 'Le Lac' or 'La Vigne et la maison', Musset in *Les Nuits*, write directly about intimate personal feelings. Self-expression is the conscious aim of the Romantic generation. Yet they rarely succeed in making poems which are a true portrait of the self. Self-consciousness gets in the way of self-revelation. Art which is conceived out of the excitement of novelty soon begins to look out of date. Lamartine in a poem like 'Le Crucifix', Musset in 'Les Vœux stériles' or 'La Nuit de mai', are more concerned with the relation between poem and public than with that between poem and experience. The poem becomes an image rather than a reflection of the self. Narcissus looks at himself not in self-security, but in self-regard. Hence the impression of complacent attitudinizing with which so many of these poems leave us. There is no essential difference here between the 'moi' of *Les Nuits* and a 'third-person hero' like Rolla, or even Vigny's Samson. Chénier's sense of the past gives a noble reality to his description of the death of Hercules, but his successors use the heroic ages of the past as a source of glamorous images of the self.

Some of the consequences of Romantic subjectivism are of course fruitful. The pathetic fallacy by which nature becomes a reflection of the poet's feelings points forward to Baudelaire's use of things to objectify the quality of a state of mind:

> . . . ciel bizarre et livide,
> Tourmenté comme ton destin . . .
> ('Horreur sympathique')

This technique, which poets like Verlaine and Mallarmé, simply by leaving out the 'comme', developed into a new way of representing psychological reality, has become one of the mainstays of modern art, whether in literature, painting, or the cinema.

Another consequence of subjectivism is that the inner world of feeling and imagination may come to seem more important than, and even independent of, the real world. The preponderant part played in 'Le Lac' by the suggestive power of the words themselves, rather than their detachable meaning, prepares for modern theories of the autonomy of the work of art. Baudelaire was born only ten years after Musset, and his poems, like Musset's, keep a strong rhetorical structure. But at the same time he sees a poem as a kind of spell, enclosing the reader in the special atmosphere, the autonomous universe of sense and sensation, which the words create. Baudelaire is much closer than his immediate predecessors to Coleridge and the English Romantics. It is Lamartine's music, not the versified philosophy of Vigny, which initiates this development. The process takes a leap forward in the work of Rimbaud, whose prose poems are to be treated as little worlds in their own right. Instead of representing an object, the work of art itself becomes an object, as in Cubism. But Picasso and Braque are a long way from Lamartine. The notion of the work of art as an autonomous object should perhaps rather be traced back to Gautier, whose poems invite us above all to admire the delicacy of their contrivance.

Subjectivism has its negative side, summarized by a sentence from Rousseau's *La Nouvelle Héloïse*: 'le pays des chimères est en ce monde le seul digne d'être habité.' Lamartine, Musset, Vigny, and even perhaps Chénier subscribe, each in his own way, to the idea that value lies in what is not. The idea leads in Baudelaire to frustration as a principle of artistic vision. Rimbaud's creation of a hallucinatory world of the mind to compensate for the dullness of our faculties is sustained by a frenzy which is close to despair and does not survive the transition from adolescence to manhood. Gautier's aestheticism and Mallarmé's view that beauty is defined by absence may appear sterile and life-denying. If, as Rilke observed, men are not very much at their ease in the world, we might think that art, instead of saying that value lies, by definition, outside our experience, should seek it in the enrichment of experience, and, by increasing our sympathetic understanding of things as they are, help us to feel more securely in possession of them.

There are two enterprises with which art is concerned, in

variable measure: our attempts to cope with life, and our desire to escape from it. If we sometimes feel impatient with French Romantic poetry, this is partly because it tends too much in the latter direction.

NOTE

Apart from adequate representation in anthologies—J. Chiari, ed., *The Harrap Anthology of French Poetry* (1958), G.-E. Clancier, *De Chénier à Baudelaire* (1963)—French Romantic poetry is largely out of fashion. General studies include P. Moreau, *Le Romantisme* (1957), P. Van Tieghem, *Le Romantisme français* (1961), and M. Gilman, *The Idea of Poetry in France* (1958). The 'Connaissance des lettres' series provides useful introductions to Chénier (J. Fabre), Lamartine (H. Guillemin), Vigny (P.-G. Castex), and Musset (P. Van Tieghem). There is a major study of Chénier, in English, by F. Scarfe (1965) and an essay, in French, by G. d'Aubarède (1970). On Lamartine, J. C. Ireson, *Lamartime: a Revaluation* (1969) and P. Viallaneix, *Lamartine: le livre du centenaire* (1971) are both worth consulting. The works of all these poets are published in the 'Classiques Garnier' and Pléiade collections, while those of Vigny and Musset have also appeared in the one-volume Intégrale collection.

ANDRÉ CHÉNIER, 1762–94, when his life ended on the guillotine, was known only as occasional political journalist and author of two polemical poems. His works were published in 1819, but not satisfactorily edited until 1908.

ALPHONSE DE LAMARTINE, 1790–1869, made his name with his *Méditations poétiques* (1820), but their effortless suavity is dispersed in the *Nouvelles Méditations* (1823), the *Harmonies poétiques et religieuses* (1830), and the two epics, *Jocelyn* (1836) and *La Chute d'un ange* (1838). After 1830 most of his energy went into politics, and the *Recueillements poétiques* (1839) contains *poèmes engagés*.

ALFRED DE VIGNY, 1797–1863, took his place in the vanguard of the Romantic movement with his *Poèmes antiques et modernes* (1826 and 1837), his translations from Shakespeare, and his historical novel *Cinq-Mars* (1826). In the didactic fiction of his middle period—*Stello* (1832) and *Servitude et grandeur militaires* (1835)—in his prose drama *Chatterton* (1835), and in the poems of his maturity, published posthumously as *Les Destinées*, he developed the myth of the great man whose vision and integrity cut him off from contemporary self-fulfilment.

ALFRED DE MUSSET, 1810–57, was flippantly and sombrely Romantic by turns in his *Premières poésies*, which included *Contes d'Espagne et d'Italie* (1830) and *Un Spectacle dans un fauteuil* (1832). His unhappy love-affair with George Sand led to a deepening of inspiration in his autobiographical novel *La Confession d'un enfant du siècle* (1836), in the tragic drama *Lorenzaccio* (1834), and in *Les Nuits* (1835–7), which figure in *Poésies nouvelles*. The blend of irony and melancholy continues in the *Comédies et proverbes* and some of the *Nouvelles*.

3. Hugo

IT is ironic that to perceive and enjoy the imagery, suggestive power, and general poetic *maîtrise* of which Victor Hugo was capable, to see why he could be considered the father of modern French poetry, we find ourselves obliged to disregard some of the traditional bases for his fame. Hugo's work is like a large city which the sophisticated traveller has deliberately avoided because of impressions gained from vulgar travel advertisements. Then, obliged to enter the city at last, he is surprised to find immensely rich and varied artistic beauty whose existence he had not suspected.

Hugo is paradoxically the best and the least-known writer of the nineteenth century. Some of the predominant trends in French literary history over the past hundred years have unfortunately contributed to the neglect of those aspects of the poet's work that a present-day reader would most enjoy. The misleading conception of literary history as a succession of homogeneous schools and movements, each a reaction to the preceding one, has compressed Hugo's dynamic and wide-ranging imagination into the mould traditionally labelled French Romanticism. Inevitably, some of the best poetry finds little or no place in such an arbitrary classification. Also, critics have tended to place greater emphasis on the author than on his writings. Admittedly, Hugo's flamboyant personality and his democratic and humanitarian militancy may make interesting reading, but they have too often overshadowed formal study of his art. Generations of both teachers and students have been nurtured on the superficial: studies of the spectators' battle at the first production of *Hernani*, shifting pauses in his alexandrine verse, and the writer's love-life with Juliette Drouet.

Above all, a century of anthologies and academic programmes has unwittingly solidified the image of Hugo as a pretentious, egocentric, verbal machine disgorging reams of melodrama, declamation,

and sentimentality. The fact that, at his worst moments, he possesses all these faults, both as man and writer, has meant that
many readers who respond to Baudelaire, Rimbaud, or Proust do
not even consider exploring his work further. Yet they might be
quite surprised, for example, to find the evocative animation of
objects in:

> L'ombre emplit la maison de ses souffles funèbres.
> Il est nuit. Tout se tait. Les formes des Ténèbres
> Vont et viennent autour des endormis gisants.
> Pendant que je deviens une chose, je sens
> Les choses près de moi qui deviennent des êtres,
> Mon mur est une face et voit; mes deux fenêtres,
> Blêmes sur le ciel gris, me regardent dormir . . .
> $\qquad$ (Fragment published in *Océan*)

or the surrealist fantasy of:

> Un sylphe bâtissait une maison sans pierre,
> Il avait pour truelle une feuille de lierre,
> Délayait des parfums mêlés à des couleurs,
> Et maçonnait gaîment son mur avec des fleurs;
> Il en bouchait les trous avec de la lumière.
> $\qquad$ (reliquat of *Chansons des rues et des bois*)

or the palpable rendering of the human condition in:

> Nous rampons, oiseaux pris sous le filet de l'être;
> Libres et prisonniers, l'immuable pénètre
> $\quad$ Toutes nos volontés;
> Captifs sous le réseau des choses nécessaires,
> Nous sentons se lier des fils à nos misères
> $\quad$ Dans les immensités.
> $\qquad$ ('Pleurs dans la nuit', *Les Contemplations*)

The point is that, whether admired for his varied imagination
or ridiculed for his oratorical pose, the poet has very rarely been
viewed with full awareness of the immense range of his art. In
fact, Hugo is one of the most complex and many-sided figures in
French literature: within each of the countless volumes of prose
and verse resulting from sixty years of prodigious literary activity
there coexist verbosity and succinctness, the melodramatic and the

realistic, the superficial and the penetrating, the banal and the suggestive. He is at once the embodiment of some of the weakest and
the best qualities of French nineteenth-century literature.

How did this paradox arise? The answer lies above all in the
interaction between Hugo's ebullient imagination and self-consciously theatrical personality, and the values and beliefs, the
linguistic and literary conventions, of his society and times. However unique an author's interweaving of feeling, thought, and
imagination, the range of literary form conceivable by him is shaped
by direct interaction with his immediate environment. Hugo's
world outlook was formed within the generation of young artists
and writers which by 1830 considered itself obliged to challenge
ideologically and artistically the neo-classical restraints on its
emotionally charged expression of new attitudes towards man,
nature, and society. In the battle which surrounded the staging of
Hernani in 1830, the militant Romantics rallied to the structural
principles on which this melodrama was based—principles that had
been vigorously formulated in the preface written by Hugo in 1827
for his first dramatic attempt, *Cromwell*. Essentially he advocated
that the criteria of literary excellence should depend less on
decorum and elegance of formulation than on the quality of the
writer's imaginative reconstruction of life. These criteria entailed
a rejection of the rigid aristocratic separation of tragic and comic
styles, a shift in emphasis from the neo-classical unities of time,
place, and action to the achievement of sensational effects, greater
flexibility in prosody, and the freer use of everyday language. Such
a literature could allow for the antithetic duality which, for Hugo,
permeates all aspects of life: the ugly and the sublime, the pathetic
and the comic, the ideal and the real, the good and the evil. Notwithstanding the ardent revolt against 'rules' that hamper the
artistic expression of feeling and imagination, Romantic writers
like Hugo retained far more than they realized of the literary forms
inherited from the *ancien régime*—particularly the taste for universal abstractions, grandiloquence, and declamation that often
offend present-day literary sensibilities. Apart from his literary
range, what most distinguishes Hugo from contemporaries such as
Lamartine, Dumas, Vigny, and Sand is the ability to give concrete

form to his extraordinary imaginative and verbal powers; to achieve linguistic effects that anticipate many characteristics of modern poetry.

Hugo possessed an encyclopedic cast of mind. He had a wide, if somewhat superficial, familiarity with history, religion, legend, and literature. He was also given to naïve philosophizing and showed an egocentric concern for his public image. Characteristics such as these go a long way towards explaining his total involvement in the political, social, and aesthetic conflicts of his times; his dedication to ideals of fraternity, enlightenment, and social progress. It was such a commitment that led him, at the age of fifty, to risk his public distinction and material success in calling for the overthrow of the authoritarian government imposed by Napoleon III's *coup d'état*. Similarly, his public expression of humanitarian pity for the defeated and persecuted Paris Communards in 1871 resulted in his violent expulsion from Belgium.

Hugo was convinced of the implacable forward movement of mankind—'ce fil qui s'atténue quelquefois au point de devenir invisible, mais qui ne casse jamais, le grand fil mystérieux du labyrinthe humain, le Progrès' (preface to *La Légende des siècles*). His idea of progress was more akin to the emotional attachment of a Michelet than to the rationalist *philosophes* of the Enlightenment. Its vehicle remained the dissemination of knowledge. But whereas many contemporary poets, such as Wordsworth, believed that scientific analysis distorted apprehension of the natural world, Hugo saw no conflict between knowledge gained through reasoned interpretation of sense data and that gained through the poet's intuition: they revealed complementary aspects of reality. Conceiving of his own role as both that of the 'philosophe du concret' and that of the 'peintre de l'abstrait', he endeavoured to fuse the imaginative expression of the real and the transcendental: 'Je cherche l'idéal, mais en touchant toujours du bout du pied le réel' (*Post-scriptum de ma vie*). Although for Hugo complete knowledge was unattainable, the great poet was a prophet—divinely endowed with both a vision of social progress and with powers of intuiting more of the mystery that lies both within and beyond our sense perception.

Since knowledge was considered the key to human betterment, the writer's responsibility was to communicate artistically his greater awareness of man's place in the universe; indeed, the poet's voice was as necessary to human enlightenment and progress as the voices of philosophers, historians, scientists, and political idealists. He describes the poet's role:

> Comme une torche qu'il secoue,
> Faire flamboyer l'avenir!
> ('Fonction du poète', *Les Rayons et les Ombres*)

As he wrote to Baudelaire in 1859: 'Je n'ai jamais dit l'art pour l'art; j'ai toujours dit l'art pour le progrès.'

To the extent that he considered his writings as arguments and trumpet-calls sounded in the ideological and political frays surrounding him, his impassioned formulations reflect the conventional oratorical style of his times; the language in which Hugo was as much at home as were his readers.

Not unlike William Blake, Hugo fused a visionary temperament with a humanitarian militancy into a single commitment to the moral, political, and metaphysical enlightenment of the people. If we blend these features of temperament and attitude with an extravagant imagination, intense visual perception, and verbal virtuosity—and place them within the framework of the prevailing literary conventions—we have the sources of his distinctive and protean art.

The principles that had been vehemently expressed in the 1827 preface to *Cromwell*—the mixture of the pathetic and comic styles, the necessity for complete linguistic freedom, the emphasis on antithesis in character, situation, and plot—continued, almost without change, to guide Hugo's dramatic and narrative output over the next fifty years. In fact, they appear again with some modification in the critical study, *William Shakespeare* (1864), accompanied by a heightened concern for the literary means of conveying the visionary outlook. Whatever evolution does occur in his work is significant only in the lyric and epic poetry. Even there, the changes are essentially a development of what is embryonically present in *Les Orientales* of 1829 and *Les Feuilles d'automne* of 1831.

For Hugo's theatre to have remained largely in the mould of *Hernani* was disastrous, for this meant that it never broke free of the 1830 taste for melodrama, declamation, and ardent emotional display. *Ruy Blas* (1838), perhaps the most effectively constructed of his plays, could be considered as one of the most typical examples of French Romantic drama—and the most typically Hugolian. In it we witness outstanding epic-size figures whose lives are marked by fate; figures who have a melancholy consciousness of the lofty social isolation that results from their superiority. Strong sensations in the mixture of love, politics, and fantasy, and a succession of incredibly melodramatic antitheses are placed in a pseudo-historical setting and are declaimed with self-conscious solemnity. Hugo's overdrawn characters are usually as unconvincing and superficial as is the action; and the present-day theatre-goer, seeking psychological subtlety or profundity, will generally be irritated and disappointed.

With the failure of *Les Burgraves* in 1843, Hugo largely abandoned the theatre in favour of those genres which afforded more fruitful opportunities to his imagination. As for the Paris audiences, their taste was in any case shifting to the comedy of manners and the *pièce à thèse*, both of which presented life-size characters in alleged everyday settings—namely the facile but well-constructed plays of Scribe and Dumas fils.

The perspectives that Hugo envisaged for the novel as early as 1823 point to the kind of narratives that he was to write during the rest of his life:

Après le roman pittoresque, mais prosaïque, de Walter Scott, il restera un autre roman à créer, plus beau et plus complet selon nous. C'est le roman à la fois drame et épopée, pittoresque mais poétique, réel mais idéal, vrai mais grand, qui enchâssera Walter Scott dans Homère. (*La Muse française*, juillet 1823)

Theatre allowed ample scope for melodrama, strong sensations, and rhetorical bombast, but in the novel Hugo was able to develop his pictorial descriptions, interpretative commentary, and, above all, epic dimensions for the action. No doubt even these works are not novels in the modern sense; the psychological depth, economy of style, chain of causality, and over-all impression of real life that many readers expect of novels would be quite foreign to these exuberant, kaleidoscopic tales that so completely embody both the charm and the weaknesses of French Romanticism. With his volcanic imagination and psychological simplicity, Hugo could hardly have thought in terms of the sophisticated irony of a Stendhal or the meticulous realism of a Flaubert; he required the sweeping panorama of myth and fantasy that we find in *Les Misérables*. This is the art of the bard spinning out his epic to spell-bound listeners for whom Quasimodo and Jean Valjean have assumed the proportions of folk heroes. The narration may be long, the subject-matter remote in time, and the moral issues over-simplified, but these stories continue to capture popular imagination the world over.

Notre-Dame de Paris (1831) reveals essentially the same traits that we find in all of Hugo's novels. Inspired by Scott, he has succeeded in creating the illusion of a historically authentic setting: the reader is plunged into the magical evocation of the cathedral and the teeming medieval life around it. This gothic atmosphere is rendered in a series of vivid tableaux that are suggestive of Villon and Rabelais, of Breughel and Callot. Into this highly evocative setting he has cast epic-size figures existing primarily in terms of the spectacular action and ultimately controlled by the workings of fate. Questions of psychological depth or analysis would be inappropriate; this is the world of fantasy, of the grotesque and the sublime, of the pure and the evil. As with Hugo's drama, we come to such a novel for entertainment and must temporarily suspend our sense of real-life probabilities in order to enjoy the performance.

In spite of the considerable digressive commentary and exposition, the descriptive images and the action possess great dramatic vitality. The intensity, rhythm, and tone of the action are strengthened by skilful shifts in point of view from narrator to characters, syntactical flexibility, highly metaphorical language, and vivid detail. A striking orchestration of sound, sight, and movement is often achieved, as in the scene when Quasimodo leaps excitedly on to the largest bell of Notre-Dame and, as it

rings out, dizzily swings back and forth above the medieval world
below:

Tout à coup la frénésie de la cloche le gagnait; son regard devenait
extraordinaire; il attendait le bourdon au passage, comme l'araignée
attend la mouche, et se jetait brusquement sur lui à corps perdu. Alors,
suspendu sur l'abîme, lancé dans le balancement formidable de la cloche,
il saisissait le monstre d'airain aux oreillettes, l'étreignait de ses deux
genoux, l'éperonnait de ses deux talons, et redoublait de tout le choc et
de tout le poids de son corps la furie de la volée. Cependant la tour
vacillait; lui, criait et grinçait des dents, ses cheveux roux se hérissaient,
sa poitrine faisait le bruit d'un soufflet de forge, son œil jetait des flammes,
la cloche monstrueuse hennissait toute haletante sous lui, et alors ce
n'était plus ni le bourdon de Notre-Dame ni Quasimodo, c'était un rêve,
un tourbillon, une tempête; le vertige à cheval sur le bruit; un esprit
cramponné à une croupe volante; un étrange centaure moitié homme,
moitié cloche; une espèce d'Astolphe horrible emporté sur un prodigieux
hippogriffe de bronze vivant.

One is reminded here of similar phantasmagoric scenes in other
novels—for example, the dynamic interplay of lights, colours, and
shapes in the setting of *Les Travailleurs de la mer* that frames the
solitary struggles of Gilliatt with the world of the sea. Thus, in the
Dover cave:

La surprenante lumière édénique qui venait de dessous l'eau, à la fois
pénombre marine et rayonnement paradisiaque, estompait tous les
linéaments dans une sorte de diffusion visionnaire. Chaque vague était
un prisme. Les contours des choses, sous ces ondoiements irisés, avaient
le chromatisme des lentilles d'optique trop convexes; des spectres
solaires flottaient sous l'eau. On croyait voir se tordre dans cette dia-
phanéité aurorale des tronçons d'arc-en-ciel noyés. Ailleurs, en d'autres
coins, il y avait dans l'eau un certain clair de lune. Toutes les splendeurs
semblaient amalgamées là pour faire on ne sait quoi d'aveugle et de
nocturne. Rien de plus troublant et de plus énigmatique que ce faste
dans cette cave. Ce qui dominait, c'était l'enchantement. La végétation
fantasque et la stratification informe s'accordaient et dégageaient une
harmonie. Ce mariage de choses farouches était heureux. Les ramifica-
tions se cramponnaient en ayant l'air d'effleurer. La caresse du roc
sauvage et de la fleur fauve était profonde. Des piliers massifs avaient
pour chapiteaux et pour ligatures de frêles guirlandes toutes pénétrées
de frémissement, on songeait à des doigts de fées chatouillant des pieds

de béhémoths, et le rocher soutenait la plante et la plante étreignait le rocher avec une grâce monstrueuse.

Or, in *Les Misérables*, the hallucinatory fright of little Cosette, alone in the forest of Montfermeil:

Nul ne marche seul la nuit dans la forêt sans tremblement. Ombres et arbres, deux épaisseurs redoutables. Une réalité chimérique apparaît dans la profondeur indistincte. L'inconcevable s'ébauche à quelque pas de vous avec une netteté spectrale. On voit flotter dans l'espace ou dans son propre cerveau, on ne sait quoi de vague et d'insaisissable comme les rêves des fleurs endormies. Il y a des attitudes farouches sur l'horizon. On aspire les effluves du grand vide noir. On a peur et envie de regarder derrière soi. Les cavités de la nuit, les choses devenues hagardes, des profils taciturnes qui se dissipent quand on avance, des échevellements obscurs, des touffes irritées, des flaques livides, le lugubre reflété dans le funèbre, l'immensité sépulcrale du silence, les êtres inconnus possibles, des penchements de branches mystérieux, d'effroyants torses d'arbres, de longues poignées d'herbes frémissantes; on est sans défense contre tout cela. Pas de hardiesse qui ne tressaille et qui ne sente le voisinage de l'angoisse. On éprouve quelque chose de hideux comme si l'âme s'amalgamait à l'ombre. Cette pénétration des ténèbres est inexprimablement sinistre dans un enfant.

Les forêts sont des apocalypses; et le battement d'ailes d'une petite âme fait un bruit d'agonie sous leur voûte monstrueuse.

While effectively colouring situations that confront the principal characters of these novels, such evocative tableaux also display the kind of imagistic intensity that one finds in Hugo's poetry. This poetry is so vast that one must patiently search out those works in which the poet's imagination broke through the patterns of oratorical grandiloquence that mark his generation, in which he succeeded in combining imagery, diction, rhythm, and sound to express the intensity of his visual and hallucinatory perception. This is the poetry that Baudelaire had in mind when he wrote:

Victor Hugo était . . . l'homme le mieux doué, le plus visiblement élu pour exprimer par la poésie ce que j'appellerai le *mystère de la vie*. . . . La musique des vers de Victor Hugo s'adapte aux profondes harmonies de la nature; sculpteur, il découpe dans ses strophes la forme inoubliable des choses; peintre, il les illumine de leur couleur propre. . . . Non-seulement il exprime nettement, il traduit littéralement la lettre nette et claire; mais il exprime avec *l'obscurité indispensable* ce qui est obscur et confusément révélé. . . . Le vers de Victor Hugo sait traduire pour l'âme humaine non seulement les plaisirs les plus directs qu'elle tire de la nature visible, mais encore les sensations les plus fugitives, les plus compliquées . . .; enfin, en d'autres termes, tout ce qu'il y a d'humain dans n'importe quoi, et aussi tout ce qu'il y a de divin, de sacré ou de diabolique. ('Réflexions sur quelques-uns de mes contemporains', from *L'Art romantique*)

Throughout Hugo's poetic output we find the presence of the pastoral idyll, of satirical vehemence, of the sweeping epic, of tender intimacy, and of visionary alchemy. As we suggested at the outset, his poetry can hardly be described within the limits of a single category or stage in the history of French poetry; it is rather an almost simultaneous expression of the major forces that were present in the nineteenth century. The range stretches from versified rhetoric to the complete subservience of language to imagination. One can accordingly discover in Hugo illustrations of the various stages through which French poetry passes during the fifty years of his poetic activity: from the pictorial to the metaphorical and the symbolic; from direct statement to oblique suggestion; from the magniloquent to the colloquial. By the 1830s most of the elements that will mark Hugo's poetic practice at its lyrical best are already in evidence, just as in the 1870s some of the most unfortunate declamation is still present. Yet one can distinguish significant over-all lines of evolution in his work: a broadening of outlook and subject-matter, a deepening of his powers of observation, an intensification of the hallucinatory, and a growing complexity of linguistic structure.

Although the visionary aspect of Hugo's poetry is already present in *Les Orientales* (1829), it assumed much greater importance after 1843 as a result of a preoccupation with the death of his eldest daughter, a greater contact with occult influences, and many hours spent in solitary contemplation during his exile in the Channel Islands. The collection of metaphysical beliefs that Hugo assembled hardly constitutes a serious philosophic system. Its importance for his poetry lies rather in the imagery and linguistic techniques by which it was given tangible representation.

The universe as seen by this *poète-visionnaire* was a strange blend of the visible and the supernatural. In it, the omnipresence of a kind of cosmic divinity is manifested in all things, animate and inanimate. There is a continual flux of interchanging forms and appearances:

... pour les esprits pensifs, toutes les parties de la nature, même les plus disparates au premier coup d'œil, se rattachent entre elles par une foule d'harmonies secrètes, fils invisibles de la création que le contemplateur aperçoit, qui font du grand tout un inextricable réseau vivant d'une seule sève, un dans la variété, et qui sont, pour ainsi parler, les racines mêmes de l'être. ('Lettre de Pasages', *En voyage*)

Both the soul within and the mystery beyond are aspects of one cosmic whole into which the *visionnaire* may be granted a fleeting glimpse by means of dream, intuition, or a kind of intense transcendental vision—what we might call hallucination:

Chose inouïe, c'est au dedans de soi qu'il faut regarder le dehors. Le profond miroir sombre est au fond de l'homme. Là est le clair-obscur terrible. La chose réfléchie par l'âme est plus vertigineuse que vue directement. . . . Ce reflet compliqué de l'Ombre, c'est pour le réel une augmentation. En nous penchant sur ce puits . . . nous y apercevons à une distance d'abîme, dans un cercle étroit, le monde immense. Le monde ainsi vu est surnaturel en même temps qu'humain, vrai en même temps que divin. Notre conscience semble apostée dans cette obscurité pour donner l'explication. ('Préface de mes œuvres et post-scriptum de ma vie' in Pauvert edition of *Œuvres dramatiques et critiques complètes*, p. 1503.)

As indicated earlier, the poet does not conceive of any opposition between the worlds of sense perception and of the *surnaturel*; one source of knowledge complements the other. But whether in the simple and delicate brush-stroke of the intimate and the pictorial, in the grandeur of the epic, or in the metaphorical interplay of kaleidoscopic visions, Hugo's poetry is always invested with pronounced emotive values. From the visual to the visionary, his unified sensibility can express artistically the delicately pathetic 'Demain dès l'aube' (*Les Contemplations*), the highly erotic 'Cantique de Bethphagé' (*La Fin de Satan*), the contemplative tableau of 'Saison des semailles — le soir' (*Chansons des rues et des bois*), the calm of 'Nuits de juin' (*Les Rayons et les Ombres*), or the magical fantasy of:

> Le carillon, c'est l'heure inattendue et folle,
> Que l'œil croit voir, vêtue en danseuse espagnole,
> Apparaître soudain par le trou vif et clair
> Que ferait en s'ouvrant une porte de l'air.
> Elle vient, secouant sur les toits léthargiques
> Son tablier d'argent plein de notes magiques,
> Réveillant sans pitié les dormeurs ennuyeux,
> Sautant à petits pas comme un oiseau joyeux,
> Vibrant, ainsi qu'un dard qui tremble dans le cible;
> Par un frêle escalier de cristal invisible,
> Effarée et dansante, elle descend des cieux;
> Et l'esprit, ce veilleur fait d'oreilles et d'yeux,
> Tandis qu'elle va, vient, monte et descend encore,
> Entend de marche en marche errer son pied sonore!
>
> (from 'Écrit sur la vitre d'une fenêtre flamande', *Les Rayons et les Ombres*)

Reference should also be made to the hallucinatory visions of 'Les Djinns' (in *Les Orientales*); something of their spirit is also conveyed in the following brief extract from *Les Contemplations*:

> Peut-être en ce moment, du fond des nuits funèbres,
> Montant vers nous, gonflant ses vagues de ténèbres,
>   Et ses flots de rayons,
> Le muet Infini, sombre mer ignorée,
> Roule vers notre ciel une grande marée
>   De constellations!
>
>   (from 'A la fenêtre pendant la nuit')

In writing of this kind Hugo directs vivid detail, dramatic intensity, synaesthetic mixtures, condensed metaphors, and imagistic concentration towards extraordinarily diversified poetic ends.

Not only do the visual and the visionary coexist in Hugo on equal terms, but many poems reflect the poet's conviction that 'une pente insensible va du monde réel à la sphère invisible'. He succeeds in fusing one with the other in a kind of metamorphosis, suggestive of cinematographic fade-in and fade-out, which he describes as follows: 'Dans le détail, dans la forme, une précision sévère, et dans le fond, une grandeur étrange et presque illimitée qu'on ne peut contempler sans y découvrir à chaque instant de nouveaux horizons pleins du rayonnement mystérieux de l'infini' (*Post-scriptum de ma vie*). It is precisely for his ability to render the supernatural experience with all the reality and concreteness of the world of the senses that Hugo stands out as a 'cosmic' poet. To express the hallucinatory in the language of visible things inevitably necessitated revolutionary changes in poetic language. Placing, as he put it, 'un bonnet rouge sur le vieux dictionnaire', he proceeded to utilize a vast number of hitherto 'unpoetic' words culled largely from his phenomenal knowledge of history and myth. Moreover, he took the familiar meanings and associative values of ordinary words and placed them in unprecedented relationships to each other and in contexts that were often quite inconsistent with the conventional linguistic depiction of reality. This linguistic alchemy of Hugo did much to develop the suggestive and the symbolic that we commonly associate with post-Romantic French poetry. However, in all his poetic innovation, Hugo avoided ambiguity and obscurity of meaning, such as in the hermetic poem of private associations. His choice of lyric techniques was guided by their appropriateness to the clear and striking communication of each experience and the direct, emotive impact of the poem on the reader.

In Hugo's hands, the poetic image frequently moved away from the traditional role of ornamentation for ideas or themes and tended to fuse with them to form metaphorical or symbolic equivalents. This is perhaps best epitomized in the philosophic poem, *Dieu*, which is organized not as a logically ordered argument but as a series of visions, each with its component images. Hugo achieved a palpable evocation of the nebulous and the abstract by such techniques as the juxtaposition of concrete and abstract words, the use of adjectives as nouns, the fluent interchanging of language between human and material worlds, appropriate effects of sound and rhythm. Examples of such techniques are widespread in his poetry:

> On entendait suinter le néant goutte à goutte.
> (*La Fin de Satan*)

Seul, sans trouver d'issue et sans voir de clarté,
Je tâte dans la nuit ce mur, l'éternité.

(*La Fin de Satan*)

—L'Invisible erre dans l'Impalpable.

(*Dieu*)

Et l'aube douce et pâle, en attendant son heure,
Semble toute la nuit errer au bas du ciel.

('Nuits de juin', *Les Rayons et les Ombres*)

La grande symphonie en ut de Beethoven, c'est une façade de cathé-
drale flottante et comme en suspension dans une brume lumineuse.

(fragment in *Tas de pierres*)

On doute
La nuit...
J'écoute: —
Tout fuit,
Tout passe,
L'espace
Efface
Le bruit.

('Les Djinns', *Les Orientales*)

Trimourti, trinité, triade, triple Hécate!
Brahmâ c'est Abraham; dans Adonis éclate
Adonaï; Jovis jaillit de Jéhovah;

(*La Fin de Satan*)

The interaction of opposites, so fundamental to Hugo's view of
the universe and to his dramatic and narrative plots, is an essential
element of his style and imagery. More specifically, the *clair-obscur*
predominates in all the poetic genres that he favoured and is particularly evocative in the imagery of his hallucinatory visions:

L'ombre était comme un temple immense aux triples voiles;
Et je voyais au fond scintiller les étoiles,
Cierges mystérieux sur le drap noir des nuits.

(*Toute la lyre*, v. xiv)

Le jour plonge au plus noir du gouffre, et va chercher
L'ombre, et la baise au front sous l'eau sombre et hagarde.

('Éclaircie', *Les Contemplations*)

Et l'on voit tout au fond, quand l'œil ose y descendre,
Au delà de la vie, et du souffle et du bruit,
Un affreux soleil noir d'où rayonne la nuit!
('Ce que dit la bouche d'ombre', *Les Contemplations*)

One characteristic method by which Hugo appeals simultaneously to the visual and contemplative responses in the reader is to create a viewpoint—situated somewhere between the reader and the poet's own immediate involvement in the scene or emotional experience which the poem conveys. This intermediary voice assumes many forms, ranging from the traditional, self-conscious first person of most Romantic poetry to that of a condensed and highly charged interjection by an implied observer. As a focal point for our attention, the intermediary voice helps to arouse in the reader an emotional response that may be only partially contained in the representation of the actual scene:

Mon esprit plongea donc sous ce flot inconnu,
Au profond de l'abîme il nagea seul et nu,
Toujours de l'ineffable allant à l'invisible…
Soudain il s'en revint avec un cri terrible,
Ébloui, haletant, stupide, épouvanté,
Car il avait au fond trouvé l'éternité.
('La Pente de la rêverie', *Les Feuilles d'automne*)

Le croissant fin et clair parmi ces fleurs de l'ombre
Brillait à l'occident, et Ruth se demandait,

Immobile, ouvrant l'œil à moitié sous ses voiles,
Quel dieu, quel moissonneur de l'éternel été,
Avait, en s'en allant, négligemment jeté
Cette faucille d'or dans le champ des étoiles.
('Booz endormi', *La Légende des siècles*)

Le noir horizon monte et la nuit noire tombe;
Tous deux, à l'occident, d'un mouvement de tombe;
Ils vont se rapprochant, et, dans le firmament,
O terreur! sur le jour, écrasé lentement,
La tenaille de l'ombre effroyable se ferme.
('Ce que dit la bouche d'ombre', *Les Contemplations*)

While the descriptive and the suggestive, the real and the imaginary, exist in varying degrees in almost all Hugo's poetry, the full dynamism of his imagination is probably most evident in the sweeping epic visions of *La Fin de Satan* and in the philosophic poem, *Dieu*, as well as in some of the poems included in *Les Contemplations* and *La Légende des siècles*. In an age in which epic and philosophic poetry were very much in fashion, these stand out from the narrative and philosophic verse of contemporaries like Vigny, precisely because of Hugo's ability to think in images, to develop or invent myths that come to life in palpable visions, to exploit to an exceptional degree the associative potential of language. Yet it would distort the total picture of Hugo's most moving poetry to reduce it completely to the expression of the hallucinatory. He will always be remembered for intimate lyrics such as:

> Demain, dès l'aube, à l'heure où blanchit la campagne,
> Je partirai. Vois-tu, je sais que tu m'attends.
> J'irai par la forêt, j'irai par la montagne.
> Je ne puis demeurer loin de toi plus longtemps.
>
> Je marcherai les yeux fixés sur mes pensées.
> Sans rien voir au dehors, sans entendre aucun bruit,
> Seul, inconnu, le dos courbé, les mains croisées,
> Triste, et le jour pour moi sera comme la nuit.
>
> Je ne regarderai ni l'or du soir qui tombe,
> Ni les voiles au loin descendant vers Harfleur,
> Et quand j'arriverai, je mettrai sur ta tombe
> Un bouquet de houx vert et de bruyère en fleur.
> ('Demain, dès l'aube . . .', *Les Contemplations*)

In a word, Hugo mastered an extraordinary range of lyric poetry from the simplest rendering of tender intimacy to the vivid action of a Delacroix painting; from the precise detail to the evocation of the infinite and the timeless. Baudelaire justly commented:

Quand on se figure ce qu'était la poésie française avant qu'il apparût, et quel rajeunissement elle a subi depuis qu'il est venu; quand on imagine ce peu qu'elle eût été s'il n'était pas venu; combien de sentiments mystérieux et profonds, qui ont été exprimés, seraient restés muets; combien d'intelligences il a accouchées, combien d'hommes qui ont rayonné par lui seraient restés obscurs, il est impossible de ne pas le considérer comme un de ces esprits rares et providentiels qui opèrent, dans l'ordre littéraire, le salut de tous . . . ('Réflexions sur quelques-uns de mes contemporains' from *L'Art romantique*)

NOTE

VICTOR HUGO, 1802–85, was the son of a Napoleonic general and a royalist mother. From the very first articles and poems, published when he was still in his teens, his literary career was marked by ever-increasing distinction and material success. By 1841 he was elected to the Académie française. His political and propagandist activities reflect the gradual evolution from a devout and ardent royalist to a socialist sympathizer. Named *pair de France* by Louis-Philippe in 1845, he was elected to the Assemblée législative as a republican after the Revolution of 1848. As a result of vigorous opposition to Napoleon III's *coup d'état* in 1851, he was obliged to live in exile in the Channel Islands. The emperor's overthrow in 1870 made possible Hugo's return and subsequent election to the Assemblée nationale. Having become a national hero and popular symbol of humanitarian and democratic ideals, he was buried in the Panthéon.

Works. The *Œuvres complètes* in the Imprimerie nationale edition, published between 1904 and 1952, are usually the most satisfactory. However, the *Œuvres complètes* published in four huge volumes by Pauvert (1961–4), and the volumes that are gradually being published in the Pléiade series, include many hitherto unpublished texts and variants. In addition, R. Journet and G. Robert have been producing first-rate definitive critical editions of individual texts.

Principal dramatic works: *Cromwell* (1827), *Hernani* (1830), *Marion de Lorme* (1831), *Le Roi s'amuse* (1832), *Lucrèce Borgia* (1833), *Marie Tudor* (1833), *Angelo* (1835), *Ruy Blas* (1838), *Les Burgraves* (1843).

Principal narrative works: *Han d'Islande* (1823), *Bug-Jargal* (1826), *Le dernier jour d'un condamné* (1829), *Notre-Dame de Paris* (1831), *Claude Gueux* (1834), *Les Misérables* (1862), *Les Travailleurs de la mer* (1866), *L'Homme qui rit* (1869), *Quatre-vingt-treize* (1873).

Principal collections of poetry: *Odes et Ballades* (1826), *Les Orientales* (1829), *Les Feuilles d'automne* (1831), *Les Chants du crépuscule* (1835), *Les Voix intérieures* (1837), *Les Rayons et les Ombres* (1840), *Les Châtiments* (1853), *Les Contemplations* (1856), *La Légende des siècles* (1859, 1877, 1883), *Chansons des rues et des bois* (1865), *L'Année terrible* (1872), *L'Art d'être grand-père* (1877), *Les Quatre Vents de l'Esprit* (1881). Published posthumously: *La Fin de Satan* (1886), *Dieu* (1891) (both unfinished), and *Toute la lyre* (1888 and 1893), *Années funestes* (1898), and *Dernière gerbe* (1902). Significant fragments gathered together as 'reliquats' (Hugo's own term) are added to some of the above volumes. Further verse has also been published under the titles *Océan* and *Tas de pierres* (1942).

Principal critical and miscellaneous writings: *Littérature et philosophie mêlées* (1834), *Le Rhin* (1842), *Napoléon le petit* (1852), *Histoire d'un crime* (1852–77), *William Shakespeare* (1864), *Actes et Paroles* (extending from 1841 to 1885). Published posthumously: *Choses vues* (1887 and 1900) and various collections grouped under such titles as *Post-scriptum de ma vie* (1901) and *Pierres* (1951) or included in *Tas de pierres* (1942). A selection of Hugo's graphic art is available in J. Sergent, *Dessins de Victor Hugo* (1955), and G. Picon, *Hugo dessinateur* (1964).

Criticism. J.-B. Barrère's *Hugo, l'homme et l'œuvre* (new edn., 1961) is a useful and up-to-date introductory biography. The following are helpful studies of aspects of Hugo's art: J. Gaudon, *Victor Hugo, dramaturge* (1955), P. Albouy, *La Création mythologique chez Victor Hugo* (1963), L. Mabilleau, *Victor Hugo* (1893), J.-B. Barrère, *La Fantaisie de Victor Hugo* (1949–60), C. Renouvier, *Victor Hugo, le poète* (2nd edn., 1897). See also H. J. Hunt, *The Epic in Nineteenth-Century France* (1941). H. Guillemin continues to publish new material on Hugo's life and thought, while the articles of M. Riffaterre focus attention on the language and imagery of his poetry. J.-B. Barrère reviewed recent studies of Hugo in 'Vingt ans de recherche sur Victor Hugo', *L'Information littéraire* (Sept.–Oct. 1961) and this can be complemented by E. M. Grant, *Victor Hugo: a Select and Critical Bibliography* (1967). In 1969 J. Gaudon published *Le Temps de la contemplation: l'œuvre poétique de Victor Hugo des Misères au Seuil du gouffre*; we await with interest his further work on Hugo's imagery, as well as J. Seebacher's study of Hugo the novelist.

4. Social Romanticism

As an earlier chapter has shown,[1] one major idea emerged from the thirty years of relative sterility and historic reappraisal that French literature endured after 1789: artistic taste had varied in the past, and in a way often closely related to the changes in the society that gave it birth. It therefore seemed to the Romantic artists that the secret of long-term success lay in being recognizably 'of their time'. Mme de Staël's pioneering study, *De la littérature considérée dans ses rapports avec les institutions sociales* (1800), had been eccentric—overstressing factors close to her heart, such as the advantages of an artistically enlightened un-Napoleonlike emperor, or the position of women in society—and, while recognizing the issues essential to each age, would seem to a modern historian to have often placed them in the wrong perspective. But the cleverness and conviction she applied to her theme, together with Sismondi's academic variations on it in his *De la littérature du Midi de l'Europe* (1813), had a profound effect on the young generation of the 1820s. Stendhal, for instance, repeats again and again in *Racine et Shakespeare* (1823) that taste is not absolute, as the classics had appeared to believe, but relative to the age.

If art is an organic part of the society or 'culture' in which it flourishes, then it is obvious that Mme de Staël's type of analysis, taken up and developed by critics such as Sainte-Beuve and Taine, will further our understanding of our literary heritage. But such a method will not necessarily lead to rules for the literature of the present day. Self-conscious involvement in contemporary problems and events contradicts the whole idea of a 'natural', therefore spontaneous and inevitable, cultural unity. The literature selected and preserved by the public approval of past centuries is only occasionally of the sort that appeared topical to its first audience.

[1] See Chapter 1, *passim*.

C

Indeed, the works that respond best to this type of historical inquiry are often those that bear fewest surface resemblances to their age. Mme de Staël uncovered this problem without solving it: 'Ces portraits d'hommes vivans, ces épigrammes sur les faits contemporains, sont des plaisanteries de famille et des succès d'un jour, qui doivent ennuyer les nations et les siècles.' The transitory works she refers to here are those that the historian interested in literature talks about with the greatest ease—yet they usually fail to satisfy Mme de Staël's own aesthetic criteria. Introducing politics into literature, Stendhal agreed, has the effect of a pistol-shot in the middle of a concert.

Though none of the Romantics doubted that they would be judged in centuries to come in terms of their response to the society around them, they were in a dilemma as to how to apply this new awareness of their own historicity. They had inherited from the eighteenth century a view of literature as a vehicle for the public debate of social issues; and the Revolution had left proof that human speculation could be stronger than tradition or divine authority, and might reshape the world. Yet in aesthetic terms it was clearly realized that the eighteenth century had been pallid and the Revolution barren. This issue was only imperfectly formulated in the early years of the Bourbon Restoration; had it been better understood, a literary historian such as Mme de Staël might well have prophesied that only two factors could lead Romanticism to choose the secular course: strong idealistic and social convictions on the part of artists, or a revolution in taste leading to a democratization of aesthetic criteria.

The first factor did not exist under either Napoleon or Louis XVIII. Belief in the constant and indefinite perfectibility of society received, during the Terror and Napoleon's aggressive militarism, as stunning a blow as at the bombing of Hiroshima. English and German observers of those events had been more outspoken than the French, but the undercurrent of bitter disappointment with the contemporary world is an essential feature of French literature in the 1820s.

Hence the dazed literary twilight of Napoleon's Empire, with its choice between false confidence dictated by the State and puzzled exile, or between safe but uninspiring classical art and new, disturbing, but as yet ill-defined sentiments and modes of expression. Hence the odd, contradictory assertions of the Romantics during the first decade after Waterloo. The successful artist is the one who first feels the pulse of his age, says Stendhal—the poet owes it to his fellow-men to delve into his private experience, answers Lamartine. Responsible intellectuals must record their novel feelings in times of change, writes Mme de Staël—let us rather soothe this change-stricken generation with the stable thoughts of the distant past, counters the young Hugo. Hence the two groups, both eventually calling themselves 'Romantics': the 'liberals', inheritors of the Encyclopedists, gravitating around Stendhal and Mérimée, and the young conservatives—'royalistes voltairiens' Hugo and Nodier called themselves. Both were in contradictory positions: the former believing in literature as a vehicle for political progress, but too conscious of the aesthetic dangers of uneducated popular control of the arts to disavow classical literature, although it bored them; the latter grasping at revolutionary literary themes and styles, yet from resignation supporting a system that acted as though nothing had happened between 1789 and 1815. Those with the literary ability to be 'of their time' gave tacit support to a reactionary regime.

A timid political change began around 1825. Interest in the liberation of Greece from the Turkish empire, a cause which fired the enthusiasm of young men all over Europe, and in the Italian struggles for political liberalism, openly connected with a young literature labelling itself Romantic, brought the two groups of French writers closer together. At the same time the *Globe*, which was known to have *carbonari* on its staff,[1] began to emerge as an organ of the new movement. Hugo's progress from 1822 to 1828, from the extreme right to tentative liberalism, can be traced, as he himself points out, through the successive prefaces to *Odes et Ballades*.[2] In 1822 he calls for moral and religious rearmament under

---

[1] The *carbonari* were the members of a secret political organization founded in Naples in 1807. From 1820 to 1850 the label was applied loosely to anyone suspected of liberal conspiracy.

[2] The four editions in question vary in either title or content: *Odes et Poésies diverses* (1822); *Nouvelles Odes* (1824); *Odes et Ballades* (1826); *Odes et Ballades* (revised, 1828).

a traditional monarchy; in 1824 he regrets the unfortunate alliance between royalism and a cadaverous literary classicism; in 1826 he separates his youthful 'political' poems from his personal ones in what almost amounts to a repudiation; in 1828 he pleads within the same paragraph for freedom in art *and* in politics.

Yet this opportunism is not necessarily as reprehensible as it might be made to appear from a purely political point of view. On the one hand, the Bourbon regime itself became progressively less liberal; on the other, an ambitious young poet in the narrow Parisian literary society of the 1820s naturally wished to please the most appreciative audience, and this audience was socially reactionary. The fear of interrupting the aesthetic harmony with a pistol-shot was to last until new literary forms appeared which allowed a man of letters to write of his real-life beliefs and ways of seeing the contemporary world without shocking the arbiters of taste. In the meantime, Romanticism went through a whole series of fashions, the bardic tale, the gothic craze, the historical romance, that were all in their time presented as 'new', and therefore connected in some obscure way with the new age.

Eventually, the second factor decided the issue: the balance of taste changed, prose fiction invaded the literary market, and the very homeliness of its appeal opened the way to the recognition of the people in literature. As long as the artist had been in a position similar to that of a court jester, depending on the whims of an aristocratic patron or a royal pension, he had naturally paid lip-service to the closed refined world he catered for, and been bound to a regulated, ceremonial form, poetry. Like many of the institutions in the old order, this bondage was also a protection, and could in many cases be fairly liberal. Between 1750 and 1830 the writer's status was gradually but completely upturned. Hugo and Lamartine, while they were receiving pensions from Louis XVIII, both still wrote for a small Parisian intelligentsia; yet a dozen years later they, like all their colleagues, were entering into industrial contracts with entrepreneur publishers and aspiring to national, even international, sales.

Various causes combined to turn literature from a rich man's pastime into a consumer industry. There was a technical revolution in printing and publishing: machine-made paper, rapid mechanical inking, improvements in communications all made it possible to widen the public. Whereas in 1820 only two Frenchmen in five could read, the Guizot and Falloux acts of 1833–5 made universal primary education a national norm, so that by 1845 an illiterate adolescent was an exception. The Romantic age saw the appearance of the first great literary and philosophic periodicals, the *Revue des Deux Mondes*, the *Globe*, the *Revue de Paris*; it also coincided with a newspaper 'explosion'. There were 11 Parisian dailies in 1810, 26 just before 1848. In 1836 *La Presse* and *Le Siècle* inaugurated the French equivalent of the 'penny press', financed by publicity and beginning to rely on popular, piecemeal sales as much as on subscriptions. These newspapers were to be of crucial importance to the development of social Romanticism, for they relied on the day-to-day type of news that brought men of letters into touch with the life of all sections of society, whilst providing them with columns which were still the only way of communicating with a comparatively wide audience.

For this was also the age of buccaneering publishers, demanding quick returns from a market they helped to create, which they analysed and coloured with the devices of the industrial age: publicity stunts, literary polemic, hack criticism, serial publication, enormous (usually whimsical) numbers of editions. The new man of letters, the Balzac, the Süe, the Dumas, the Zola, wrote for so much a page, sometimes for so much a line, and he had only this for a living: for this reason alone it is not surprising that he abandoned the more rigid and selective forms of poetry for lengthy verse or prose fiction. The world-wide sales figures of *Childe Harold* and *Waverley* were in everyone's minds. But none of this existed at the time when Hugo was pondering over the prefaces to his *Odes et Ballades*. It was not until well after the 1830 revolution that a Frenchman was able to afford a book any more readily than a pair of hand-made riding-boots.

It is small wonder then that the literature of the 1820s should have been so indecisive about plunging into the new century. Paris was once again, as Mercier had pointed out in his *Tableau de Paris* before the Revolution (it was first published in 1781), the rallying-place of a large marginal population of would-be intellectuals. But patronage was hard to come by, for the leading classes were not as opulent as of old; whilst the economic potential of the provincial middle class had hardly begun to be tapped, except by hawkers of pulp literature. Ambitious artists were forced into boisterous originality, then if this did not earn quick recognition, into puzzled protest against the callousness of society, illustrated by Vigny's *Stello*. This personal cause was to open the way towards a wider protest, on behalf of other categories of people also suffering from the new order. But this was not to be yet. For a long time the murmurings of novel thoughts and images were sacrificed to a long-ingrained aristocratic detachment that demanded that poets fall eloquently in love with well-to-do ladies, retire to their castles, or manor houses, to meditate, and indulge in expensive voyages to forget.

It is indeed striking how attached the young Romantics were to their noble antecedents. Henri Beyle hid a shamefully common name behind a fashionably Germanic title and pseudonym. Though the literary historians of the Third Republic have abbreviated these names for us almost beyond recognition, Stendhal's contemporaries were actually called François, vicomte de Chateaubriand; Germaine, baronne de Staël-Holstein; Alfred, comte de Vigny, seigneur d'Émerville; Alphonse de Lamartine de Prat; Victor-Marie comte Hugo. On 4 January 1831 Amantine Aurore Lucile Dupin, baronne Dudevant made both literary and social history by leaving her small-time provincial baron to his horses and hounds, and travelling alone to Paris to try to make a living writing novels under the plain plebeian pseudonym of George Sand.

This gesture was perhaps more prophetic than well-informed; but no lucid observer of the time could fail to see that the people of France were about to assume a new importance on the national scene: the dominant issues of a century heralded by a popular revolution were to revolve around the work, the living conditions, the social organization, and the opinions of large masses of people. 'Quelle sera cette civilisation moderne dont le romantisme serait l'expression littéraire?' The critic who in 1825 thus voiced the main preoccupation of the Romantics answered rightly that it was the people who would characterize the age.

In numbers first: the French population had been stagnant throughout the eighteenth century, when what minute measure of control the government had was always used to restrain it, because of the widespread belief that the country was overpopulated. From 1820 it rose sharply: by one million or almost 5 per cent in the next half-decade, by three million in the twenty years after 1830. Mortality dropped with vaccination, the beginnings of hygiene, the first steps of scientific medicine. Large sections of society also benefited from improved methods for producing cereals and new, cheaper commodities, such as clothes. But the distribution of the population changed even more influentially than its numbers. In 1831 one-sixth lived in towns of over 5,000 inhabitants; by 1851 this had increased to one-fifth. This shift was mainly to four centres, Paris, Lyon, Marseille, and Bordeaux. But Bordeaux and Marseille had no authors to write of their wharves and docks, Lyon had no poet to sing of its civil wars. The literary trade remained concentrated in the capital even though its customers were beginning to be nation-wide: the social Romanticism stemming from the people was to be mainly preoccupied with Paris.

Societies have a limitless fund of passive hypocrisy where differences in living conditions are concerned: individuals in the upper reaches can genuinely live in thoughtless acceptance of the existence of another class, caste, or race, and believe it to be destined by Nature to live in a world apart. Fortunately Nature, more of an egalitarian, provided in the great cholera epidemic of 1832 the strongest possible reminder that the conditions of physical morbidity amongst the people were a danger and a disgrace to all, and the clearest token of tragic inequality of conditions. Many rich people took refuge in the provinces, but all classes were affected in some way. There had been epidemics before, but not in such close proximity to the normally immune upper classes. 'Nous allons essayer de mettre sous les yeux du lecteur quelques épisodes de la vie d'autres barbares, aussi en dehors de la civilisation que les peuplades sauvages si bien dépeints par [Fenimore] Cooper. Seulement les barbares dont nous parlons sont au milieu de nous.' This is Süe's introduction to *Les Mystères de Paris*.

The Romantic writers were not the first to discover the shocking conditions in certain parts of Paris: at most, they publicized facts studied under both Charles X and Louis-Philippe by a number of social scientists, mostly members of the civil service, that lasting legacy of the Empire. Their conclusions and statistics have been more widely used by modern historians than they could ever have been by the politicians of their time. But Dr. Parent-Duchatelet's reports to the Conseil de salubrité of Paris and his journal *Annales d'hygiene publique et de médecine légale* provided Hugo with the material for his famous descriptions of the sewers in *Les Misérables*, and Süe with limitless information on the lives of prostitutes and watermen. The annual *Recherches statistiques sur la ville de Paris* began in 1817, the year that Hugo chooses as the object of a complete survey of society in his novel. The same is true to a lesser degree of many other works, such as those of Villermé on poverty, or of Moheau, Bigot de Morogues, and Buret on social hygiene.

The men of the time only understood the economic causes of these conditions imperfectly, but they were very clearly faced with a mass germination of humanity similar, on a small scale, to that of south-east Asia today, and they were acutely conscious of the problems of organization and coexistence that this implied. Paris was more and more a city of dreadful night. People living near the Champs-Élysées had thirty times more floor space each than the inhabitants of the Cité and the Hôtel de Ville districts. Here tall buildings lined dark narrow streets with open drains and littered with rubbish. Around Montfaucon the easiest way to get rid of the carcase of a horse was to leave it out in the street overnight: by the morning the rats had stripped the skeleton clean.

Overpopulation and creaking townships would of course have been lesser evils had they not been accompanied by that intense urban poverty which, in Europe as a whole, marked the switch from the agricultural to the industrial system. The agony was if anything longer, though rather less acute, than in some other countries, because France was slow to industrialize. Napoleon had developed a technological élite and an efficient system of commercial credit, but, partly because of the political turmoil of the revolutionary period and the blockade of the Continent, there were hardly any machines in France in the 1820s, and heavy industry only became a significant factor after 1845. But a serious depression in wages, probably caused by the disorganized labour market and by foreign competition after 1815, led to the large-scale migration of marginal, unskilled rural workers towards the towns in the hope of finding employment. Their legal status there was extremely unjust. France retained the infamous Le Chapelier law of 1791, adverse to any form of union or association, until the Third Republic. Not only was collective bargaining denied them, but they had to carry passports countersigned by their former employer in order to get a job. As a result their conditions did not improve when trade was good, and they were the first to suffer in any crisis. Wages in textiles (still a luxury industry in 1815) dropped by four-fifths between 1823 and 1840. The general drop was of about one quarter. A few stark facts have to be added before we, in our modern affluence, can really picture the consequences of these conditions. In 1830, we should remember, about one Frenchman in four could not afford to eat bread. One in three could occasionally eat meat. *Before* the most startling drops in wages, a Parisian woman worker could earn 75 centimes for an eleven-hour day, a labourer up to 2 francs. A four-pound loaf of bread (food for two people for one day) cost 85 centimes at that time. Similar conditions had in all probability existed at certain periods in previous centuries. But families living in towns in small units have a less flexible budget and less varied resources than farming communities; and, more important still, the poor could not fail to be more conscious of their difference in station now that they were living so close to the rich.

To the middle class, which did not venture readily into the slum areas, the most obvious effect of these conditions was an unparalleled rise in crime and immorality. Police and census records of the 1840s show that at one time, of 900,000 adult inhabitants of Paris, only a third earned their living in identifiable ways, and these included begging and prostitution. Fifteen thousand prostitutes were registered with the police, and of these one in eight was under the age of twelve. Between 1820 and 1830, one child out of three born in Paris was illegitimate, one out of four abandoned, over half died before the age of one. Statistics on crime are hard to come by; but it is worth remembering that a convict was fed and clothed and made to work twelve hours a day, whereas a free man in the textile industry could work fourteen and a half hours and be unable to feed his children. 'Il y a un point', writes Hugo, 'où les infortunés et les infâmes se mêlent et se confondent dans un seul mot, mot fatal, les misérables.' A characteristic feature of the period was the public interest in crime. One of the most popular newspapers was the *Gazette des Tribunaux*, which provided, from 1825 onwards, regular accounts of awful happenings and grounds for periodic scares of organized gangs in the underworld. When the popular dailies began to appear in the 1830s, such items of news were a boon to them: they provided the cheap everyday suspense, drama, and violence that is catered for in so many ways in our own world and is at once an apology and a compensation for secure and drab urban lives. This and a less wholesome taste for publicly enacted horror, in part a heritage from the days of the Revolution and subsisting in those famous festivals, the public executions in the Place de la Grève, first found literary recognition in 1829 in the *Mémoires* of Vidocq. All the thrills of the popular romances to come had been experienced and recorded by this extraordinary master criminal (the model for Balzac's Vautrin), who had been in turn a galley prisoner, a chief of police, an industrial speculator, a bankrupt, and a policeman again, this time as a cover for his gang. A few weeks after the publication of the first volume, Hugo took up the new popular idiom and began to write his protest against the death penalty, *Le dernier jour d'un condamné* (1829).

But the daily reports on crime are connected more narrowly with the works of Eugène Süe. His was the first really popular literature in that it was read by Parisians and provincials, intellectuals, and working men alike. A few weeks after it began to serialize *Les Mystères de Paris* (1842–3), the *Journal des débats* found its circulation doubled, from 50,000 to 100,000. *Le Constitutionnel*, which bought *Le Juif errant* (1844–5) two years later, jumped similarly from 3,000 to 40,000. Süe's sudden success (these were not his first serial novels) was achieved partly by his creating an ambiguous link between his two audiences. His *Mystères* set out to shock the gentle reader by a straightforwardly melodramatic tale of a modern knight errant venturing into the gutters to punish the wicked and save

various relations and a few deserving acquaintances from the
clutches of a group of criminals who are evil incarnate. The background is one of sordid places and customs which exist, the reader
is supposed to learn, only a few miles away from him. The mur-
derous gangs of cut-purses, quack doctors, money-lenders, and
kidnappers, using shady cafés and sordid apartment buildings as a
cover, are vividly depicted. But for the other class of reader, who
may also wish to escape from his own surroundings, Süe provides
an equally picturesque account of the high society his hero really
belongs to. He thus, half unwittingly, stresses the enormous contrast between the living conditions of the poor and the rich.
Encouraged by the success of some pathetic descriptions of a poor
family, he devotes large sections in the second half of the work to
comments on social conditions, and gives precise information on
wages and costs, language, and customs. Süe himself, like his hero
Rodolphe, penetrated the Hôtel de Ville district disguised as a
worker, but accompanied by a couple of athletic friends. It was
whispered with a thrill in the literary salons that his story sometimes reached real prostitutes, watermen, and cut-throats, through
cafés and reading societies, and that they wrote to him to praise or
correct his information. It is indeed refreshing to see *grisettes*
represented, not in the rosy tones of Musset or Murger, but realistic-
ally, as poor working girls having to prostitute themselves to rich
young gentlemen; or *tapis francs* for what they were, not the dens
of comic-opera thieves, but sordid filthy holes in the ground. Yet
in the last analysis, Süe always remained a dandy and an entertainer,
presenting these facts as curiosities. The bearded woman may be
the wonder of the fair, but no one takes steps to cure her.

It was immediately after Süe's success that Victor Hugo wrote
the first version of *Les Misérables*, but, characteristically, he only
published his novel twenty years later (1862). He had eventually
come round in 1853 to agreeing with Stendhal that 'les poètes sont
aux écoutes des grands événements et les précèdent', but had never
really made up for lost time. In the 1830s, while people were being
slaughtered at Lyon and in the Rue Transnonain, he had timidly
suggested, in *Claude Gueux* (1834), that the penalties for stealing
to feed one's children were rather high. During the Orléans

monarchy, under the enormous strains of *laissez-faire* industrializa-
tion, his only pronouncement was, in the preface to *Ruy Blas*, that
the people were the key to the future. The 24th of February 1848
found him trying to persuade the crowd at the Bastille to support
the duchesse d'Orléans at the very moment when Lamartine was
helping to inaugurate the Second Republic at the Chambre des
députés. A year later, when the wind was veering towards socialism,
he directed a newspaper that saw no harm in the rising star of
Louis Napoleon. After his exile, he was right in pointing out that
he had evolved romantically from legitimism to a form of socialism—
but so had France, and he was constantly behind, not ahead, although he camouflaged the fact by writing retrospective prefaces
and backdating poems. This too is a way to popularity, though with
a rather less progressive public.

Les Misérables is, however, a salutary reminder that it is possible
to inquire into social questions without being a socialist, even in the
wide sense that word had in the mid-nineteenth century. Hugo's
debt to Süe is obvious: the stolen babies, the convicts in disguise,
the redeemed guttersnipes, the realism, and the melodramatic
shock tactics are used for a similar purpose. Hugo is addressing the
widest possible public. He too is concerned mainly with the seamy
side of Paris, though perhaps more with the causes of crime than
with its horrific interest. But it would be useless to look for a social
policy in this famous book; it is moved purely by the spirit of
humanitarianism. The very success of *Les Misérables*, which for
decades was a rallying work for the poor and the oppressed everywhere in Europe, under all political regimes, shows that it has an
idealistic rather than a practical appeal. Hugo was very far from
being a socialist; but he was moved by individual plights to generous
protests, which catalogued unhappy situations rather than suggesting a coherent view of society. In the last resort, he trusts to human
nature rather than to social organization to put things right. The
same appears in his poetry. 'Melancholia', in *Les Contemplations*,
is characteristic: it lists nine scenes arousing the poet's pity, but
this is their only link. Some are genuine social ills: children at work
in factories, women with undeserving husbands unjustly held to the
marriage bond, over-luxurious balls in time of poverty. But a plea

for kindness to animals, and questions of personal morality—an adulteress is redeemed because she has sinned for love—are also included. Hugo never confined himself to being the 'echo of his time'. In the poem 'A quoi songeaient les deux cavaliers dans la forêt', when Hermann, his 'other self', calls his attention to the sufferings of the living, he answers that he is more preoccupied with those who are dead.

Though the political fruits of the 1830 revolution turned bitter so quickly, to many intellectuals it appeared to herald the coming of a new age. In an article, published in 1831, entitled 'Espoir et vœu du mouvement littéraire et poétique après la révolution de 1830', Sainte-Beuve pointed out that during the Restoration art had been content to survey life as if from the esplanade at Saint-Germain. Now, however, 'peuple et poètes vont marcher ensemble, une période nouvelle s'ouvre pour la poésie; l'art est désormais sur le pied commun, dans l'arène avec tous, côte à côte avec l'infatigable humanité'. Sainte-Beuve was wrong in supposing that poetry could fulfil this role. There was too large a breach between the language of poetry and the tastes of the people. The renewal of prose fiction at the popular source proved in the end an indirect answer to his wishes.

It was, however, suggested earlier that the dilemma of artists in the 1820s could also be solved by a strong spiritual renewal urging them to set themselves up as leaders of taste above the arbiters of taste, and to adapt fashionable aesthetic demands to the aspirations of the age. In the general intellectual unrest of Charles X's reign this began to take place, albeit muffled under an ostentatious campaign for the reform of certain apparently trivial rules of classical drama. The Romantic battles culminating in the victory of *Hernani* consecrated the right of the artist to be respected as an intellectual able to lead society. The stage—that symbolic place where the poet, dressed up as his hero, sways the people dressed up as his audience—was an appropriate scene for this achievement. It points to a new era, in which the intellectual herald will express the highest hopes and ideals of humanity and his own society. Hugo drummed this conception into his readers in the opening poems of all his collections after 1830; it helps to explain the idealistic vein which, in *Les Misérables*, runs parallel with the popular inspiration and causes the story to jump constantly between dramatic realities and abstractions. This stream too, though it looks on society from a higher level and sometimes prefers ideals to facts, deserves to be called social Romanticism.

The year 1830 symbolically freed France from all the spectres of 1793 and 1815. A limited revolution had been achieved without uncovering pits of evil; progress could now be resumed. A book such as *La Légende des siècles*, resting on the assumption that mankind generally moved forward, was again possible. The difficulties of the industrial revolution were at hand, but in certain moods the human mind soars above the challenge of everyday realities and constructs ideal models for the society of the future. We will find this in certain novels of George Sand and Balzac; it is also eminently true of the social Utopias that must be described first.

The sense of renewal, which was for a time called 'l'esprit de 1830', runs through all the ideas of men such as Saint-Simon, Fourier, and Proudhon, whom Marx later labelled Utopian socialists. Though widely divergent in their diagnosis and prescriptions, they shared a fundamental assumption of Rousseau's, discredited by the Revolution but now able to emerge again: the 'natural' state of Man was good; the evils of modern society could be corrected by a return to the intermediate stage at which things had started to go wrong, and a fresh start taking into account the experience now gathered. The French Revolution was proof of the feasibility of such an enterprise, even though its particular model had not proved viable; it should also be remembered that the men of the time felt less cramped than we do by State restrictions, all-embracing communications, and sheer numbers—virgin lands still existed in the New World and community experiments in the countryside were conceivable.

According to Henri de Saint-Simon, descendant and editor of the eighteenth-century chronicler, society, which goes through periods of organization and of criticism, had now reached an organic period, in which a renewal would be made possible by scientific production and distribution. Saint-Simon was a prophet

of the capitalist era. His early plans for a Panama canal, his successful speculations on *biens nationaux* during the Revolution, show him
as an early model of the capitalist entrepreneur. His followers,
who at one time formed a semi-monastic order which was to replace
Christianity, later became, as economists, engineers, and financiers,
the moving spirits behind such monuments of nineteenth-century
capitalism as the Paris–Lyon–Marseille railway and the Suez
Canal. Saint-Simon advocated an economy planned by pro-
ducers—on the assumption that this would automatically be in
the best interests of consumers. He also wanted this new basis of
society to be acknowledged in the organization of power and status
by the introduction of an industrial and scientific government and
hierarchy in place of the old aristocratic and spiritual ones. His
famous parable of 1819, which almost took him to gaol, argued that
if the royal family, the aristocracy, the leading politicians, and the
ecclesiastics of France were to disappear, nothing much would be
lost, whereas if the same happened to her leading scientists, artists,
bankers, doctors, and industrialists, the country would suffer
greatly.

Charles Fourier considered social reform from the point of view
of a tradesman and travelling salesman rather than as a financier.
He saw social wrongs as deriving essentially from the top-heavy
system of distribution that leads an apple to centuple its price between the farm and the table of a fashionable restaurant. The cure
he suggested consisted in a corporate community, where individual
property and profit, the source of anarchy and misery, would be
integrated into a harmonious system based on the proper understanding of agriculture and of human nature. Property is also the
main bugbear of Pierre-Joseph Proudhon, whose ideal system
consisted in federations of small communist units which would
eventually replace national states. Many other radical idealistic
thinkers, such as Pierre Leroux, director of the literary and Saint-
Simonian *Globe*, were active in the 1830s. There was a lively movement towards Catholic socialism under the impulsion of Lamennais.
'Quelque part où l'on marche,' wrote Musset sarcastically, 'on met
le pied sur un messie.' But the feeling of renewal was shared by all,
by Marcelle de Blanchemont for instance, an emancipated woman

like her creator George Sand: 'Elle savait donc bien que ce présent engourdi et malade est aux prises avec le passé qui le retient et l'avenir qui l'appelle. Elle voyait de grands éclairs se croiser sur sa tête, elle pouvait pressentir une grande lutte plus ou moins éloignée.'

Though George Sand believed she was more concerned with the ideal future than with the struggle to achieve it, to a modern reader she cannot fail to appear gripped by the past. Late nineteenth-century Utopias accept the need for modern machines and constitutions, and show them tamed; but for Sand the ideal is a return to a pre-industrial, at times idyllic, society close to Nature and a rejection of two main evils, towns and money. In *Le Compagnon du tour de France* (1840) and *Le Meunier d'Angibault* (1845) the glimpses of the ideal consist in a patriarchal scene in an orchard and an evening meal of the community at the mill, symbol of plenty. Sand's heroines, Marcelle de Blanchemont and Yseult de Ville-preux, though not feminists, find themselves, because of family circumstances, in a responsible situation; both discover, by falling in love with craftsmen, that money and social position are only valid as symbols of the work that produces them. Marcelle's lover refuses to marry her while she is heiress to a fortune she has not earned herself. Yseult's lover, Pierre Huguenin, is more pre-occupied with the proper organization of work. He tries to persuade the ancient guilds, or *corporations*, prevented by cruel, useless traditions from agreeing on the proper rights and status of their members, to associate and set an example to the rest of society. Unjust property and harmful ambition would disappear if all were made to experience the rewarding nature of work.

The starting-point of Balzac's 'Scènes de la vie de campagne' is very similar to that of George Sand. Mainly concerned with individual behaviour when he describes urban environments, he too has in *Le Médecin de campagne* (1833) a brief vision of regeneration through Nature. The country as it exists is spiteful, cruel, and degenerate, mainly because land-owners have refused to do their share of work and to deserve their share of wealth, and the peasants are exploited either by feudal-minded proprietors or by land speculators. Organization is necessary, on Saint-Simonian lines, with a knowledge of technology and economics. Balzac stresses above all the part to be played by the 'supériorités sociales', men with a professional training, priests, doctors, and lawyers. Thus Bénassis, the country doctor, takes over a depressed mountain village and rebuilds it into a scale model of a capitalist-mercantilist state. Primary, secondary, and tertiary production are organized in turn on modern principles, and there is not a moment's doubt that as general wealth increases, that of the rich will increase more, yet the social question will resolve itself. These hopes of Balzac's were still alive when he wrote *Le Curé de village* (1839), but they had disappeared by the time he started *Les Paysans* (1844), originally entitled 'Qui terre a guerre a'. Here he despairs of human nature amongst peasants reduced to an animal existence and animal viciousness. The reformer can do nothing which does not crumble under century-old spite and prejudice.

The French countryside, from which the waves of urban immigrants came, was indeed in the grip of a social crisis. Most peasants at least ate bread with their roots and acorns. But those who had subsisted as dependants during the age of 'wasteful' aristocratic exploitation were in many cases eliminated now that large estates had been divided by the Revolution into medium-size units exploited frugally and sometimes managed personally by a new rural middle class. Dissatisfaction at this, suspicion of any kind of modernization or intervention, and bitterness because peasant property and methods were shockingly inefficient and rural credit facilities non-existent, contributed to make the country a very un-idyllic place. Balzac's progress from idealism to the realism of *Les Paysans* is a step towards the truth; yet in a sense it oversteps, for the picture is as black as the previous one was rosy. It is the novel of a disenchanted idealist. For a sober portrayal we have to wait yet another twenty years for the arrival of Zola.

In a sense it is unfair to apply to the populist literature modern standards of sophistication that it consciously avoided, or to the idealist authors concepts that their contemporaries did not possess. The Romantics themselves instructed us to judge them in relation to their time. Yet, paradoxically, we know many things about their time that they themselves did not know or chose to disregard. To stress these is in fact to replace the Romantics more justly in their age.

The sensibility and literary style of the Romantics gave them one enormous advantage: the power to appreciate individuals. Where society tended to shut itself off from the undifferentiated mass of the poor, the Romantic could translate the idea of misery into an individual case and make it live as a person, far more understandable to an audience with a built-in passivity towards statistical information. In this the social novel rendered invaluable services—there can be no doubt that the readers who wrote to Süe asking for the address of the Morels so that they could come to their aid were better members of society thereafter. But the individualism of the authors themselves has less flattering aspects. One cannot help suspecting that the novelist is often using exemplary situations and events in order to return quickly to his idea and strike up a virtuous attitude. Never does Hugo let an episode of *Les Misérables* speak for itself—he always imposes on us a long-winded humanitarian rhetoric of the obvious. Süe openly symbolizes this attitude in the character of Rodolphe, who is not a social worker but, like Süe, a dandy dabbling in the underworld and handing out rewards and punishment to all who cross his path. The very heroic nature of Rodolphe the beneficent, Valjean the martyr, Bénassis the economic conjuror, Huguenin the angelic, diminishes their claim to universality, and indeed to realism.

It is obvious to us now that the crucial problem in the society of the time was that of poverty. Change the economic distribution of wealth and products, and it is only a matter of time before issues such as the death penalty, feminine rights, crime, the condition of children are solved. But whereas some of these aspects of the problem were conscientiously attacked (Lamartine pleaded many times for reforms at the Chambre under Louis-Philippe; Hugo's *Le dernier jour d'un condamné*, his most precise work, is probably also his most effective), whereas Süe's accounts of Paris slums and Hugo's protests on behalf of exploited women and children undoubtedly helped the growth of a social conscience in France, their analysis of poverty itself was curiously reactionary. The poor in their novels are almost a different species. In Hugo they are always seen through a rich person's eyes. In Süe one hears of them, but only the representatives of Evil have a part in the story. If a prostitute is rescued from her sordid life, she shows sudden gifts for learning and virtue and turns out to have been the daughter of a prince; similarly, if George Sand introduces a working man of virtue, he will almost certainly marry money or position. These two examples illustrate a characteristic nineteenth-century myth, which is more than a device of romance: it expresses an underlying belief in a moral difference between rich and poor and a confidence in the ultimate value of the present social organization. If someone climbs in society the fact is quickly justified by the discovery of a latent difference in status; conversely, if someone shows promise society will recognize this with symbols of success, matrimonial or financial. It follows that if someone stays poor, he deserves it. Though this may not appear on the surface, Sand, Hugo, and Süe are not only of their age, but largely in agreement with it: at least as much so as Balzac, whose studies of individual fortunes capture the very essence of bourgeois social mobility, but who, one could argue, was perhaps at heart protesting against the individualist system which he saw and portrayed as a destroyer of personalities.

Our own explanations of the poverty in France would be very different: we would point to unchecked fecundity, insecure and irrational conditions of employment, even perhaps to the whole concept of *laissez-faire* economy. But the authors we are considering did no such thing, and where they were led to suggest solutions these usually amounted to plain unquestioning Christian charity. 'La charité, c'est le socialisme', wrote Lamartine in 1834. He is echoed by Bishop Myriel, that allegory of Virtue who, at the opening of *Les Misérables*, gives Valjean his candlesticks so that he should make a fresh start; as well as by Süe's Rodolphe, when he distributes Ruritanian gold to his poor. In charity the conflict between the self and others can be resolved without detriment to the self. Voluntary charity on a large scale was of course characteristic of the nineteenth-century upper middle class; we can hardly expect its spokesmen to have thought of social security—in this the Romantics also succeeded in being 'of their time'.

Yet from another point of view three out of these four novelists were considerably behind the times—Hugo, Sand, and Süe all agree in their condemnation of the grasping, avaricious lower middle class. The Thénardiers in Hugo, the Bricolins, Sand's 'paysans parvenus', all the middle layers of caretakers, small-holders, pseudo-professional men in Süe, are painted in the blackest colours. Their ambition to rise alienates them from both rich and poor. Good is done, if at all, over their heads, by Sand's country barons, Süe's German prince, Hugo's bishop or general. Balzac, on the other hand, saw society guided by the responsible middle class thanks to its professional or commercial ability: yet even he intro-duced Napoleonic officers as a new responsible élite and petty bourgeois profiteers as villains. The Romantics were after all brought up as entertainers of the aristocracy. Some, like Musset and Vigny, remained in aristocratic aloofness and did not even attempt to socialize. Those who did all looked back to a mythical time before Figaro came between the count and his villagers, when it was the function of the great to do good paternally. Hugo, on leaving a royal ball at Vincennes in 1847, notes with irritation the lines of bystanders grumbling and shouting their childish hatred and envy as the embroidered and glittering coaches draw away from the château, and remarks that they ought to be pleased with such lavish expense because it puts hundreds of thousands of francs into circulation.

It was at once courageous and rather useless to attack the lower middle class, to which the audience of the Romantics now extended. A group is only sensitive to attacks of this sort if they are made in front of a tribunal not its own, and though some members of the working class undoubtedly read Sand and Süe, the great majority obviously did not. Imaginative literature is essentially a luxury industry, and can only deal with poverty at a distance as long as it is financed by free enterprise.

Yet Saint-Simon, who had the greatest influence on these writers, both because he believed in progress without revolution and because he allowed artists an important place in his ideal society, did so presumably because they could develop an unbiased imaginative awareness of all its reaches. Why did the Romantics not achieve this, though others like Zola have come very near to doing so since? Partly, no doubt, because of their very eagerness to be of their time. In doing so one can be forced into contemporary prejudices. Stendhal, because he did not appear to be topical, and Zola, because he tried to be dispassionate, were both more successful in depicting their age.

Balzac partly escapes this criticism. Engels said that Balzac had taught him more than all the economists, statisticians, and socialists put together. But this was precisely because Balzac was not a socialist. Neither, for that matter, were any of the Romantics. Where they protested, it was on behalf of individuals against the unjust restrictions that are to be found in any social code.

NOTE

GEORGE SAND, 1804-76, became a successful novelist almost immediately after beginning her emancipated life in Paris. Her first romances were concerned with the efforts of individuals, usually women, towards self-definition against a hostile family or social background. The best-known are *Indiana* (1831) and *Consuelo* (1842). In 1839 she was deeply impressed by *Le Livre du compagnonnage*, an account of the medieval craftsmen's guilds and secret societies still flourishing illegally in France. Its author Agricol Perdiguier, himself a craftsman, introduced her to progressive workers' circles; he is portrayed as Huguenin, the hero of *Le Compagnon du tour de France* (1840). George Sand also broached the social question in *Le Meunier d'Angibault* (1845) and *Le Péché de M. Antoine* (1847). In 1848 she took an enthusiastic part in revolutionary politics, but was soon disenchanted and retired to her estate at Nohant; her later works were accounts of simple emotions in an idyllic setting: *La Petite Fadette* (1840), *La Mare au diable* (1847), *François le Champi* (1850), *Les Maîtres sonneurs* (1853). The voluminous literature on her has been concerned almost entirely with her passionate affairs with Alfred de Musset, Frédéric Chopin, and others. But E. Dolléans's *Féminisme et mouvement ouvrier: G. Sand* (1951) deals with her response to social problems. For general biographical and critical summaries see P. Salmon, *George Sand* (1953), or E. Thomas, *George Sand* (1959). Some previously unpublished texts by George Sand, as well as a number of essays on her work, will be found in L. Cellier (ed.), *Hommage à George Sand* (1969).

EUGÈNE SÜE, 1804-57, was the most successful popular novelist of the 1840s. After losing a fortune as an extravagant Parisian dandy, he regained it by prolifically exploiting the vogue for serialized romances in newspapers. He too, after meeting socialist workers, introduced social issues into stories previously concerned only with the exotic or the horrific: this led to his greatest successes, *Les Mystères de Paris* (1842-3, reprinted by Pauvert in 1963) and *Le Juif errant*

(1844-5, reprinted in 1965). J.-L. Bory gives an account of his brilliant career in *E. Süe: le roi du roman populaire* (1962).

VICTOR HUGO deals with social problems mainly in *Le dernier jour d'un condamné* (1829), *Claude Gueux* (1834), *Les Contemplations* (1856), and *Les Misérables* (1862). Two voluminous theses have dealt with this side of his work: M. Ley-Deutsch, *Le Gueux chez V. Hugo* (1936), and P. Savey-Casard, *Le Crime et la peine dans l'œuvre de V. Hugo* (1956). A good introduction is provided by R. Journet and G. Robert, *Le Mythe du peuple dans 'Les Misérables'* (1965).

BALZAC's social theories are best illustrated in *Le Médecin de campagne* (1833), *Le Curé de village* (1839), and his last, unfinished work, *Les Paysans* (1855). He too has been the object of exhaustive commentary by B. Guyon, *La Pensée politique et sociale de Balzac* (1947; 2nd enlarged ed., 1967), and J. H. Donnard, *Les Réalités économiques et sociales dans la 'Comédie humaine'* (1961). A. Wurmser's synthesis of 1964, *La Comédie inhumaine*, is illuminating on this topic; one may also consult the collection of essays presented to H. J. Hunt and edited by D. G. Charlton and others under the title: *Balzac and the Nineteenth Century* (1972). The social works of Hugo and Balzac are dealt with in detail in two special numbers of the left-wing review *Europe* (Feb.-Mar. 1962 and Jan.-Feb. 1965).

For background works on the social and political history of the period, see J. L. Talmon, *Romanticism and Revolt: Europe 1815-1848* (1967); P. Vigier, *La Monarchie de Juillet* (1965); P. Plamenatz, *The Revolutionary Movement in France* (1952); J. Aynard, *Justice ou charité* (1945); L. Chevalier, *Classes laborieuses et classes dangereuses* (1958). The 'socialist' theories of the period are best approached through selected readings, for instance *Fourier: textes choisis*, ed. F. Armand (1953), *Pour connaître la pensée de Proudhon*, ed. G. Guy-Grand (1947), and *Henri comte de Saint-Simon 1760-1825: Selected Writings*, ed. F. M. H. Markham (1952). See also J.-B. Duroselle, *Les Débuts du catholicisme social en France: 1822-1870* (1951); A. Cuvillier, *Hommes et idéologies de 1840* (1956); D. G. Charlton, *Secular Religions in France: 1815-1870* (1963).

The topic outlined in this chapter can be pursued through H. J. Hunt, *Le Socialisme et le Romantisme en France: étude de la presse socialiste de 1830 à 1848* (1935), and A. J. George, *The Development of French Romanticism: the Impact of the Industrial Revolution on Literature* (1965). See also J. Michelet, *Le Peuple* (1846; ed. L. Refort, 1946); J.-P. Sartre, 'Qu'est-ce que la littérature?', in *Situations*, vol. ii, 1948; and the informative critical bibliography in D. O. Evans, *Social Romanticism in France: 1830-1848* (1951).

5. Stendhal

IN describing the rise of social realism in the novel, critics often quote a comment addressed to the reader by the self-conscious author-persona in *Le Rouge et le Noir*:

. . . un roman est un miroir qui se promène sur une grande route. Tantôt il reflète à vos yeux l'azur des cieux, tantôt la fange des bourbiers de la route. Et l'homme qui porte le miroir dans sa hotte sera par vous accusé d'être immoral! Accusez bien plutôt le grand chemin où est le bourbier, et plus encore l'inspecteur des routes qui laisse l'eau croupir et le bourbier se former.

Stendhal was not mistaken in anticipating that his 'Chronique de 1830' would displease a reading public drawn largely from what he considered to be a stagnant aristocracy and a parvenu bourgeoisie: a public which delighted in Chateaubriand's melancholy, Hugo's melodrama, and George Sánd's sentimentality. Unlike the 'Happy Few', such readers could scarcely be expected to appreciate a novel in which situations, behaviour, and events were so heavily charged with political and ideological significance. As he explained to his worried publisher, it was 'presque impossible de bien écrire sans rappeler plus ou moins indirectement des vérités qui choquent mortellement le pouvoir'. These 'vérités' were of course nothing more than Stendhal's own assessment of his society. His energy and talents had thrived in the revolutionary ferment that extended into much of the Napoleonic age. Notwithstanding his inability to loosen the magnetic hold that sophisticated Paris had on him, he now found post-Waterloo French society restrictive, dull, hypocritical; never rising above its engrossment in the manoeuvres of an unprincipled and crude bourgeoisie jostling with a stultified and pretentious aristocracy for political hegemony. For a more spontaneous and unaffected expression of emotions, an energetic enthusiasm, and an uninhibited response to beauty and art he turned to

Italy and to the Italian character. A kind of latter-day humanist, he admired the Renaissance ideals of life and art that he associated with Benvenuto Cellini, Boccaccio, and Michelangelo.

He was, as well, a rare surviving son of the French Enlightenment, with an analytical mind and aesthetic sensibilities that had been nurtured by *le naturel* of Rousseau, the materialist rationalism of Condillac and Helvétius, and the satiric wit of Voltaire and Diderot. The pursuit of happiness, a major concern of Enlightenment thinkers, demanded, according to Stendhal, continual self-analysis accompanied by the free expression of the imagination and sensibilities. Hence his contempt for the studied affectation and inhibiting social conventions of contemporary Parisian society. Specifically, convinced that love is central to the 'good life', he sought (notably in his essay *De l'amour*, 1822) to analyse it, to determine the attitudes that hinder or contribute to love's natural development and expression.

While he delighted in keen observation of man as a social animal, he was also intensely interested in that more complex and uncertain area of observation, namely, the study of the self. His lasting preoccupation with analysis of his own make-up, evident in the unfinished autobiographical manuscripts of *La Vie de Henry Brulard* and *Souvenirs d'égotisme*, for example, resulted in a rare ability to view with objectivity his own behaviour in relation both to the contemporary social context and to his readers of the future. In *La Vie de Henry Brulard* we read:

. . . j'écris ceci, sans mentir j'espère, sans me faire illusion, avec plaisir comme une lettre à un ami. Quelles seront les idées de cet ami en 1880? Combien différentes des nôtres! . . . parler à des gens dont on ignore absolument la tournure d'esprit, le genre d'éducation, les préjugés, la religion! Quel encouragement à être vrai, et simplement *vrai*, il n'y a que cela qui tienne.

The convivial and sincere manner which permeates these endeavours to place himself and his times in historical perspective contributes not a little to the continuing persuasive quality of his insights.

Convinced of the relativity of criteria for beauty, morality, and truth, he is one of the few among his contemporaries to perceive the instability of the institutions and values that dominated his society;

one of the few intellectuals to retain Condorcet's firm confidence in ultimate human progress, although he saw no significant political group on the horizon capable of bringing about effective change in his own day. He perceived too much hypocrisy and opportunism in the 'liberal' political groups to expect much from them and he was not so naïve as to be taken in by the utopian visions of George Sand and Victor Hugo. While avoiding romantic idealization of the lower classes, his sensitivity to the humiliation suffered by them as a matter of course accompanied his opposition to any idea of inherent class superiority or privilege. But in the 1830s the only example of a democratic society was the culturally empty life of frontier America. Hence the paradox that Stendhal expressed quite frankly: while believing strongly in political and social equality, this *homme du monde* could only be truly happy in the society of a refined and 'enlightened' salon. His predicament was expressed, for example, in the second preface to *Lucien Leuwen*:

Entre deux hommes d'esprit, l'un extrêmement républicain, l'autre extrêmement légitimiste, le penchant secret de l'auteur sera pour le plus aimable. En général, le légitimiste aura des manières plus élégantes et saura un plus grand nombre d'anecdotes amusantes; le républicain aura plus de feu dans l'âme et des façons plus simples et plus jeunes. Après avoir pesé ces qualités d'un genre opposé, l'auteur, ainsi qu'il en a déjà prévenu, préférera le plus aimable des deux; et leurs idées politiques n'entreront pour rien dans les motifs de sa préférence.

In the sophisticated salon the conversation—unhampered, he thought, by prevailing social conventions, prejudices, or material concerns—would be marked by wit, cultivation, and grace; his own vivacity of imagination, his taste for the improvised repartee, his *esprit raffiné* would be fully at home. As he tells the reader in *La Vie de Henry Brulard*:

Un salon de provinciaux enrichis qui étalent du luxe est ma bête noire par exemple. Ensuite vient un salon de marquis et de grands cordons de la Légion d'honneur qui étalent de la morale.

Un salon de huit ou dix personnes dont toutes les femmes ont eu des amants, où la conversation est gaie, anecdotique, et où l'on prend du punch léger à minuit et demi, est l'endroit du monde où je me trouve le mieux. . . .

In the 1820s it was Stendhal the critic who was best known to Parisian literary circles—'le hussard du romantisme', as Sainte-Beuve later called him. But the romanticism that he defended in *Racine et Shakespeare* (1825) had little in common with the 'volupté mélancolique' of Chateaubriand: 'Le *Romantisme* est l'art de présenter aux peuples les œuvres littéraires qui, dans l'état actuel de leurs habitudes et leurs croyances, sont susceptibles de leur donner le plus de plaisir possible.' The crucial issue for Stendhal was the artist's freedom to express his view of life in the language of his contemporaries. If he took Shakespeare as a model, it was not to suggest imitation of his plots and style: 'Ce qu'il faut imiter de ce grand homme, c'est la manière d'étudier le monde au milieu duquel nous vivons.' In other words, the imaginative vision that gives shape to the great work of art is rooted in reality, speaks its idiom, and has relevance to its specific traits.

Although he never developed a coherent aesthetic system, Stendhal left ample indications of his views in marginalia and notes, in correspondence, and in critical articles. The key word in his approach to art, as to life, is 'le naturel': 'le beau idéal' to which he frequently refers is precisely 'le *naturel* dans les façons, dans les discours . . .'. Rejecting, he tells us in *La Vie de Henry Brulard*, 'l'affectation qu'on appelle bien écrire en 1825-36'—from the *exagérations colorées* of Chateaubriand to the flowery sentimentality of George Sand—he endeavoured to shape a style which would be both lucid and appropriate to the substance of the work in question. As he observed when working on *Lucien Leuwen*: 'La première qualité d'un roman doit être: raconter, amuser par des récits, et, pour pouvoir amuser les gens sensés, peindre des caractères qui soient dans la nature.' And on numerous occasions he reiterates this need for all art to imitate reality. It is quite evident, however, that he does not have in mind a literal imitation. His own fiction is not a 'miroir qui se promène sur une route', as the author-persona in each novel would have us believe, but a consciously selected *interpretation* of reality. As he stresses in *Écoles italiennes de peinture*: '. . . il est presque impossible que la nature présente une action telle qu'on n'ait qu'à la copier pour faire un tableau.' Quite the contrary, he comments in a marginal note of *Lucien Leuwen*, 'tous les arts sont fondés sur un certain degré de fausseté'. This distortion is directed at creating the over-all *impression* of being true to life: 'En général, *idéaliser* comme Raphaël idéalise dans un portrait, pour le rendre plus ressemblant.'

Stendhal ridiculed the attempts of some novelists, in the manner of Walter Scott, to create the illusion of authenticity by means of copious detail. Where Balzac firmly believed that 'les détails constitueront désormais le mérite des ouvrages improprement appelés *Romans*', Stendhal had, in writing *Le Rouge et le Noir*, deliberately rejected any use of 'deux pages à décrire la vue que l'avait [*sic*] de la fenêtre de la chambre où était le héros; deux autres pages à décrire son habillement, et encore deux pages à représenter la forme du fauteuil sur lequel il était posé'.

While he did employ physical detail to recreate the society encountered by his heroes, he did so with the intent of capturing only the essence of each scene by the skilful use of the 'petit fait vrai' that characterizes its particularity most suggestively. His manner calls to mind the bold lines of a Daumier lithograph—selected concrete traits instantly evoking in the reader the character's real-life counterpart.

Just as he could not accept the reliance on copious detail to render the 'reality' of a scene, he attached little importance to the traditional concern for removing the author's voice—the preoccupation which was to culminate a generation later in the *impassibilité* of *Madame Bovary*. He did not see the active presence of an author-persona as being inherently harmful to the impression of real life. There was only one sense in which the author had to be absent from the novel: it must never be evident that the autonomy of the characters had been violated, or that the course of events resulted from the author's manipulation—as in the manner of Hugo's novels. The story must appear to evolve exclusively from the interaction of the characters and situations.

Drawing on the tradition of Rabelais, Cervantes, Sterne, and Diderot, Stendhal mocked the very contrivances by which fiction is supposed to achieve the illusion of authenticity. In his own novels, the reader is invited to join the author in a game in which the rules for representing reality are patently lax, in the interests of intensifying the breadth of life and of making the work more entertaining and immediate.

Apart from the 'Happy Few'—'ces êtres malheureux, aimables, charmants, point hypocrites, point moraux, auxquels je voudrais plaire'—the reading public failed to respond to *Le Rouge et le Noir* or to *La Chartreuse de Parme* during Stendhal's life-time. This is not because social satire and comic irony were foreign to the French literary tradition, although it is true that at this time Rabelais and Voltaire were hardly the most respectable authors. What was probably most shocking was the unprecedented use of the contemporary political and social scene as the playing-field for ebullient young heroes who challenged not only the rules of the game but the integrity of the players as well. While it is true that the more popular Balzac was also beginning to draw socially relevant, life-size portraits, at least his *roman-feuilleton* plots and moral abstractions were more palatable to prevailing tastes. Stendhal, on the other hand, with his distinctive approach to fictional representation of 'l'âpreté du réel de la vie', rooted his plots in recognizable actuality and derived the attitudes and behaviour of his characters directly from their social and political situations, thus forcing his audience into a more active confrontation with the issues posed. Yet this does not mean that he conceived of the novel as a *conte philosophique*, that is, as a vehicle for the explicit presentation of political or philosophic ideas, in the manner of *Gulliver's Travels* or *Candide*. The interpretation of society underlying *Le Rouge et le Noir* or *Lucien Leuwen* is, in fact, just one of their basic ingredients, indispensable and integral to the author's art as a novelist.

It is not surprising that ever since he was 'discovered' in France, towards the end of the nineteenth century (as he had anticipated), the novels have been more often studied for their historical insights and their resonances of the intriguing personality of the author than for their artistic merit. Unfortunately, this has sometimes resulted in mechanical identification of Stendhal with the fictional characters, such as Mosca in *La Chartreuse de Parme*, or most often the dramatized author-persona that does the narrating in each novel. I am not suggesting that there exists a divorce between Stendhal and his novels. Nothing could be farther from the truth: Stendhal's personality unquestionably permeates everything he ever wrote and his personal values inform each novel very directly. But while Stendhal, like most novelists, draws from himself to construct various fictional characters, the nature and behaviour of each one, including the mock author, are ultimately determined by the exigencies of the narrative and not by the author's intention to dramatize himself.

When he wrote in 1823 that 'le public français attend encore son Fielding', Stendhal may not have been aware that he would later, as a novelist, aspire to that very distinction; but certainly *Le Rouge et le Noir*, and above all *La Chartreuse de Parme*, immediately remind the reader of some characteristic features that are associated with the author of *Tom Jones*. Indeed, the influence exerted by Fielding was quite obvious to Stendhal himself. Their novels reveal a similar taste for comic irony and colourful verve; satiric attacks on the vanity, hypocrisy, and affectation around them; the elevation of an engaging author-persona to a major role in the novel.

Stendhal did not write *Armance* until 1827, when he was forty-four, but this first novel marked the completion of an apprenticeship begun in his prodigious autobiographical, descriptive, and critical writings and in his interest in the theatre, where he had hoped to become the Molière of his generation. In any event, once initiated, Stendhal realized that he had at last found his true métier.

By the time he wrote *Le Rouge et le Noir*, about three years later, he had arrived at the pattern which he was to apply in each future novel: that well-known blend which includes the unpredictable young hero (or heroine, as in *Lamiel*) placed in a tragi-comic confrontation with the satirically rendered image of contemporary reality *pris sur le vif*, the values and attitudes of the hero finding their nemesis in the upper classes among whom he plays various roles, and set in ironic relief by a witty and perceptive narrating 'author'.

In *Le Rouge et le Noir*, this confrontation of hero and society takes the form of efforts made by Julien Sorel, following a humiliating and loveless childhood, to rise in the wealthy and aristocratic circles that he despises, by donning 'l'uniforme de mon siècle'— hypocrisy. The author-persona indulgently 'assures' us at the beginning of this career:

Il ne faut pas trop mal augurer de Julien; il inventait correctement les paroles d'une hypocrisie cauteleuse et prudente. Ce n'est pas mal à son âge. Quant au ton et aux gestes, il vivait avec des campagnards; il avait été privé de la vue des grands modèles. Par la suite, à peine lui eut-il été donné d'approcher de ces messieurs, qu'il fut admirable pour les gestes comme pour les paroles.

And with amused malice, he adds at one point: 'Julien atteignit à un tel degré de perfection dans ce genre d'éloquence qui a remplacé la rapidité d'action de l'empire qu'il finit par s'ennuyer lui-même par le son de ses paroles.' Personal ambition for the Stendhalian hero never becomes a drive for purely material gain; it remains always the expression of his adolescent ideal of a worthy and meaningful existence, a strategy for asserting his dignity and proving the superiority of 'le mérite' over 'le rang'. In this solitary war against the upper classes waged from within their midst, Julien's naïve conception of Napoleon and Rousseau provides the military guide and the inspiring ideal. Since he is propelled in his ambitious career by 'le sentiment vif de sa pauvreté et de sa bassesse aux yeux du monde', he wears his humble origins as an assertion of his dignity:

Si je veux être estimé et d'eux et de moi-même, il faut leur montrer que c'est ma pauvreté qui est en commerce avec leur richesse, mais que mon cœur est à mille lieux de leur insolence, et placé dans une sphère trop haute pour être atteinte par leurs petites marques de dédain ou de faveur.

In each situation that confronts him he feels the need, as do all Stendhal's heroes, to get his bearings, endeavouring to base his behaviour upon logical analysis. After each encounter the basic question that obsesses him in the evaluation of his conduct is whether he has acted according to his 'devoir': 'Comme le soldat qui revient de la parade, Julien fut attentivement occupé à repasser tous les détails de sa conduite. N'ai-je manqué à rien de ce que je me dois à moi-même? Ai-je bien joué mon rôle?'

However, hypocrisy never comes easily to Julien; he knows only too well that the principal threat to the success of all his strategems emanates from himself. To his great discomfort his *cœur sensible* is forever asserting itself unexpectedly. In his eyes, the danger to his newly won advances is secondary to his fear that these outbursts of sensibility will expose him to the contempt and disdain of his enemies:

... j'ai le cœur facile à toucher; la parole la plus commune, si elle est dite avec un accent vrai, peut attendrir ma voix et même faire couler mes larmes. Que de fois les cœurs secs ne m'ont-ils méprisé pour ce défaut! Ils croyaient que je demandais grâce: voilà ce qu'il ne faut pas souffrir.

Until the last section of the novel, Julien's encounters with the upper-class Establishment are always projected into his consciousness as a quasi-comic tension between his true self and his public mask, between *l'imprèvu* and the calculated: '... il avait les manières mais non pas encore le cœur de son état. Malgré toute son hypocrisie si souvent exercée il sentit une grosse larme couler le long de sa joue.' The author-persona, whose role we shall discuss later, frequently appears to deplore and to apologize for Julien's 'failure' to suppress this sensibility in the interests of his career. Yet he can recognize with delight, for example, that '... l'adresse dont nous lui reprochons l'absence aurait exclu le mouvement sublime de saisir l'épée qui, dans ce moment, le rendait si joli aux yeux de mademoiselle de la Môle'. Ironically, Julien's successes are in fact more often the result both of his impulsiveness and of chance than of his carefully worked-out tactics. The mock-author, concerned as he pretends to be about Julien's ability to learn the methods of success, frequently interjects his indulgent 'criticism': 'J'avoue que la faiblesse dont Julien fait preuve dans ce monologue me donne une pauvre opinion de lui'; or: 'On voit que Julien n'avait aucune expérience de la vie, il n'avait pas même lu des romans. . . .' The deliberately transparent admonitions obviously reassure us that Julien's character is basically good and that his 'weaknesses' are in fact a manifestation of the permanence of his virtuous qualities. 'The author' is obliged to confess with a smile: 'Jamais il ne fera ni un bon Prêtre, ni un grand administrateur. Les âmes qui s'émeuvent ainsi sont bonnes tout au plus à produire un artiste.'

As we might have expected, the passionate and susceptible nature which Julien could never hold in check for long, asserts itself once and for all and precipitates the 'état de demi-folie' in which he wounds Mme de Rênal.

At this climactic point in the story there is a change in the dominant tone of the narration and in the consciousness of the hero. The author-persona dispenses with the comic note, bringing us closer to Julien's point of view.

He now records the process of self-analysis with a discreet absence of comment. The detached and calm existence of prison life preceding the judgement and the expectation of the death-sentence heighten the sobriety and pathos of the hero's efforts to assess his short life. 'Notre héros' is no longer the adolescent peasant who, upon gaining an early success over M. de Rênal, 'ne voyait rien entre lui et les actions les plus héroïques, que le manque d'occasion'. He is at last 'fatigué d'héroïsme': 'Il n'y avait plus rien de rude et de grandiose en lui, plus de vertu romaine; la mort lui apparaissait à une plus grande hauteur, et comme chose moins facile.' Julien's approach to death is a manifestation more of moral courage than of the heroic bravado it might have been at the beginning of his career. He has no illusions about the horror of death: the visit by the broken and dying old abbé Chêlan 'fut le plus cruel qu'il eût éprouvé depuis le crime. Il venait de voir la mort, et dans toute sa laideur. Toutes les illusions de grandeur d'âme et de générosité s'étaient dissipées comme devant la tempête.'

Life in prison has finally completed his release from the pursuit of illusions. No longer could he wonder, as when he first arrived at the Hôtel de la Môle, 'Comment peut-on être malheureux... quand on habite un séjour aussi splendide!' In fact, the process of dis-illusionment began almost immediately afterwards, when he perceived that in this most aristocratic of salons:

La moindre idée vive semblait une grossièreté. Malgré le bon ton, la politesse parfaite, l'envie d'être agréable, l'ennui se lisait sur tous les fronts. Les jeunes gens qui venaient rendre des devoirs, ayant peur de parler de quelque chose qui fît soupçonner une pensée, ou de trahir quelque lecture prohibée, se taisaient après quelques mots bien élégants sur Rossini et le temps qu'il faisait.

Like Lucien Leuwen and Lamiel, Julien might also have remarked 'N'est-ce que ça?' as he experiences more and more of life among the social and political élite. He soon perceived that 'dès qu'il cessait de travailler il était en proie à un ennui mortel'. The sympathetic guidance received from knowledgeable informants such as the abbé Pirard ultimately contributes more to his rejection of that society than to his easy progress to the top. Now, realizing that he has been deceived by appearances, he at last can say that 'l'ambition était morte'.

When Mme de Rênal visits him in prison he tells her of the understanding he has acquired: 'Autrefois . . . quand j'aurais pu être si heureux pendant nos promenades dans le bois de Vergy, une ambition fougueuse entraînait mon âme dans les pays imaginaires.' Only the precious moments spent with her have survived in him: 'Les moindres incidents de ces temps trop rapidement envolés avaient pour lui une fraîcheur et un charme irrésistibles. Jamais il ne pensait à ses succès de Paris; il en était ennuyé.'

This is a lesson learned by all of Stendhal's heroes: happiness can be achieved not in the realization of ambition but when, as we read in *Lucien Leuwen*, 'deux âmes de même portée . . . se rencontrent et se reconnaissent au milieu des masques de cet ignoble bal masqué qu'on appelle le monde'. The resulting passionate love provides the only situation in which the Stendhalian hero can be fully himself: no political or social intrigue ever manages to mobilize his energy and imagination so completely. In a society where the relationships between men and women tend towards the superficial and the calculating, love becomes a testing ground on which the heroes reveal the extent of their generosity and sensibility.

In a more general sense, what has emerged from Julien's quest for happiness in 'ce siècle si moral, si hypocrite, et par conséquent si ennuyeux' is his growing conviction that the very qualities—intelligence, imagination, and vitality—which in another age might bring gratification and happiness can now provide only a painful understanding of why it is that they must be frustrated. When his beliefs and personality, which he has hitherto kept integral and independent from the self which engaged in social advancement, are permitted to shape his behaviour, a tragic ending becomes inevitable. Refusing any longer to compromise his integrity, he forces the climax by turning the tables and passing judgement on

D

the jury which has been called to judge him, thus deliberately provoking the death sentence, the only decoration 'qui ne s'achète pas':

L'horreur du mépris, que je croyais pouvoir braver au moment de la mort, me fait prendre la parole. Messieurs, je n'ai point l'honneur d'appartenir à votre classe, vous voyez en moi un paysan qui s'est révolté contre la bassesse de sa fortune.

Je ne vous demande aucune grâce, continua Julien en affermissant sa voix. Je ne me fais point illusion, la mort m'attend: elle sera juste. J'ai pu attenter aux jours de la femme la plus digne de tous les respects, de tous les hommages. Madame de Rênal avait été pour moi comme une mère. Mon crime est atroce, et il fut *prémédité*. J'ai donc mérité la mort, messieurs les jurés. Mais quand je serais moins coupable, je vois des hommes qui, sans s'arrêter à ce que ma jeunesse peut mériter de pitié, voudront punir en moi et décourager à jamais cette classe de jeunes gens qui, nés dans une classe inférieure et en quelque sorte opprimés par la pauvreté, ont le bonheur de se procurer une bonne éducation, et l'audace de se mêler à ce que l'orgueil des gens riches appelle la société.

Voilà mon crime, messieurs, et il sera puni avec d'autant plus de sévérité, que, dans le fait, je ne suis point jugé par mes pairs. Je ne vois point sur les bancs des jurés quelque paysan enrichi, mais uniquement des bourgeois indignés.

In definitively rejecting any question of compromise with this society Julien has defined his identity. His historical moment precluded attainment of happiness, but the final moral triumph belongs to him.

The hero's gesture of defiance and the resulting execution are a fitting denouement for the novel that initiated what Auerbach described in *Mimesis* as 'modern tragic realism based on the contemporary'. What a contrast with the self-conscious lyrical melancholy of the heroes of Byron and Chateaubriand! In Stendhal's fictional world there are no ambiguities about the nature of everyday reality, no means of transcending the specific historical moment or of retreating from it. It is there and must be dealt with. But Julien Sorel is not Oedipus facing the inexplicable will of the gods; nor is he 'man' confronting profound metaphysical abstractions. He has not called into question, in the manner of Camus's Meursault, moral and social values in general. He has, simply, challenged the

values of the upper classes in a particular society. He is well aware
that it is not human nature which is responsible for his frustration,
but the facts of life in the France of 1830.

In Stendhal's other novels the protagonists possess a similar
consciousness of the distance between their approach to life and the
avenues of personal fulfilment attainable in their society. Easily
achieving distinction among the upper-class milieux which they
despise, they find no more happiness than did Julien. As Lucien
Leuwen recognizes: 'Moi, plébéien et libéral, je ne puis être
quelque chose au milieu de toutes ces vanités que par résistance.'
Because such heroes are such pure and passionate extremes, pre-
servation of their distinctive identity provokes a denouement which
effectively removes them from the social scene in one way or
another: in *Lucien Leuwen* and *La Chartreuse de Parme* the hero
largely fades away, while in *Lamiel*, according to the author's working notes, the heroine goes off with the bandit who loves her
passionately. It is only in *Le Rouge et le Noir* that Stendhal resolved
the confrontation of the hero with his society in a tragic gesture of
defiant self-assertion.

It is quite evident that such a tragic note would be out of place in
La Chartreuse de Parme (1839), for the progressive disillusionment
of Fabrice is set in a framework of high comedy. In what Henry
James considered to be 'a novel which will always be remembered
among the dozen finest novels we possess', Stendhal came closest
to the comic-epic style that he admired in *Tom Jones* and which was
singularly suited to his own rich imagination and satiric wit.

Unlike the realistic context of his other novels, Parma is an auto-
cratic state of lilliputian dimensions in which nineteenth-century
events take place in a sixteenth-century Italian décor: Machiavellian
intrigues unfold with mock heroics and humorous melodrama.
Although it is Fabrice's adventures that carry the action forward,
the intricate and finely constructed plot ties together the consciousness and experience of several major protagonists, each of whom is
placed at a different level of involvement with the corrupt and
insipid court life of the despotic Ernest IV, a ruler who,

la nuit . . . tremble dans sa chambre. Toutes les portes fermées à dix
verrous, et les pièces voisines, au-dessus comme au-dessous, remplies

de soldats, il a peur des jacobins. Si une feuille du parquet vient à crier, il saute sur ses pistolets et croit à un libéral caché sous son lit.

However, the reader's attention is generally focused less upon the amusing action-packed plot than upon the contrast between the extraordinary energy and imagination of these major characters and the corrupt, boring court life about them.

Far more than Stendhal's other heroes, Fabrice can never suppress his *élan*, for he has an 'Italian' character. He too learns, by the time he has become archbishop of Parma, that for all his success, the only happiness he experienced was in the moments spent near his beloved Clélia, a heroine in the tradition of Armance and Mme de Rênal.

The *Chartreuse* has sometimes been referred to as the supreme nineteenth-century example of a political novel. While his other explicitly political work, *Lucien Leuwen*, involves a recognizable contemporary situation, Stendhal failed in this case to integrate the political content with other elements. In the *Chartreuse*, however, politics are integral to the entire novel. Above all, the highly imaginative setting heightens the effectiveness of the parody of European political life under the reactionary Holy Alliance.

There is of course the danger, not always avoided by some critics, of reducing a novel by Stendhal to its theme, such as the hero's realization of his identity, or to the underlying ideological implications. There is also the other pitfall which consists of taking the impressions and reflections of a Julien Sorel or a Fabrice del Dongo at their face value as the 'message' of *Le Rouge et le Noir* or *La Chartreuse de Parme*. But Stendhal's art is far more complex than this, interweaving, as it does, objective reality, the hero's consciousness of this reality, and the author-persona who observes the action alongside the reader. The last of these is the principal instrument in the ironic juxtaposition of the other two.

This author-persona has been cast so convincingly that some critics have unfortunately attempted to merge him, as we suggested earlier, with what is known of the life of Monsieur Henri Beyle. To do this is to overlook the dramatic function of the author-persona. This role is the key to the entire rhetorical apparatus for securing the reader's acceptance not only of the interaction of the hero and the fictional world, but also of the underlying social critique. This mock-author never participates in the action, never detracts our attention from the hero, is unknown to the other characters, and, with no more than a sly nod to the acquiescent reader, respectfully shifts his position and viewpoint from omniscient reporter to fellow spectator. His presence in the novels adds a piquant dimension which has become a hallmark of Stendhal's narrative style, and the thinly disguised rhetoric is one of its most appealing characteristics. Thus at one moment he accepts full responsibility for the narrative structure and style; the next, he is brazenly asserting that he has not invented the events, that he can exercise no control over them, nor can he foresee what will happen from one moment to the next. Similarly, this author-persona may reassure us that he would have preferred to omit certain conversations or behaviour which could bore or annoy the reader, excusing himself in *Le Rouge et le Noir*, for example, by placing the onus on the 'éditeur': 'Si vos personnages ne parlent pas politique, reprend l'éditeur, ce ne sont pas plus des Français de 1830, et, votre livre n'est pas un miroir comme vous en avez la prétension.'

Much of the effectiveness of the author-persona role is due to the distinctive ironic manner that it assumes in most of Stendhal's novels. This is evident in the transparent apologies for the 'flaws' in behaviour of each hero: 'Lucien [Leuwen] avait encore la mauvaise habitude et la haute imprudence d'être naturel dans l'intimité. . . .' And it is present as well when the 'author' supposedly expresses the viewpoints of characters, as in these examples from *La Chartreuse de Parme*:

Ces messieurs [the party of 'la réaction'] fort honnêtes gens quand ils n'avaient pas peur, mais qui tremblaient toujours, parvinrent à circonvenir le général autrichien: assez bon homme, il se laissa persuader que la sévérité était de la haute politique, et fit arrêter cent cinquante patriotes: c'était bien alors ce qu'il y avait de mieux en Italie.

Bientôt on les déporta . . . et, jetés dans les grottes souterraines, l'humidité et surtout le manque de pain firent bonne et prompte justice de tous ces coquins.

Ce mot dur et le ricanement général qui le suivit accablèrent Fabrice.

La guerre n'était donc plus ce noble et commun élan d'âmes amantes de la gloire qu'il s'était figuré d'après les proclamations de Napoléon!

At other times Stendhal uses his author-persona in what might best be described as dramatic *reportage*: in the manner of a film editor he selects and arranges a sequence of shifting viewpoints provided by two cameras. Achieving this dual view appears to have been a constant concern in both the writing and the projected revision of his novels. Thus he places a reminder in his working notes for *Lucien Leuwen*: 'En relisant, se faire toujours la double question: de quel œil le héros voit-il ceci? De quel œil le lecteur?' One camera is set within a particular consciousness and interprets events and situations accordingly, while the other provides us, either directly or obliquely, with the more 'objective' comment on the same scene. Thus in *Le Rouge et le Noir*, for example, without diverting us from the character we are following at the moment, we are provided with an unillusioned insight or a suggestive comment: 'Depuis longtemps, elle [Mme de Rênal] désirait sincèrement la mort . . . cet être affaibli par un malheur trop constant. Ce malheur était l'absence de Julien; elle l'appelait, elle, *le remords*'; or: 'Les enfants étaient ravis de ce seul mot "cabaret", que prononce avec tant de plaisir la pruderie moderne'; or: '[Julien] était mortellement dégoûté de toutes ses bonnes qualités, de toutes les choses qu'il avait aimées avec enthousiasme; et dans cet état *d'imagination renversée*, il entreprenait de juger la vie avec son imagination. Cette erreur est d'un homme supérieur.' Moreover, in each novel, the implicit guidelines for the reader are complemented by the numerous occasions when 'information' about society is directly presented by the author-persona asserting his full authority, usually in the guise of one who has intimate contact with these circles in the real world:

Ce raisonnement, si juste en apparence, acheva de jeter Mathilde [de la Môle] hors d'elle-même. Cette âme altière, mais saturée de toute cette prudence sèche, qui passe dans le grand monde pour peindre fidèlement le cœur humain, n'était pas faite pour prendre vite le bonheur de se moquer de toute prudence, qui peut être si vif pour une âme ardente. Dans les hautes classes de la société de Paris, où Mathilde avait vécu, la passion ne peut bien rarement se dépouiller de prudence, et c'est du cinquième étage qu'on se jette par la fenêtre.

Whatever the particular stances assumed by the author-persona in his variegated pattern of intervention, there is no ambiguity regarding the judgements he wishes us to make. They are even present when he is at pains to insist upon the impartiality of his 'reporting', as in *La Chartreuse de Parme*:

Pourquoi l'historien qui suit fidèlement les moindres détails du récit qu'on lui a fait serait-il coupable? Est-ce sa faute si les personnages, séduits par des passions qu'il ne partage point malheureusement pour lui, tombent dans des actions profondément immorales? Il est vrai que des choses de cette sorte ne se font plus dans un pays où l'unique passion survivante à toutes les autres est l'argent, moyen de vanité.

Often, however, such judgements emerge directly from the action and are related by experienced and wise *raisonneurs* such as Mosca in the *Chartreuse*, Sansfin in *Lamiel*, or Leuwen *père* in *Lucien Leuwen*. The following is from *La Chartreuse de Parme*:

— Mais savez-vous que ce que vous me proposez là est fort immoral? dit la comtesse.
— Pas plus immoral que tout ce qu'on fait à notre cour et dans vingt autres. Le pouvoir absolu a cela de commode qu'il sanctifie tout aux yeux des peuples; or, qu'est-ce qu'un ridicule que personne n'aperçoit? Notre politique, pendant vingt ans, va consister à avoir peur des jacobins, et quelle peur! . . . Tout ce qui pourra diminuer un peu cette peur sera *souverainement moral* aux yeux des nobles et des dévots.

The authorial intervention in Stendhal's novels is indeed extensive, but that it never becomes objectionable is in part due to the intimate relationship established between 'l'auteur' and 'le lecteur bénévole'. The reader accepts the former as a genial, perceptive, and worldly-wise travelling companion, one whose brief asides— always fresh, candid, and knowledgeable—discreetly illuminate the events of the novel. When the attitudes he expresses are patently not his own, the insincerity is often made just evident enough for the reader to feel a measure of complicity in detecting the innuendo. Even the reader does not escape inclusion in the narrative. Although more passive than in Sterne's *Tristram Shandy* or Diderot's *Jacques le fataliste*, he is endowed with distinct attitudes which the author-persona takes into consideration. Demonstrating the highest regard for the reader, our artful teller of anecdotes pretends to draw him into the élite circle—the 'Happy Few'—since he is 'obviously' also a discerning *esprit*, free of conventional prejudices.

The confidence that we are induced to place in the narrating author-persona is very much bound up with the characteristic Stendhalian diction: the casual, chatty manner—an extension of urbane speech. Recreating the flavour of his own conversation, Stendhal evolved a style appropriate to the quick aside that is juxtaposed to a character's reflections or behaviour. This illusion of having written *à l'improviste* is of course part of the pose of being indifferent to stylistic rules: as though considerations of style were mere affectation and the only stylistic requirements were lucidity and wit. But Stendhal did not indulge in improvisation to the extent that he would have us believe. We know from his notes and first editions that he crowded margins with criticisms and possible changes for later editions, partly with the aim of achieving that very spontaneous, casual air.

While narrative style is integral to the conception of any novel, in the case of Stendhal it is very much the key to that very distinctive tone that Valéry once described as 'le plus individuel qui soit en littérature'. The ever-present perceptive and ironic author-persona, the lively conversational manner, the shifting angles of dramatic *reportage*, the flashes of insight into characters and situations—these are fundamental to that air of intense life which informs Stendhal's fiction. If I suggest that he is a supreme realist, it is not in the manner of Balzac's precise observation or Flaubert's meticulous constructions. It is not to place him in a conventional category of literary history, for his novels cannot be defined in such narrow terms. I mean rather that his fiction dramatizes and assesses the *essence* of contemporary social values and behaviour.

The absence of pretence, the ubiquitous humour, the delicate susceptibility are intrinsic to the art that emerged from his profoundly civilized approach to life. Here was a solitary but confident and vigorous echo of the Enlightenment, a singularly imaginative affirmation of the dignity of intellect and sensibility whose insights into behaviour and attitudes are still relevant to our own society.

NOTE

STENDHAL (pseudonym of Henri Beyle), 1783-1842, was born and educated in Grenoble. From 1800 to 1802 and from 1806 to 1813 he was an officer in Napoleon's army, first in Italy and then in Germany, Russia, and Austria. Having spent seven years in Italy pursuing his interests in art, literature, and music, he was obliged to leave in 1821 because, in the eyes of the Austrian police, he was 'un ennemi irréligieux, immoral et dangereux de la légitimité'. In Paris, from 1821 to 1830, he devoted himself to extensive writing, including critical articles for British journals, autobiographical studies, and fiction. In 1831, under the more liberal July Monarchy, he was appointed French consul at Trieste and then at a small port not far from Rome—the post which he held until his death. During this period he continued his writing career and made visits to Paris.

Works. The rough draft of *La Vie de Henry Brulard*, the *Journal*, and the *Souvenirs d'égotisme* contain valuable autobiographical observations, especially for the period up to 1830. Like most of Stendhal's works, they were published posthumously. Miscellaneous observations on literature and the arts, on places of interest, and on society can be found in such works as *Filosofia nova* (posth. publ., 1931), *Vie de Haydn, Mozart et Métastase* (1815), *Histoire de la peinture en Italie* (1817), *Rome, Naples et Florence* (1817), *Promenades dans Rome* (1829), *Mémoires d'un touriste* (1838), and *Courrier anglais* (posth. publ., 1935-6), a collection of his articles in British journals. *De l'amour* (1822) is Stendhal's study of this 'maladie de l'âme', while the two pamphlets making up *Racine et Shakespeare* (1823 and 1825) are basic documents of Romanticism. Stendhal's fiction consists of *Armance* (1827), *Le Rouge et le Noir* (1831), *La Chartreuse de Parme* (1839), a collection of Renaissance Italian tales entitled *Chroniques italiennes* (1839), and short stories assembled posthumously in *Romans et Nouvelles*. The manuscripts and notes for the unfinished novels, *Lamiel* and *Lucien Leuwen*, illustrate Stendhal's problems in writing fiction.

Editions. No definitive critical edition will be possible until the Stendhal library, now in private possession, is made publicly available. The 'Divan' edition (1927-37) prepared by the indefatigable Henri Martineau is at present the most complete. It is now being re-edited and brought up to date by V. del Litto and E. Abravanel. H. Martineau also prepared the excellent Pléiade edition of Stendhal's principal works, including a volume of the *Correspondance* (from 1800 to 1831) which he edited with V. del Litto.

Criticism. Making excellent use of the fundamental research of H. Martineau and following the course charted by J. Prévost, *La Création chez Stendhal* (1942, 1951), and M. Bardèche, *Stendhal romancier* (1946), G. Blin has produced the most thorough and penetrating analyses in *Stendhal et les problèmes du roman* (1953) and *Stendhal et les problèmes de la personnalité* (vol. i, 1958; vol. ii to appear in 1968). Illuminating chapters can be found in E. Auerbach, *Mimesis* (1946); I. Howe, *Politics and the Novel* (1957); H. Levin, *The Gates of Horn* (1963); G. Lukács, *Studies in European Realism* (1950); M. Turnell, *The Novel in France*

(1950). Useful studies include J. Atherton, *Stendhal* (1965); V. Brombert, *Stendhal et la voie oblique* (1954); F. W. J. Hemmings, *Stendhal, a Study of his Novels* (1964). V. del Litto, *La Vie de Stendhal* (1965), H. Martineau, *L'Œuvre de Stendhal: histoire de ses livres et de sa pensée* (1945), and P. Martino, *Stendhal* (1934) are among the better biographical studies. The social background to Stendhal's work is considered by F. Rude, *Stendhal et la pensée sociale de son temps* (1967), while recent books in English are Joanna Richardson, *Stendhal* (1974), G. Strickland, *Stendhal: the Education of a Novelist* (1974), and Margaret G. Tillett, *Stendhal: the Background to the Novels* (1971). Stendhal bibliographies are published periodically by V. del Litto.

6. Romanticism and History

IF a serious literary critic had had to consider history as a worth-while pursuit before 1800, he might well have placed it, aesthetically, in a niche between the funeral oration and the philosophical treatise, and said that its purpose was an eloquent chronological account of recorded events. By 1830 it had undergone a swelling change and was buttressed by careful discussions of method and purpose, while at the same time imaginative literature had become increasingly affected by a kind of knowledge towards which it had previously remained aloof. 'Par une sorte de *fusion* qui a produit la *confusion*', wrote Vigny to posterity in that historical genre so fashionable in his time, the artist's journal, 'l'œuvre d'*imagination*, le roman, a emprunté à l'histoire l'*exactitude* et la *réalité* des faits, tandis que l'histoire, œuvre de la *mémoire* et du *jugement*, a pris au roman quelque chose de sa passion, de ses allures tragiques et comiques et ses descriptions détaillées. . . . Or l'historien est coupable et le romancier ne l'est pas.' Here was one aspect of that revolution which, as Renan observed in 1848, 'a changé complète-ment la face des études historiques, ou pour mieux dire qui a fondé l'histoire parmi nous'. And if, after the mid century, history changed yet again, under the challenge of German 'scientific' methods, nevertheless the study of history, as still widely understood today, may reasonably be taken to have been born in the early nineteenth century, and some of its purposes and methods to have been formulated then. And certainly an extensive interest in history dates from that time. For all the devoted erudition of the Benedictines, and despite the pregnant examples of Montesquieu and Voltaire, the history of Europe—Rome was another matter—had never attracted widespread attention in France. Quite suddenly after 1815 this situation was transformed. Clamorous demands for history were made by a public for whom memoir-reading very quickly became a passion—so much so that memoirs by Robespierre and Condorcet, by Napoleon's valet and Marie-Antoinette's modiste, were manufactured to satisfy this appetite. Genuine memoirs, too, poured forth, in single volumes or great collections: 160 volumes, edited by Petitot and Guizot, concerned with the kingdom of France before 1660; 26 on the English revolution; 80 or more on that in France. Meanwhile Augustin Thierry, Barante and Quinet, Mignet and Guizot, Thiers and Michelet began to draw attentive audiences to their lectures, eager readers to their books. Forty million pages of history, Stendhal's uncle estimated, were printed in 1825, as against three million in 1811.

There is no single explanation for this, and the multiple reasons one can proffer combine in different blends as one considers this or that section of the public, or as one moves through time: for it was a rapidly changing concept of history, and not a single fashion, that earned recognition. Men were now more curious about the past. Thierry, one of the foremost theoreticians active in this historical revolution, suggested that in the relatively humdrum days of the Restoration there was time for inquiry, whereas under the Empire action rather than contemplation had been the necessity of the hour. Besides, the cataclysmic years just past forced men to face the fact of change. A society that in living memory had seemed so stable that it was assumed by some to have extended back indefinitely had suddenly jolted through a series of violent shifts; national frontiers had bubbled out and collapsed; religion, property, even the Gregorian calendar had been proved impermanent. It was now impossible for ordinary educated men to think in static terms as they could when no clearly recognizable shift occurred within the lifetime of one observer. Acutely aware of change, it was natural for them to think in historical terms.

But a sense of transience can have other outlets: in Romantic poetry we see it expressed as an awareness of change in love and weather, of life giving way to death; and social Utopian thinkers, speculating about the future, were encouraged to do so by the fact of change in recent memory. This turn to the past, and not only to the immediate past, but to history as a whole, needs to be explained in more general terms.

It must first be pointed out, though this is a generalization rather than an explanation, that the French Revolution only finally consummated the turn, long preparing in the European consciousness, from ideas to facts. The eighteenth century in its down-to-earthness had already questioned the value of universals, and the old Christian suspicion of the impure material world. And to those who still doubted, the Terror proved conclusively that purely rational attempts to build up a model for life and government were ill-fated: they had not equipped France to deal with the malignant forces that had submerged her. History was one aspect of the growing tendency to grasp reality in its diversity through an empirical study of objective facts, now that so many ideals had exploded.

A new trend of thought needs guiding principles. As usually happens, these appeared simultaneously from several quarters; yet it is more than mere convenience that often points to two significant sources, the work of the German Herder, *Philosophy of the History of Humanity* (1791), and that of the Italian Vico, *Principles of Historical Philosophy* (1744), since both were translated into French in 1827, the first by Quinet, the second by Michelet. The significance of Herder, whose works are said to have prompted Goethe, and through him Walter Scott, to make extensive imaginative use of history for the first time, lies in his break with the traditional conception of the past as a number of brilliant periods separated by barbarism. Societies, he said, did not all seek the same static perfection, but developed organically one from another in a sequence determined by cause and effect. His comparison, incidentally, between the history of human society and the growth of an individual man was to be essential to the imagery of Romantic poetry. From his conception of the past stemmed the plan for a synoptic explanation of civilizations by what went before, together with the theory, already sketched out by Montesquieu, that all the different features of a period or civilization were linked mystically in the 'atmosphere of the epoch', or the 'national character'. After Herder it was possible to explain the national present by the national past. The ideas of Vico were more general, but in a sense complementary. First, all primitive cultures were the same, and developed according to similar laws but in various circumstances; second, the history of their transformations is that of a steady improvement of men and their institutions. Hence Vigny's request, in 1827, for 'l'étude du destin *général* des sociétés'; hence too the general thesis of Chateaubriand's *Génie du christianisme*—that, contrary to what had often been said, Man had progressed since antiquity.

Progress, development—these were not abstract considerations kept for the study, but concepts rehearsed and disputed as men confronted with the fact of the Restoration defined their own attitudes to it and to that recent tumultuous past which the Bourbons, largely, sought to reject. Here three tendencies may be discerned. The first, best illustrated by Chateaubriand, was that of men who, having witnessed France torn apart and Europe convulsed for a generation, needed to explain to themselves how it had happened. Besides, their intellectual optimism, inherited from Condorcet and Helvétius, urged them to salvage the achievements of the Revolution from the general disgust at the Terror, by comparing elements in it with other more reputable revolutions. In the spirit of Chateaubriand's early *Essai sur les Révolutions* (1797) all the main historians attempted to explain either the English revolutions (Villemain, 1819; Guizot, 1826–7) or the French ones (Mignet, 1824; Thiers, 1823–7; Michelet, 1847–53). Time and again in Romantic writings sententious phrases such as 'dans les époques des révolutions' occur, and they express the very same search for lost confidence.

The second tendency is closely linked with the attitude of the aristocrats who returned in 1815, having 'understood nothing, forgotten nothing'. To them the recent past was an appalling aberration, an opinion that could best be justified by demonstrating what the proper order of things had been in history. The more perceptive (Vigny represents them) realized that their position in the new order was a fated anachronism, but nevertheless wished to celebrate the glories of the bygone system in which they would have had a place. Louis XVIII's and especially Charles X's governments were eager to associate themselves with any memory of past Bourbon glory, for instance by brilliant performances of seventeenth-century drama at Court; while the aristocrats back from an ignominious exile turned all the more readily to memoirs concerning episodes (the Fronde, the wars of religion, even the Crusades) in which their ancestors had apparently played a more scintillating role. Furthermore, Napoleon had inaugurated the era of official propaganda with a picturesque national mythology, and there was an obvious political advantage to be gained by refurbishing a few colourful royalist legends such as those of Saint-Louis and Joan of Arc: both were the subjects of plays performed in Paris in 1818. The aristocracy sought roots even for its literary activity in the distant past. Several young writers, among them Hugo, were encouraged in their vocation by the revival of interest in the troubadours and sixteenth-century poets, most of whom had been aristocrats, some even princes. The 1821 'prospectus' of the ultra-monarchic and classical Société Royale des Bonnes Lettres (where what was to be the first Romantic *cénacle*, consisting of Chateaubriand, Deschamps, Hugo, Lamartine, Nodier, Vigny, associated itself unashamedly with most of the aristocratic members of the Académie) stresses the importance of preserving the literature of the past, then finds political grounds for historical studies in that they teach the people 'les rapports qu'il y a entre les institutions présentes et les institutions anciennes. Il faut leur apprendre que la patrie, ou d'après le sens littéral du mot, le pays des aïeux, n'existe pas dans le sol, mais dans les souvenirs; que la gloire d'un peuple ne se trouve que dans ses annales, et que l'expérience, si nécessaire aujourd'hui, est dans la mémoire des temps passés.' Memoirs, usually arranged by reigns, are appropriate if not always edifying fodder for such hopes.

But those who knew their Mme de Staël could answer that liberty had as fine a pedigree and was as much a part of France as the Bourbons. This was the attitude of that third group of intellectuals whose main concern was the building of the future in accordance with lessons learned from the past, a past which included the Revolution. This too was a political posture, and two of the outstanding historians of the time were, indeed, active politicians: Thiers and Guizot. And there were good reasons why they should choose to express themselves in historical works. First, purely ideological argument had been largely discredited during the Revolution; secondly, if one's opponents were citing the past in support of their theories in the Chambers, in pamphlets, and in the Press, then one could not be outdone; thirdly, the stringent literary censorship that operated almost continuously until the Third Republic, with short gaps only in 1830-1 and 1848-50, made it necessary for liberal thought, indeed sometimes any real political thought, to camouflage its references to the present. When Mérimée, who, together with Stendhal, led the liberal group of Romantics in the 1820s, published, during the reign of Charles X, a historical study of France's weakest and most unfortunate king, the *Chronique du règne de Charles IX* (1829), only the censor can have been misled. And in all the accounts of troubled times, which were legion, one recognizes clearly the situations of the period 1789-1830.

The enormous impact of the Revolution on historical writing made for a predominant interest in periods of transition. Significantly, not until 1856 did Tocqueville, in his *L'Ancien Régime et la Révolution*, compare two forms of society, rather than analyse the machinery of change. The Romantics for their part seized upon transience and the attendant feelings of nostalgia and regret as eminently suited to the uncontrolled emotional treatment now fashionable in poetry: so that even when they looked back towards feudalism, chivalry, and the spiritual security of the Christian Middle Ages, or to the political or cultural hegemony of their nation or class, they still usually pictured these things against the decline and fall of some lost cause.

On the specifically literary scene, France was no longer the 'onlie begetter' of the arts. In the same year, 1820, for instance, translations were published of Goethe, Schiller, and Shakespeare; all three playwrights used national historical material for its own sake (and all three belonged to the winning side at Waterloo). Over a total of ten months, between 1827 and 1829, Kean's company performed Shakespeare in English on the Parisian stage, and one of the most widely acclaimed pieces was *Richard III*. Meanwhile, the novel was electrified by the success of Walter Scott. Stendhal ironically tells, in *Racine et Shakespeare* (1823, 1825), how respectable literary circles scoffed at the historical novel and at Chateaubriand's paltry attempt, in the preface to *Les Martyrs* (1809), to find in Aristotle authority for calling his work a prose epic—until they learned that Scott's British publisher had died a millionaire,

and therefore decided that the time had come to put into practice
the Romantic principle of writing to suit present-day taste. From
1820 onwards Scott's novels were translated as they appeared;
there were costume balls à la Scott, members of secret societies
chose the names of his characters as pseudonyms; Heine noted that
30 paintings in the salon of 1830 had been directly inspired by him.
Here were dramatic, eminently readable stories appealing both to
'romantic' imagination and to the current taste for the concrete
through their detailed descriptions of period buildings and costumes.
They appealed, also, to that wider public which now sought in
literature relaxation and entertainment rather than prestige;
besides, to use a Marxist notion, the rising middle class was seeking
its roots, and historical panoramas now were likely to mention the
crowds who were kept out of sight in the old aristocratic tragedy.

Partly for these reasons, partly too because of a structural evolution, both the novel and the drama were in a receptive state at this
time. The former had still not answered satisfactorily the old
accusation of untruth and the subsequent charge of immorality.
Real-life portraits (for which the novelist could be sued), or elbow-
shoving à la Sterne, were not respectable enough; the novel by
letter and the forged autobiography prolonged the fable that novels
were based on fact, but only through the tacit understanding that
they were genuine stories with the names changed (*La Nouvelle
Héloïse*, *Adolphe*). History brought two advantages: first, a morally
impregnable framework of harmless facts within which romanesque
invention, the constant if unavowed mainspring of interest, was
permissible; second, an omniscient narrative technique—instead
of pretending to be writing a diary or to have discovered a drawer-
full of letters, the novelist could now play at being a historian, a far
more respectable fantasy. The device was not entirely new: Mme
de La Fayette had written ostensibly about a former reign; *Fara-
mond*, a seventeenth-century novel by La Calprenède, in a style
borrowed from Plutarch and Xenophon, had been sub-titled
'Histoire de France'. But 'history' here was a grandiose name for a
mere device; only after their great flowering in the early nineteenth
century could historical studies be a really worthwhile patron for
the novel.

It was, at any rate, with these claims in mind that Vigny attempted to justify *Cinq-Mars*, by prefacing it with some 'Réflexions sur la vérité dans l'art'. Assuming, he writes, that it will be of use to the reader to know of the decline of the feudal system in seventeenth-century France, a novel is a more palatable pill to swallow. Besides, historical accounts are frequently too diluted to provide practical lessons, and thus the novelist's generalizations about 'le vrai' will be in a sense truer than 'le vrai visible' of the historian. What is more, the historian must both narrate and interpret, whereas the novelist can give free rein to 'ce grand bon sens qu'est le génie'. It will be noticed first that Vigny's argument is practically circular, and secondly that what he describes as the difference between the historical novel and history is also the line dividing two conflicting conceptions of history whose merits were being debated at this very time in the prefaces of Thierry, Guizot, and their colleagues. Obviously, fiction in a historical setting and historical narrative were by no means clearly distinct in some people's minds. Thierry's *Récits des temps mérovingiens* included as much fantasy as fact; and Barante, the author of the dramatized *Histoire des ducs de Bourgogne*, helped to popularize the phrase 'couleur locale'.

The theatre is not so organically linked with history, from which it can only borrow plots and personalities—yet the 'drame histori-que' too was one of the banners of the new movement. The controversies of the seventeenth century had long settled that history should be quoted in learned prefaces and used in its outline to give a glitter of 'vraisemblance' to a play, but that dramatists had a free hand in interpreting motivation, which history in any case rarely analysed. Ironically, these debates, originally prompted by a mistrust of imagination, had finally led, in the eighteenth century, to the abuse of history as a formal excuse for 'romanesque' plots. Therefore the new emergence of historical material under the Restoration gave the theatre a chance to renew its discredited sources. The abbé Duclos had perhaps been right to suggest that this is a regular cycle: fiction must periodically pay homage to truth. Indeed, Musset remarked that the change in fashion boiled down to calling one's characters Charlemagne, François I, or Henri III, instead of Amadis, Oronte, or Saint-Albin.

Yet the very nature of the new history was to change the kind of subjects staged. For one thing they had to be more 'democratic': a critic remarked in 1826 that no play could qualify as Romantic if it did not include at least one scene on the barricades. An audience who had heard the crowd yelling in the streets was no longer to be fooled by rosy pictures of civil wars decided in ladies' antechambers. The other feature was that most of the new material related to French history—and this fitted the principle, learnt from Shakespeare, Schiller, Mme de Staël, Stendhal, that the new literatures should be concerned with national subjects instead of the common Graeco-Roman inheritance. It was even suggested, though no one achieved quite such modernity, that France could find material for its own *Iliad* in the exploits of Kléber, Murat, or Desaix. These were heroes, *our* heroes, the heroes of France, of *our* nation—a nation with roots, with a glorious past. And Frenchmen were not unique in possessing such pride. All over Europe nationalistic sentiments had been galvanized by the trumpeting of the revolutionary principle of self-determination, and fed by patriotic reactions to Napoleon's rapacity and the assault which his Empire made on old customs and laws, on frontiers and institutions. Nationalistic sentiments, the very concept, indeed, of 'nation', foster the study of origins, encourage (and are encouraged by) publications such as Marchangy's *La Gaule poétique* (1813-17), a series of drafts for plays and poems on France before 1600, seen as the cradle of modern poetry. Here again we find a literary theory marrying with the subject-matter and preoccupations of some of the new historical inquiries, without our being able to tell whether one was cause and the other effect. Herder's suggestion that a whole civilization could be shaped by one of its primitive poets (his examples were Homer and the Old Testament) led the Romantics not only to write 'primitive' poetry, but to want to be considered subsequently as the prophets of their nation and culture. For the Christian revivalists such as Chateaubriand, and to some extent Hugo, this might be achieved by writing in praise of primitive and medieval Christianity since the classical blinkers had prevented anyone doing this before —hence *Le Génie du christianisme* (1802) and the original framework of *La Légende des siècles* (1859, 1877, 1883). The more secular and progressive believed that the Revolution would provide the imagery for the religion of the future: Vigny's *Stello* is, amongst other things, a self-conscious rendering of recent history for future use as a myth.

Romantic pulp literature had perhaps as great an influence on historical writing as Herder's lofty principles, but it, too, can be profitably described as a function of the society in which it appeared. One of the crosses the new movement had to bear was its association with the vogue for 'blood and thunder' fiction, labelled at the time 'roman frénétique'; here, as one still sees in present-day horror films, the historical setting is merely an excuse for pictures of depravity and violence. Fear breeds on the unknown, and a defence mechanism leads bourgeois audiences in particular to want to believe that such hair-raising events as they revel in could not occur in their enlightened times. Eugène Süe was to dispel effectively in *Les Mystères de Paris* (1842–3) the illusion fostered by Hugo's *Notre-Dame de Paris* (1831) by 'revealing', to a public who had secretly known it all along, that horror and crime were in the present. But for some time, the new material satisfied the popular taste: memoirs usually refer to troubled times, and of course the Romantics wanted all passions to be developed to the full. The very same unhealthy interest in blood and horrors that inspired the 'roman frénétique' accounts to a great extent for Hugo's long and boring, but seething and cankering *Notre-Dame*, and for the luxurious catalogues of brutalities that make up Mérimée's *Chronique du règne de Charles IX* or his later *Histoire de don Pèdre I er, roi de Castille*. And we should not forget that even memoirs may serve, like Job's lament, not so much to prompt philosophic thoughts on the destiny of men as to provide the reassuring spectacle of others suffering and failing—and beheaded too.

Though straight history too undoubtedly had its roots in contemporary quarrels and memories, it very quickly reached a different and more serious pitch. Thierry confessed that in 1817 he had turned to historical works to find corroboration of his political beliefs. Mignet and Thiers also consciously searched for ammunition to use against the regime. But later, their consciences pricked,

such liberals often returned to the discovery of the past for less
crude reasons.

Guizot, for instance, was a committed 'liberal', and might be
read with comfort by men of his persuasion. But there was more to
it than this when his magisterial lectures were acclaimed. Here was
a supremely intelligent attempt to answer two great questions pre-
occupying that change-conscious generation—'D'où venons-nous,
où allons-nous?' And yet his answers could not satisfy every
inquirer. One of Chateaubriand's complaints about the older
historians had been that when they had produced conclusions,
these were only too often conducive to a fatalistic attitude. Sainte-
Beuve criticized Guizot in the same spirit because his history, 'sans
faits, sans dates, sans noms', seemed 'too logical to be true'. As
Vigny perspicaciously observed, this was a time when many felt in
their hearts 'deux besoins qui semblent opposés, mais qui se confondent . . . dans une source commune, l'un est l'amour du vrai,
l'autre du fabuleux'. There was nothing of the latter in Guizot nor
in the 'well-manufactured gridiron' (Carlyle's phrase) of Mignet's
history. And as for 'le vrai', was not the past more 'knobbly', more
awkward than it appeared in the inexorable, fatalistic prose of
Guizot? Certainly these were not historians of the old style—Velly
or Anquetil 'embaumant [Manzoni's phrase] avec leur encre les
entreprises des princes et potentats'. But even if princes were not
their sole subject-matter, where were the people, the living masses
who had erupted in '89 and who had been there, pullulating, active,
for long centuries? 'Existe-t-il une histoire de France qui repro-
duise avec fidélité les idées, les sentiments, les mœurs des hommes
qui nous ont transmis le nom que nous portons et dont la destinée
a préparé la nôtre?' Thierry was quite entitled to answer, in 1820:
'Je ne le pense pas.' And where could it be found, '[cette] vraie
histoire nationale, celle qui mériterait de devenir populaire'? 'Dans
la poussière des chroniques contemporaines . . . [d'où] personne
[encore] ne songe à l'en tirer.'

In the course of the next twenty years, however, many did turn
to these chronicles whose texts were being assiduously reprinted and
read by a public which was devouring Scott and had savoured the
picturesque, the concrete, living descriptions in Chateaubriand's

Martyrs. 'Le roman', observed Barante, 'a été absorbé par l'intérêt historique. . . . Une telle disposition des esprits doit encourager à écrire l'histoire'—and preferably colourful, 'realistic' history. In 1824 Thierry planned a thirty-volume *Histoire de France* unmarred by comment and modern reflections, a history taken from chronicles which would be 'la représentation immédiate du passé'. It was never published, but Thierry himself and Barante, with their *Conquête de l'Angleterre* and the twelve-volume *Histoire des ducs de Bourgogne* showed what could be done with a combination of old chronicles and latter-day imagination. 'Il y a sept cents ans', wrote Thierry, 'que ces hommes ne sont plus, que leurs cœurs ont cessé de battre pour l'orgueil ou pour la souffrance; mais qu'importe à l'imagination? Pour elle il n'y a point de passé. . . .'

Imagination could, of course, if it was uncurbed, easily lead the historian away from that truth which it was his duty to try to attain; and chronicles had their limitations and demanded from the historian that critical scrutiny which was increasingly recognized as essential. But the great thing was that an impulse had been generated to go to the sources, to listen and learn with sympathy, to study the archives which were being listed and published and classified all over France in the 1830s. 'Armée de documents certains qu'ignore [la chronique], l'histoire'—and the personified image is typical of its author, Michelet—'la tient, pour ainsi dire, sur ses genoux comme un petit enfant dont elle écoute volontiers le babil, mais qu'il lui faut souvent reprendre et démentir.' The facts of the past were re-emerging in ever increasing quantities now, yet not to the detriment of the power to recreate, to reanimate the living past. It was his ability to 'resurrect' (to use his own word) the past, a past crammed with detail and colour, which made Michelet's *Histoire de France* so popular with his generation. Here was a history of a people in all its rich diversity, and yet no mere ragbag of picturesque details, but as full of those 'vues d'ensemble' as it was the result of erudition. And his history was the story of France, of a nation made not by its kings or its church or its soil, though these were powerful influences, but made by herself—her own creation through the centuries. 'L'histoire est un roman', Vigny had said, 'dont le peuple est l'auteur.' Here at last were the people enthroned as the hero of a vast achievement. 'La France a fait la France . . . [car] dans le progrès humain la part essentielle est à la force vive, qu'on appelle homme. L'homme est son propre Prométhée.' No wonder George Sand approved, exulting: 'Vous élevez les cœurs dès que vous placez les faits de l'histoire sous nos yeux. Vous ne touchez point au passé sans nous faire embrasser les pensées qui doivent nous guider vers l'avenir.'

No wonder, either, that almost at once it was questioned whether Michelet's vision was really anchored in the documents. Referring to vol. iii of Michelet's work, Thierry understandably suggested in some alarm that perhaps history had here 'passé du domaine de l'analyse et de l'observation exacte dans celui des hardiesses synthétiques'. In this type of history there is certainly too much sensibility, too little objectivity, too much premature synthesis, not enough scrupulous analysis. And yet this manner of approach has its relevance in part of the legacy left by the revolution in historical studies which took place in France. That legacy did not merely consist of institutions—chairs, government commissions publishing documents, learned societies with their journals. It also consisted in part of an example, a grandiose purpose, and an approach. First, the historian had to go to the documents of the age he studied; this was the age of 'la première ruée vers les archives', followed by a growing concern for the way in which documents should be scrutinized. Secondly, Michelet had proclaimed as the seductive purpose '[la] résurrection de la vie intégrale [du passé]'. And thirdly, historians began to reconstruct by using their imaginations. Vigny of course was right: too many historians of the time were guilty of coming too close to the style and methods of the novelist; but nevertheless, for all its dangers, the 'resurrectionist' approach had its positive lessons for the future. As well as 'science', accuracy, and objectivity, the historian needs a dose of imaginative sympathy —not so strong as to curb the all-important search for the truth, but enough for him to begin to understand and not merely see. He needs a living sense of the past. 'Et en ce sens', to quote one of Michelet's own teachers, Villemain, 'l'on peut dire que [l'historien] a besoin d'être poète, non seulement pour être éloquent, mais pour être vrai.'

But too strong a dose of poetry meant that much of the history written then is no longer acceptable as such (save, perhaps, in the case of Michelet, by over-patriotic Frenchmen); though it partly explains the wide audience of the time. Boring chronicles of kings and battles were avoided, but only for certain 'romantic' individuals to be overstressed or wrongly stressed. In France as all over Europe, 'national romanticism' fed dangerously and over-confidently on national historians. Also, where poetry was indeed made to serve eloquence, this could hardly lead to level-headed conclusions, but rather to the dangerous recourse to aesthetic rather than exact standards in determining the interest of a piece of historical evidence.

Nevertheless, history did take two real steps forward during this period of cross-fertilization. First, the obvious threats to historical impartiality and the great attention paid to history for the first time by literary critics led to the first comprehensive and public debate in France on methodology, which is still of interest to historians today. Secondly, 'couleur locale', at least in part developed by Romantic writers, caused the historians themselves—sometimes for the wrong reasons and always imperfectly, for lack of proper tools, but for the eventual good of their science—to make imaginative use of environmental factors in historical explanation.

History's gifts in return to imaginative literature were equally ambiguous. They certainly did not, as the Romantics had hoped, endow it with any lasting charm. The historical drama, for instance, was short-lived. For one thing, revolutionary crowds are unwieldly on the stage: over half the historical plays of the 1820s and 1830s, including Hugo's *Cromwell* and Musset's *Lorenzaccio*, have never been produced in full. Then an interested audience was not necessarily an informed one, and it is very difficult in the short space of a play to provide enough basic information for any valid ideas on an alien country or epoch to be understandable. Hugo complained that his audiences always had to read the following morning's paper before even grasping the plot. Both these difficulties led naturally to the writing of plays to be read and not acted, and this is a considerable step towards the historical novel. The only alternative was to stress 'couleur locale' merely for the sake of escaping the present. Hugo's plays are a case in point: *Cromwell*, a full scale historical reconstruction, could not be staged; *Marion de Lorme* was convincing with lesser means, but it did not convince the censor that it was really about Louis XIII's reign at all; *Hernani*, his first success, puts forward a real, if clumsy, theory on an individual, but in doing so neglects all historical atmosphere beyond the most superficial features; *Ruy Blas* succeeds purely because of its human and dramatic interest—it is no more informed an image of historical Spain than *Le Cid*. Meanwhile, less worthy dramatists were tempted to use history for its easy pageantry. The vague and hollow associations of great names became, for Scribe, merely a backcloth against which he demonstrated (many times) how small details such as a glass of water can change the outward course of events—such subjects are obviously of manageable dramatic size, but no longer of historical interest.

Other difficulties were common to plays and novels. The first derive from the Romantic conception of the hero. He must stand above the crowd, for he is a projection of that aloof aristocratic figure, the Romantic poet; but when the crowd is a revolutionary one (it usually is), he is led to despise its shouts and passions—so that works appearing to revel in progress are led to present a reactionary image of the people. The hero, whether imaginary or, worse, real, must also stand foremost among the other figures, and as a result there is always either too much history or not enough of it: either history is distorted to serve a fashionable psychological or social pattern, or complete verisimilitude is made impossible by hard historical facts that cannot entirely be left out. This dilemma spoils even the carefully documented and purposeful *Cinq-Mars*, where Richelieu is grossly over-romanticized and Cinq-Mars's historical career is too contradictory to make for a satisfactory plot. 'The crowd', wrote Hugo, 'will read it as a novel, the statesman as history.' Unfortunately it was too expensive for the crowd to buy, and statesmen who knew their memoirs had no need for it. Theoretically, of course, Hugo's point was still worth making. The casual reader of a novel can retain a far more human and vivid image of, say, war or slavery, which might otherwise be no more than abstract problems. Hugo's own *Bug-Jargal* was a good instance. But an essential danger remains: even if the novelist is genuinely exercising the critical judgement of a historian, which must be rare, his reader is still at a lower level of critical awareness than he would be if reading a book of history.

Besides, the critic in search of works of permanent value has an ambiguous task here; Romanticism itself has taught us that the novelist continually fails to disguise his own experience, which, whatever his erudition, is essentially of his own time, so that historical novels and plays are usually not really 'about' what they pretend to be. *Ruy Blas* was an idea of Rousseau's in fancy dress; Vigny's 'populace' clamouring at the trial of Urbain Grandier is the self-same crowd of extras who are dressed up as 'medievals' at the foot of Hugo's Notre-Dame—in real life they are *sans-culottes* of 1793 or *canuts* of 1834; d'Artagnan, the young Gascon musketeer, is only one of the wave of immigrants to Paris in the 1830s and 1840s. These amateur historians, to an even greater extent than the professionals, look into the past through lenses shaped by their own age.

Where they recognize this, it can become a virtue; it is significant that the four historical novels of this period that can still claim an audience are *Servitude et grandeur militaires*, *Stello*, *Les Chouans*, and *Quatre-vingt-treize*. They have an obvious feature in common: they partly dropped the cloak of history. All referred to events almost within their author's lifetime. Vigny and Balzac especially (Musset and Hugo worked on secondary sources) had enough first-hand documents or accounts to be able to write as if the events they described belonged to their own, and real, experience. It is equally obvious to us now that this was only the first step. The second is described by Balzac in the *Avant-propos* to the *Comédie humaine*: 'La Société française allait être l'historien, je ne devais être que le secrétaire. . . . Avec beaucoup de courage, je réaliserais, sur la France au 19ᵉ siècle, ce livre que nous regrettons tous que Rome, Athènes, Tyr, Memphis, la Perse, l'Inde, ne nous ont malheureusement pas laissé sur leurs civilisations.' Stendhal, as usual with less emphasis but equal point, had already subtitled *Le Rouge et le Noir*, published in 1831, 'Chronique de 1830'. Novelists, indeed, soon gave up trying to be historians and decided instead to write historical documents.

NOTE

Historians' attitudes to the past, like those of other writers, changed rapidly in the course of the early nineteenth century—and Europeans generally became 'historical' in their thinking. G. P. Gooch, *History and Historians in the Nineteenth Century* (2nd ed., 1952), considers this revolution in Germany and England as well as in France, whereas L. Halphen and P. Moreau concentrate on France—(Halphen) *L'Histoire en France depuis cent ans* (1914) and (Moreau) *L'Histoire en France au XIXᵉ siècle* (1935). A more succinct account is provided in the introduction to a book which has gone through several editions since it appeared in 1897, C. Jullian, *Extraits des historiens français du XIXᵉ siècle*. Here passages are reprinted from some of the works which are exemplars of, or milestones in, this historiographical revolution. Such works include, for example, Jules Michelet's *Histoire romaine* (2 vols., 1831); *Histoire de la Révolution française* (7 vols., 1847–53); and his monumental *Histoire de France* (17 vols., 1833–67; see the preface to the 1869 edition). This last, or indeed any of the histories mentioned here, may be compared with, say, either the *Histoire de France* of P. F. Velly, etc. (33 vols., 1769–99) or another standard, and typical before-the-revolution-type history, that by L. P. Anquetil (14 vols., 1805). Some other consequential works were F. Guizot, *Essais sur l'histoire de France* (1824), *Histoire de la civilisation en Europe* (1828), and *Histoire de la civilisation en France* (5 vols., 1829–32); E. Quinet, *Les Révolutions d'Italie* (2 vols., 1848–51); F. Mignet, *Histoire de la Révolution française* (2 vols., 1824); A. G. de Barante, *Histoire des ducs de Bourgogne de la maison de Valois* (12 vols., 1824–6); and J. N. A. Thierry, *Récits des temps mérovingiens* (2 vols., 1833–40). Thierry actively encouraged this revolution in attitudes and techniques, and he reflected on it in his *Lettres sur l'histoire de France* (1820—later revised and enlarged), *Dix ans d'études historiques* (1834), and 'Considérations sur l'histoire de France' (written 1838–9, and printed in his *Temps mérovingiens*).

Revolutions, or changing societies, are an essential preoccupation of these works and also feature predominantly in the many historical novels and plays that appeared mainly between 1820 and 1835: the fall of the Roman Empire (Chateaubriand, *Les Martyrs*, 1809), medieval uprisings (Mérimée, *La Jacquerie*, 1828; Hugo, *Notre-Dame de Paris*, 1831), the troubled politics of the Renaissance (Musset, *Lorenzaccio*, 1834), the French wars of religion (Dumas *père* was one of five playwrights to write on Henri III in 1826–30), the Fronde (Vigny, *Cinq-Mars*, 1826 and *La Maréchale d'Ancre*, 1831; Hugo, *Marion de Lorme*, 1831), the English revolutions (*Cromwell* by Mérimée, 1824; by Hugo, 1828), the French revolutions (Balzac, *Les Chouans*, 1829; Vigny, *Stello*, 1831; Hugo, *Quatre-vingt-treize*, 1874), even the Dominican slave revolt of 1804 (Hugo, *Bug-Jargal*, 2nd ed., 1826).

For some interesting general views on the relationship between history and Romantic literature see E. Neff, *The Poetry of History* (1947), and G. Lukács, *The Historical Novel* (1962).

7. Balzac

THE spirited opening of Dickens's *Hard Times* is memorable for its expression of a view so much at variance with the novelist's own comic or pathetic distortions of the natural world:

Now, what I want is, Facts. Teach these boys and girls nothing but Facts. Facts alone are wanted in life. Plant nothing else and root out everything else. You can only form the minds of reasoning animals upon Facts: nothing else will ever be of any service to them . . .

Balzac knew Mr. Gradgrind's world of 'facts' but, like Dickens, his own creative impulse as a writer was to go beyond it. He is not a simple chronicler of the surface movements of society (though he was touched by the prevailing craze for satirical sketches of social types), but an artist struggling to make experience meaningful. Balzac's novels faithfully register significant aspects of the life of French society under the Restoration and July Monarchy, but everything is refracted through a personal vision which reorders the social history of the times in terms that are ultimately satisfying to his sensibility and to his moral and aesthetic sense. In effect, Balzac's fiction is constantly poised between a sociological and a supernatural mode of rendering experience. He is superbly gifted at showing how men are shaped by their social medium, but he also sees them in the perspectives of a larger reality which, for all the vulgarity with which he so often depicts it, we must call 'religious' or, at least, 'sub-religious'.

Much of Balzac's equipment in his familiar role as social novelist comes, of course, from his fascinated scrutiny of his fellow citizens, but this vein of observation is supported by a genuinely reflective intelligence attuned to the contemporary climate of ideas. Thus, he owes something of his vital interest in the economic organization of society to the writings of Utopian socialists like Saint-Simon,

Fourier, and Leroux. In the same way, he is heavily indebted to Walter Scott's Waverley Novels for showing him how the past can be recovered by an art of imaginative synthesis and for revealing man in his public and social aspects, man as shaped by his place and function in society and his relation to a historic past. Balzac does not copy Scott, but it is through coming to grips with Scott's historical romances that he forged his own conception of the novel as the history of contemporary life and learned to dramatize the organic relationship of the present to the recent past. The 'recent past' which Balzac used as the context for a number of his important novels was the period of the Restoration. Nothing is more striking than the sociological tact, the sensitivity to the nuances of economic and social life of the period which are displayed in these novels, unless it is the skill with which economic realities are made to serve as the natural framework for individual characters who perform actions consistent with their nature, in a distinctive fusion of personal and social life.

The idealism of Dr. Benassis in *Le Médecin de campagne* (1833) is rooted very specifically in a half-derelict canton which he makes it his mission to reclaim. Shaken out of inertia by the doctor's energy and practical good sense, this community begins its painful climb to prosperity with the making of a much-needed road connecting it with Grenoble. This humdrum detail illustrates very well how Balzac tends to link his fictional invention (the doctor's earlier desertion of a virtuous woman and his desire to atone for it) to a typical problem of the 'real' world: in this case, the poor internal communications of Restoration France which modern historians judge to be one of the main causes of its economic stagnation. Elsewhere, a memorable episode in *Eugénie Grandet* (1833) further exemplifies Balzac's manner of creating a situation in which a chosen character acts out his given nature at a precise historical moment and within a clearly specified economic and social pattern. The miserly old Grandet, in an episode charged with mystery and excitement (if only because we see it through the innocent eyes of the hidden Eugénie), leaves Saumur at dead of night, in a fast carriage, to convey a keg of his hoarded gold coins to Angers. He has found out that the ship-builders at Nantes need funds for fitting out new vessels and, because of the shortage of ready money, the price of gold is rising among the speculators at Angers. Grandet's secret expedition is thus used as a convenient device for connecting a piece of psychological insight about his avarice and business acumen to an economic and social fact about the Restoration's inadequate system of public credit.

This play of economic self-interest on the part of certain characters is often given additional solidity by being shown as conditioned by a historical process. What frequently happens is that a historical retrospect, occupying the opening chapter or chapters of a Balzac novel, initiates the reader into the earlier life of an individual or social group and serves, because of its quasi-objective status as a narrative summary of the 'real' past, to guarantee the authenticity of the conflicts that follow or, at least, to make them plausible. Again, *Eugénie Grandet* offers a typical example. The novel opens with a masterly short sketch, resting on careful period detail and informing us of Grandet's purchase of confiscated lands ('biens nationaux') under the Revolution of 1789, his profits from supplying wine to the Republican armies, his advantageous marriage to the daughter of a prosperous timber-merchant, and his skill as a time-serving mayor in managing public funds to serve his private interests. As the narrator drily remarks: 'Il avait fait faire, dans l'intérêt de la ville, d'excellents chemins qui menaient à ses propriétés.' The relationship between the movement of history and the course of private fortunes is here established with deft economy, and Grandet emerges both as an opportunistic and astute individual and as a characteristic product of his times. The novel's principal intrigues, and his part in them, consequently appear to stem naturally from a living past.

The life of society, as Balzac describes it, is so nearly inexhaustible in its historical resonances, in the variety of its urban and rural scenes, its kinds of furniture and architecture, its range of trades and professions, its dense web of personal and family bonds, that we must see it as the central and animating force of *La Comédie humaine*. Indeed, the collective life of society not only provides a continuum for the characters who reappear at different points in Balzac's fictional scheme, but is itself a 'character' that endures, rivalling in interest the vicissitudes of individual lives and surviving changes of regime, local strains and conflicts, and the erosion of private ambition and appetite.

Nowhere, perhaps, is this collective life more strongly felt, and nowhere does the idea of the novel as an imaginative sociology impose itself more forcibly on us than in *Les Paysans* (1844-55), the novel left unfinished at Balzac's death and completed from his rough proofs. The plot of *Les Paysans* is almost schematic in the degree to which it makes characters serve as convenient embodiments of more general conflicts affecting three well-defined social groups. The first is represented by the Comte de Montcornet, a retired and *nouveau riche* Napoleonic general of plebeian origins who buys up the country estate of Les Aigues in Burgundy, together with its château and handsome park, and who typifies the interests of the great landowner. This new lord of the manor, lacking the authority which birth and custom had conferred on the nobility of the old regime, is soon subjected to a guerilla war of poaching, thieving, intimidation, and violence at the hands of the sly and greedy peasant-proprietors of the neighbourhood, avid to dismember the estate so as to enlarge their own holdings. They are backed by the sinister and powerful money-lender, Rigou, and secretly supported by the middle-class notables and politicians of the nearby towns. The peasants' campaign of violence and depredation reaches a climax with the death of Montcornet's faithful estate-warden, Michaud, and with Montcornet's own virtual capitulation. He is forced to sell at a loss to Rigou who accommodates his middle-class allies by sharing some of the estate with them while he splits up the rest into small lots and makes them over to the peasants at extortionate rates of interest. The capitalist speculator triumphs, a neo-feudal tradition of social obligation is defeated, and the peasants exchange one master for another, at least as exigent as the first and less involved in their daily concerns.

In spite of some lively portraiture of the more wily and subversive peasants—the cunning and promiscuous Tonsard family at the local inn, or the conniving ex-schoolmaster, père Fourchon— *Les Paysans* does not derive its main interest from the skill with which Balzac handles the psychology of individuals, but from his understanding of the grosser influences that shape men's lives. *Les Paysans* is pre-eminently about collective issues—the decline of the old aristocracy, the Revolutionary land settlement, the problem of authority—and about large, impersonal forces which condition men's behaviour, such as the pressures of a rural environment or the group-psychology of the peasantry. For these reasons, it is easy to see why this novel has remained a favourite with Marxist critics, even when they dissent from the conservative values it implies. Indeed, in showing how capitalism, in the form of Rigou, replaces a living social bond by what Marx termed the cash-nexus, Balzac's analysis approaches that of Marxism. And yet, a closer look at the novel in its more purely imaginative aspects suggests that, for all the weight of sober sociological detail, it is chiefly moved by powerful images, the total effect of which is to create a fundamentally un-Marxist picture of social conflict.

Some sense of how this image-making faculty threatens by its power to distort or even displace the specifically social analysis is already present in the preface to *Les Paysans* with its highly emotive references to the peasants. The peasantry is either a conspiracy ('la conspiration permanente de ceux que nous appelons encore les faibles'), a revolutionary monster ('ce Robespierre à une tête et à vingt millions de bras'), or a sinister rodent undermining the foundations of property ('cet infatigable sapeur, ce rongeur qui morcèle et divise le sol'). These images are reinforced in the course of the narrative. The elaborately developed contrast between the grace and charm of the great house and its superb park and the squalid tavern of the Grand-I-Vert sets the opulent image of an Arcadia of social order and congenial culture against a den or lair whose denizens are constantly diminished to the level of predatory animals, all appetite and cunning. Indeed, the Montcornets' Parisian guest Blondet, a journalist of royalist sympathies, thinks of the local peasants as Fenimore Cooper's redskin savages transposed into a French setting, and the narrator supports this by physical descriptions which caricature their animality: Tonsard's canine teeth and flattened ears and nose, Vermichel's huge swollen head. In the same way, the struggle between landed proprietor and peasants is not seen simply as arising from the defects of a particular

economic system but as a wicked plot in which the animal nature of
the peasants is allied to the diabolical nature of Rigou who is,
significantly, an unfrocked monk, a kind of sub-Lucifer in a provincial setting, and who endows what a Marxist critic would surely
judge to be a purely economic struggle with the dimension of evil.

If Rigou is not conceived as a fully demonic figure in *Les Paysans*
(the potentialities of his role as the embodiment of evil being checked
and contained by the elaborate economic and social detail surrounding him), this dimension is still present, though not as powerfully
rendered as in other novels where the characteristic Balzacian
themes of power, corruption, and evil elude or even transcend
strictly social explanations of human behaviour. Certainly, this
sense of straining beyond the limits of the natural and social worlds
is shown to be not incompatible with Balzac's remarkable flair for
identifying the role of money in modern society. One has only to
recall the leisurely and intricate account of Grandet's liquidation of
his dead brother's debts or the descriptions of the pushing scent-
merchant's battles with his creditors in *Histoire de la grandeur et de
la décadence de César Birotteau* (1837). In these aspects of his art,
Balzac makes us as readers uniquely aware of the cash-nexus and
compels us to see its social and moral consequences in terms of
individual lives rendered so vividly in their material context that
we cannot imagine them anywhere else or at any other period. But
money, seen in these examples as part of banal economic processes,
is also seen as a powerful myth. Usury, speculation, investment,
alliance of private fortunes, all tend to assume in Balzac's work the
status of occult forces shaping the whole life of society, and are
given magical rather than practical influence because they are
connected with wild dreams of power, with brilliant and total
success on the one hand, or utter degradation on the other. Viewed
in this way, they animate a kind of moral melodrama rather than a
pondered social vision, so that, if we compare Balzac with a stren-
uously serious novelist of social and moral life like George Eliot, we
are struck by his enormous theatricality.

The conception of money as an animating spirit is linked in
Balzac to a sharp sense of how frequently the source of money is
tainted. One recalls how his brief topography of the dwellings of the

E

different social classes of Paris (which opens *La Fille aux yeux d'or*, 1834–5) leaves one with an image suggestive of more than inadequate public hygiene: 'La moitié de Paris couche dans les exhalaisons putrides des cours, des rues et des basses œuvres.' The description points to that other underworld of vice and crime upon which the city is built and, though it never attains in Balzac the fully expressive symbolism of the 'Mounds', those huge heaps of refuse and human excrement which loom over the landscape in Dickens's *Our Mutual Friend* and are the origins of Mr. Boffin's wealth, this image serves to characterize the equivocal sources of Parisian life in Balzac's fiction. Indeed, one often encounters in his novels examples of dazzling social figures whose wealth and position derive from fraud or confidence-trick or crime, in much the same way as the social graces of the Popinots' drawing-room in *Le Cousin Pons* (1847) rest on the legal spoliation of the poor, bewildered Schmucke and are bought at the expense of his innocence. The fertile Balzacian notion of the 'vol décent' (of acting criminally *within* the law), which owes so much to observation of the economic sharp practice of the times and which was expressed by him in his early satirical sketch, *Le Code des gens honnêtes* (1825), is here rendered with imaginative force.

To have recognized this principle of social life is the peculiar distinction of the arch-criminal Vautrin who pushes the governing impulse of the acquisitive society to its limit, exploding its contradictions and revealing its moral squalor. By inflating the principles of economic liberalism (Guizot's 'Enrichissez-vous') to the ultimate degree, this sinister and ambiguous figure serves as a curiously Brechtian critic of capitalism. This is made clear in the derisive expression of his political creed which enlivens the pages of *Le Père Goriot* (1834–5) and which combines a sense of outrage at the privileges of wealth and class with a cynical, compensatory gospel of power:

Pourquoi deux mois de prison au dandy qui, dans une nuit, ôte à un enfant la moitié de sa fortune, et pourquoi le bagne au pauvre diable qui vole un billet de mille francs avec les circonstances aggravantes? Voilà vos lois. Il n'y a pas un article qui n'arrive à l'absurde. . . . Méprisez donc les hommes, et voyez les mailles par où on peut passer à travers le réseau du Code. Le secret des grandes fortunes sans cause apparente est un crime oublié, parce qu'il a été proprement fait.

It is illustrated in even more spectacular fashion by the audacious manipulation of law and the machinery of justice which eventually permits Vautrin (in *La Dernière Incarnation de Vautrin*, 1847) to invert all moral authority and replace Bibi-Lupin as head of the criminal police.

The apotheosis of Vautrin, criminal, outcast, and model of destructive energy, takes us beyond explanations of the human adventure that are based on purely social or economic motives. One imagined world here merges imperceptibly with another: the play of economic and social interest recedes so as to reveal, in a fitful and lurid light, a transcendent but equivocal struggle between good and evil—equivocal because the values presented are as uncertain and confused as the distribution of punishments and rewards. No doubt Vautrin's triumph is an extreme case, but it provides a clinching image of the moral ambiguity inherent in much of Balzac's fiction. It frames a great and central contradiction at the heart of the *Comédie humaine*, the contradiction between Balzac's worship of the will and his craving for a satisfying moral and social order. The ambiguous level of reality on which Vautrin moves is intensified for us by the verbal aura with which Balzac surrounds him, an aura that is consciously demonic. He is persistently seen in the light of the stock formulas of the sensational serial novels of the period (such as Eugène Süe's celebrated *Les Mystères de Paris*, 1842-3) and incarnates the folk-villain with paralysing magnetic eyes, super-human strength, and mastery of disguise. This supernatural element in Vautrin is precisely that contrived by Balzac for the appalling concièrge, Madame Cibot, of *Le Cousin Pons*, who makes a tacit pact with Dr. Poulain to influence the dying Pons in her favour and is then projected in a diabolical light: 'cette affreuse lady Macbeth de la rue fut éclairée d'une lueur infernale.'

Nor is this the only or even the most potent melodramatic convention at work in Balzac's *Comédie humaine*. The idea of a mysterious and providential retribution recurs still more per-sistently. It is central to that curious novel *Ursule Mirouet* (1841) which hinges upon the theft of Dr. Minoret's will by the ambitious postmaster Minoret-Levrault. In the end, the virtue of the chaste, if insipid, Ursule is rewarded by marital bliss and a solid income whilst her would-be despoilers are condignly punished. The postmaster's son, Désiré, dies, as foreseen by Ursule in one of four prophetic dreams; his wife goes mad; he himself turns to good works, and the villainous and conniving lawyer's clerk, Goupil, lands up with an ugly wife and deformed children. Here, the rivalry for status and the acquisitive appetites of the protagonists are explored with a genuine feeling for the social realities of the period, but human depravity and materialism are inflated for moralizing purposes and shown to be judged by a larger law of life, depicted only in the most arbitrary and factitious terms. The social analysis may convince us at the level of common experience, but the supernatural elements and edification are offered to us for acceptance on the same basis of plausibility. Admittedly, *Ursule Mirouet* is a bad novel, as was to be expected from a fiction packed with phrenology, second-sight, and mesmerism and which could, without a trace of irony, refer to 'magnetism' as 'the favourite science of Jesus', but its use of retribution as a dramatic device rather than a theological model has unhappy parallels elsewhere. It can be found in the galloping consumption mechanically visited on the passionate and unconventional Louise de Chaulieu in *Mémoires de deux jeunes mariées* (1841-2), in the fate of Rosalie de Watteville, the satanic young forger of *Albert Savarus* (1842), who is mutilated and crippled in an accident, and, not least, in the repulsive deaths engineered in *La Cousine Bette* (1846) for the retired scent-manufacturer Crevel and his depraved mistress, Valérie Marneffe.

No account of Balzac's fictional world can be adequate that does not try to come to terms with the presence within it of this uneasy supernatural realm. In part, Balzac simply responds to notions that are in the air at the time he is writing. The ideas of redemption, regeneration, and atonement, which he recast in forms assimilable to his own eccentric Catholicism, are important period ideas, whether he derives them from the spiritualist system-builders (illuminists like Saint-Martin and Swedenborg, visionaries like

Ballanche) or from his contact with that kind of evangelism about the future unity of mankind which is a feature of the ideologies of Utopian socialism. But, if Balzac shows himself responsive to these key ideas and gives them new (and changed) life in his own novels, it may be because they suggest a possible escape from his political dilemma. He is a severe critic of the anarchy and inhumanity of 'liberal' capitalism who can accept neither the remedies of the Utopian socialists nor, in spite of sympathizing with the humane protest of old-style legitimists like Villeneuve-Bargemont (royalist prefect of the Nord under the Restoration), the attitudes and policies of the surviving French nobility who form the Crown's traditional support. In fact, in his pitiless dissection of the figure of the marquis d'Esgrignon in *Le Cabinet des antiques* (1836-9), Balzac uses an imaginary character to indict the egoism, snobbery, irresponsibility, and political impotence of the aristocracy. Between visionary socialists on the one hand, and blind and incompetent nobles on the other, there is little to choose. It is the lesson W. B. Yeats felt able to draw from his reading of the *Comédie humaine*: 'Balzac who saved me from Jacobin and Jacobite'; an example of one profoundly conservative mind commenting approvingly upon another.

The d'Esgrignons of Balzac's fictional world cannot contain his banker-villains, like Nucingen, who embody the immoral power of money, or his ambitious and unscrupulous journalists, like Étienne Lousteau, who symbolize the debasement of culture to a market commodity. Both visionary and reactionary critics of the new industrial regime are powerless to check the financial, commercial, and professional middle classes who are its real beneficiaries and the legitimate targets of Daumier's savage cartoons. Though these classes are shown to have their merits, their virtues are rarely enough to live by, as the career of César Birotteau implies. The mock-heroic title of the novel in which he appears (with its Gibbonian echo of 'decline and fall'), already suggests as does his grandiose imperial name, something of Balzac's reservations. César is certainly portrayed as a martyr to an ideal of commercial probity, but he is also shown as a jumped-up tradesman infected with the greed and folly of the times. Nor is it easy to believe, at the end of the novel,

that the traditional bourgeois virtues of thrift and industry (em-
bodied in César's wife) represent an adequate or persuasive scale
of values to set against the ferocious pursuit of power and material
possession. The life of trade does not emerge as a sufficient model
of the moral life, and the struggle with creditors to keep out of the
bankruptcy court cannot really aspire to moral grandeur when the
victim has accepted so much of the philosophy of the bigger sharks
who finally swallow him. 'Bankrupt' may be intended to convey
the authentic thrill of horror and to displace other terms of moral
reprobation, but it is too uncertain in the values it implies to
convince us.

There seems no convincing way out of the desert of competitive
greed in Balzac's *Comédie humaine*. The old regime is effectively
dead, the new acceptable in certain respects to one of Balzac's
temperament, but intolerable in others. He responds to its energy
and innovation, its creation of social and economic opportunity
because, in these ways, it is consistent with his own cult of the will;
but he is horrified by its inhumanity, its destruction of valuable
social bonds, its moral bankruptcy. Perhaps Balzac's escape into
melodrama and a sub-religious realm of sin, expiation, regeneration, and retribution is a poetic way out of the impasse confronting
him as a creative writer, part of whom registers the new world of
industrial capitalism, detests it, cannot come to terms with it, and
yet knows he cannot reverse it at the historical level. He transcends
it, so to say, vertically, leaping out of history into religious myth,
out of the re-creation of social experience into a supernatural
dimension which situates that experience in the context of higher
values, invoked in arbitrary fashion so as to restore the moral
balance that has been destroyed by his apostles of the will. Some
part of the pressure behind these scenes of retribution, in which
the moral equilibrium is re-established, derives, no doubt, from
Balzac's sense of guilt at his own fascination with power and fame,
his own complicity with material success and pleasure, but it is
also drawn from his conception of religion as a means of coping
with human depravity rather than a way of releasing the energies
of human love.

The fact is that Balzac is moved by a fundamentally Manichean vision of life in which the forces of evil, the demonic presences, are capable of triumphing over the good. Consequently, the emotional temper of the novels is often that of horror combined with astonished admiration at the power and success of the great demonic figures. The energy of evil tends to win the world and the novels often make it appear natural that it should. One might say that the imaginative logic of novels like *La Dernière Incarnation de Vautrin* demands the triumph of evil. The attempts to qualify this triumph through the intercession of terms of conventional moral reprobation ('horrible' is positively abused in this connection) or through scenes of supernatural retribution are simply not adequate, *in imaginative terms*, to counter the evil that has been evoked with such vividness. Indeed, such scenes offer an uncertain melodramatic device that rarely rises to the level of the sheer expressiveness displayed in the narratives concerned with the progress of the demonic 'heroes'. One has only to recall here how, in *La Rabouilleuse* (1841-3), the death of the near-gangster Philippe Bridau at the hands of Arabs in Algeria is not rendered with anything like enough imaginative force to efface the glitter of his peerage and great wealth or the engrossing will-power that has brought him from next to nothing to a pinnacle of worldly success. The very uncertainty of the retributive device in Balzac's hands is what prompts one to qualify the supernatural dimension in his work as essentially 'sub-religious'. He strains, in fact, to produce the properties of religious belief within a fictional context conspicuously confused in the religious values it displays and not articulated about a body of coherent Christian doctrine or a seriously pondered set of spiritual insights. Finer moral discriminations tend, at these moments in the narrative, to be sacrificed to a Manichean dualism which draws much of its vitality from a long folk tradition, very much in evidence in the melodrama and prose thriller of Balzac's day, through which the popular mind sought, in episodes of crime, pursuit, capture, and punishment, to approximate to the moral and emotional satisfactions of religious myth.

In the sense that they transcend the flat social documentation of 'realists' of the 1850s and 1860s, like Champfleury and Duranty, Balzac's novels are 'idealistic'. Their personal and social action is always related to a larger moral or religious framework, implied when not emphatically stated. Whereas the realists tend to restrict themselves to a kind of photographic reproduction of the physical facts of existence among the depressed classes, with increasing emphasis on low life, Balzac's densely rendered physical settings and economic and social scenes are frequently viewed in the light of what he conceives to be eternal truths, though that light is intermittent. Stylistically, therefore, Balzac's is a technique of distortion, created so as to support an underlying Manichean conflict. Goodness is sentimentally inflated, wickedness made more terrifying and grotesque. It is also a technique of contrast in which sacred and profane, material and spiritual are juxtaposed so as to dramatize their perennial conflict.

When, in *Eugénie Grandet*, Eugénie's nascent love for Charles infuses new colour and life into the straggling garden of her father's house in Saumur, the novelist-narrator cannot resist appealing to a facile rhetoric of sentiment: 'Quand le soleil atteignit un pan de mur d'où tombaient des cheveux-de-Vénus aux feuilles épaisses à couleurs changeantes comme la gorge des pigeons, de célestes rayons d'espérance illuminèrent l'avenir pour Eugénie. . . .' That 'célestes' is a fatal index to Balzac's vulgar confusion of the sacred and profane, his proneness to the 'ineffable' which is, perhaps, the stylistic evidence of his attempts to connect mechanically the material and spiritual worlds. The equivocal effect of this kind of language is reinforced for us by his later comparison between Eugénie's awakening to love and the Virgin Mary's Immaculate Conception. The same straining of language makes itself felt in the sensational scene of *Le Père Goriot* where Vautrin is betrayed to the police at the 'pension Vauquer':

Le bagne avec ses mœurs et son langage, avec ses brusques transitions du plaisant à l'horrible, son épouvantable grandeur, sa familiarité, sa bassesse, fut tout à coup représenté dans cette interpellation et par cet homme, qui ne fut plus un homme, mais le type de toute une nation dégénérée, d'un peuple sauvage et logique, brutal et souple. En un moment Collin devint un poème infernal où se peignirent tous les sentiments humains, moins un seul, celui du repentir. Son regard était celui de l'archange déchu qui veut toujours la guerre.

Here the accumulation of epithets and the ready invocation of supernatural power ('épouvantable grandeur', 'poème infernal', 'archange déchu') are not simply devices for intensifying the emotional impact of the passage. They point by implication to the writer's sense that his language is inadequate to meet the exigencies of the lurid reality in which the world is bathed for him. The verbal energy at work here suggests that Balzac's demonic universe, however vulgarly conceived, necessarily tends to challenge the resources of language, and that the 'ineffable' may perhaps be the only appropriate idiom for this universe.

Balzac's creative struggle with language is not confined to these heightened and melodramatic scenes. It is present too in his rendering of the material setting of his novels. The eighteenth-century picaresque novel and the semi-romanced account of low life do, of course, offer passages of vivid and particularized description, but these are usually incidental or fragmentary, and none of them gives to environment or to physical objects the importance which Balzac accords them in his fictional scheme. As we have seen, Eugénie's love re-orders the familiar garden in a new and glowing perspective, but this is an unusual feature of Balzac's descriptive art. Normally, things in nature or physical objects are not shown in the perspectives created by different moods and sensibilities. Rather, they are revealed in all their stubborn and alien particularity, their objective permanence, as contrasted with the transience of human lives that burn themselves out in pursuit of obsessions. The strength, solidity, and density of Balzac's physical world spring from the energy of the imagination which vivifies them. The inanimate is often animated, the natural world endowed with anthropomorphic life. Objects vibrate with a kind of hidden energy and possess their own aura. All possession of material things in Balzac has something of the quality of sexual possession, so that the abbé Birotteau's coveting of Chapeloud's furniture and effects (in *Le Curé de Tours*, 1832) is not too far removed in feeling from the sensual thrill experienced by the miserly art-collector, Eli Magus, when confronted with the pictures in Pons's collection.

The extended description of material settings is sometimes used by Balzac to explain the nature of the characters who inhabit them.

For example, Grandet's cold, dank house not only offers a kind of metaphor for the moral life played out within its walls, but persuades us, through the detail with which it is described, of an almost organic connection between environment and character. It would, however, be wrong to exaggerate the degree to which Balzac exploits this pseudo-scientific convention. If he borrows the transformist theories of the zoologist, Geoffroy Saint-Hilaire, it is because they confirm his own imaginative insights, lend seriousness to a still uncertain fictional mode, and feed his analogical faculty, rather than because he needs them as a mechanical formula for creating character, though the affinity he develops between human society and the animal kingdom represents a fruitful fictional convention. Indeed, it frequently happens that the elaborate detail with which Balzac renders a given physical setting goes beyond the functional needs of mere representation and even beyond the needs of analogy. He manifests a keen delight in particulars for their own sake and, consequently, his achievement is sometimes purely aesthetic. For example, his rendering of sensuous particulars in the exotic boudoir of *La Fille aux yeux d'or* is so intense that it blurs the scene and almost effaces the human figures. Colour, shape, texture become the proper subjects of this scene as Balzac attempts to recreate verbally something of Delacroix's graphic effects. Similarly, in *Le Père Goriot*, the exhaustive description of the physical structure of the 'maison Vauquer' is initially intended to prepare us for the kind of life lived by its denizens, but this attempt to show the influence of environment is distorted by moments of sheer verbal inventiveness and poetic fancy, as when the furniture ceases to be a set of artefacts and parodies human decay: 'ce mobilier . . . vieux, crevassé, pourri, tremblant, rongé, manchot, borgne, invalide, expirant'.

These stylistic notations simply emphasize the persistent tendency of Balzac's fictional creation to move beyond the level of the social document, even when society itself is most fully represented with an abundance of social, economic, and topographical detail. Balzac's imagined world is at once less random than the one we normally inhabit and more intense, unified, and charged with meaning. Through this world move bankers, soldiers, politicians, civil servants, judges, lawyers, peasants, whores, social butterflies, young men on the make, ambitious doctors, secular saints, gangsters: characters in such profusion and variety that they represent one of the great imaginative feats of the nineteenth-century novel. In general, they are viewed with what has been called 'pastoral consistency', which is to say that they always act 'in character', in a way perfectly appropriate to their age and social rank and setting, though some are, in fact, capable of acting 'out of character', displaying an openness to experience that reaffirms the essential mystery of personality. In general, too, they are seen by an omniscient narrator who approaches their minds and sensibilities from outside, from the densely figured material context in which they are set. The comparison with Flaubert is instructive. What unifies *Madame Bovary*, for example, is not its formal devices like the symbolic return of the beggar when Emma is dying, however brilliantly innovating these may be and however much they conduce to that end, but a prevailing ironic *tone* which speaks of the distance between the novelist and his material, of his tendency to manipulate character in the light of his own controlled derision. By contrast, part of Balzac's strength as a novelist (though part of his weakness too) is to be found in the degree to which he understands, because he so often shares, the aspirations, energy, optimism, and inventiveness of his characters, and the whole bourgeois craving for business, speculation, and social status. This large sympathy with his own creation is, perhaps, what lies behind Balzac's ability to bring to life the massive and elaborate structure of his fiction, to raise it above its serious incidental flaws of feeling and moral discrimination, its uncertainties and ineptitudes of tone and expression, and, ultimately, to compel us to assent to it and to take his reliability on trust, as only a major and confident creator can. He allows his characters to move through an autonomous imaginary world, sustained by his own vital and equitable interest in them, by what Henry James once called 'this love of each seized identity'. Fascinated by the possibilities of this dramatic world, we follow in the wake of the author's love.

NOTE

HONORÉ DE BALZAC, 1799–1850, was born at Tours and educated at the Collège des Oratoriens at Vendôme (1807–13). This was a period of intense and precocious reading, followed by further private schooling in Paris and entry into a lawyer's office where he acquired the grasp of legal procedure that marks his work. Quitting law for literature in 1819, he wrote several trashy novels under pseudonyms and began the wild commercial speculations and mania for collecting bric-à-brac which characterized his entire career. Spurred on by failure, he wrote his first successful novel, *Les Chouans*, and published it under his own name in 1829. Thereafter, his output was prodigious: some ninety or so novels and stories between 1829 and 1848, quite apart from extensive journalism. He was constantly in debt and his health became ruined through excessively long and intense bouts of work by which he tried to meet his publishing commitments. He was very alert to the scientific and intellectual trends of his time and reflects them in his novels. Women played a prominent part in his life, but none was as influential as Mme Hanska, the wealthy Polish countess he married in 1850, after a long liaison, traceable in their fascinating correspondence.

Editions. The standard critical edition remains: *Œuvres complètes*, ed. M. Bouteron and H. Longnon (40 vols., 1912–40). Excellent and convenient is the Pléiade edition of the *Comédie humaine*, ed. M. Bouteron (11 vols., 1935–58). A useful and inexpensive edition of the *Comédie humaine* is that of the Intégrale collection (7 vols., 1965–6). Valuable critical editions of individual novels, published in the 'Classiques Garnier' series, include *Les Illusions perdues*, ed. A. Adam (1956); *Les Chouans*, ed. M. Regard (1957); *Splendeurs et misères des courtisanes*, ed. A. Adam (1958); *Le Père Goriot*, ed. P.-G. Castex (1960); *Les Paysans*, ed. J.-H. Donnard (1964); *Eugénie Grandet*, ed. P.-G. Castex (1965); *Le Lys dans la vallée*, ed. M. Le Yaouanc (1966); *La Rabouilleuse*, ed. P. Citron (1966). Another useful edition of *Eugénie Grandet* is edited by H. J. Hunt (1967).

Correspondence. The fullest edition is *Correspondance*, ed. R. Pierrot (4 vols., 1961–6). This needs to be supplemented by *Lettres à l'Étrangère*, ed. Spoelberch de Lovenjoul and M. Bouteron (4 vols., 1899–1950), until the revised and enlarged edition of these letters, currently being undertaken by R. Pierrot, is completed on the model of his *Lettres à Madame Hanska, 1832–1840* (1967).

Criticism. W. H. Royce's *A Balzac Bibliography* (1929) is still valuable, but needs updating. The best and most succinct biography in English is H. J. Hunt's *Honoré de Balzac: a Biography* (1957), while the fullest biographical treatment is André Billy's *Vie de Balzac* (1944). F. Lotte's *Dictionnaire biographique des personnages fictifs de la Comédie humaine* (1967 ed. in 1 vol.) is an indispensable guide to Balzac's reappearing characters. F. Longaud, *Dictionnaire de Balzac* (1969) may also be consulted.

The most useful general introductions are P. Bertault, *Balzac* (revised ed., 1962), and H. J. Hunt's judicious *Balzac's 'Comédie humaine'* (revised ed., 1964); while one of the best all-round critical studies is S. Rogers, *Balzac and the Novel*

(1953). Of specialized studies, M. Bardèche's *Balzac romancier* (1940) is a masterly account of the novelist's early development, and the following are authoritative for the fields they cover: P. Bertault, *Balzac et la religion* (1939); B. Guyon, *La Pensée politique et sociale de Balzac* (2nd ed., 1967); J.-H. Donnard, *Les Réalités économiques et sociales dans la 'Comédie humaine'* (1961); J. Borel, *Médecine et psychiatrie balzaciennes: la science dans le roman* (1971); M.-C. Amblard, *L'Œuvre fantastique de Balzac: sources et philosophie* (1972); J. Forest, *L'Aristo-cratie balzacienne* (1973); Diana F. McCormick, *Les Nouvelles de Balzac* (1973). P. Laubriet's *L'Intelligence de l'art chez Balzac* (1961) is very helpful on Balzac's conception of art, and G. Mayer's *La Qualification affective dans les romans d'Honoré de Balzac* (1940) on his use of language. Particularly suggestive critical essays are: A. Allemand, *Unité et structure de l'univers balzacien* (1965); A. Béguin, *Balzac visionnaire* (1946); F. Marceau, *Balzac et son monde* (1955). Three works by P. Barbéris also merit attention: *Balzac et le mal due siècle: contribution à une physiologie du monde moderne* (2 vols., 1970), *Mythes balzaciens* (1972), and *Le Monde de Balzac* (1973). Valuable chapters devoted to Balzac are to be found in M. Beebe, *Ivory Towers and Sacred Founts* (1964); Henry James, *French Poets and Novelists* (1878); H. Levin, *The Gates of Horn* (1963); G. Lukács, *Studies in European Realism* (1950); G. Poulet, *La Distance intérieure* (1952); and M. Turnell, *The Novel in France* (1950).

8. Violence and Identity in Romantic Drama

THE survival into the nineteenth century of the conventions of French neo-classical tragedy of the seventeenth century owes more to sociological than to aesthetic factors. An arrested conception of 'good taste' (what Vigny in his 'Lettre à Lord * * * sur la soirée du 24 octobre 1829' refers to as 'la Politesse') gives a kind of borrowed life to these conventions, especially under the First Empire and the Restoration. The prestige of neo-classical tragedy in the first fifteen years of the nineteenth century owed little to popular support. The official subsidized theatres simply reflected the pressures of Napoleon's cultural chauvinism which deliberately exploited the traditional artistic forms of the past as a means of affirming the continuity of the Napoleonic regime with the legitimate monarchical rule of the past. The performance of tragedies by Corneille, Racine, and Voltaire under the Restoration was, of course, an expression of taste, but 'taste' was inseparable from a tendency to view such performances as a social ritual in which the 'restored' aristocracy and gentry could publicly assert their identity and cohesion. Such plays were cherished as the cultural model of the society of the old regime. They offered consolation to a fossilized social class in a changing and treacherous world, and even appealed to those aspiring to gentility and status.

This tendency to identify certain theatrical forms and conventions with certain social and political interests helps to explain something of the vivacity with which the polite public of the 1820s reacted against attempts to reform the tragic conventions, though it is important to recognize that mild innovations had been introduced into the tragic form as early as Népomucène Lemercier's *Christophe Colomb* (1809) and Benjamin Constant's *Wallstein* (1809).

By 1819, with the staging of Casimir Delavigne's 'national tragedy', *Les Vêpres siciliennes*, the conservative playgoing public found it possible to accept a tragedy which offered rather more colour, movement, and variety of interest and character than was common in traditional tragic forms. Delavigne did not invent modern 'historical' or 'costume' drama, but he found a formula for reconciling cautious novelty of subject, plot, and language with the traditional virtues of neo-classical tragedy: high seriousness of theme, decorum of tone, and formal regularity.

Even so modest a departure from tradition could scarcely have succeeded had not the critical climate gradually altered between 1809 and 1814, with the diffusion of knowledge about foreign dramatists which resulted from the writings of critics, such as Mme de Staël's *De l'Allemagne* (1810), Sismondi's *De la littérature du Midi de l'Europe* (1813), and Schlegel's *Cours de littérature dramatique* (1814). Further changes in the climate of opinion helped to prepare the ground for the radical innovations of the young Romantic playwrights of the late 1820s and 1830s. Here, the influential factors contributing to the intellectual reorientation of the period must include Guizot's more virile translations of Shakespeare (from 1821); the bookseller Ladvocat's publishing venture, *Chefs-d'œuvre des théâtres étrangers* (1822), which opened the eyes of cultivated French readers to the richness and variety of the theatrical heritage of England, Spain, and Germany; the great season of English plays in Paris (1827-8), to which I shall return; and a handful of literary manifestos, written with polemical verve, and ranging from Manzoni's *Lettre à M. Chauvet sur l'unité de temps et de lieu dans la tragédie* (1820) and Stendhal's *Racine et Shakespeare* (1823) to Hugo's famous preface to the drama *Cromwell* (1827).

So far, I have tended to emphasize the ways in which the arrival of Romantic drama can be viewed as a response to an initially 'frozen' cultural scene, centred on revivals of the seventeenth-century French classics and nineteenth-century imitations of tragedy, and modified by changes in educated opinion. Such an emphasis ignores a large theatre public which coexists, in the 1820s and 1830s, with the cultivated and conservative public while remaining distinct from it in taste and, to a great degree, in social composition. This second public is chiefly drawn from the growing class of small manufacturers, shop-keepers, and middlemen thrown up by the expansion of industry and commerce, from the mid twenties on. It is a public without taste, in the traditional sense, eager to be distracted from the tedious routine of its humdrum working life by fast-moving and exciting entertainments, recognizably related to its own concerns but less mundane. This public sought in the theatre not insight, but release from care, not truth, but glamour and an image of the social poise and accomplishments which it lacked.

This is the natural public for Scribe's light comedies of intrigue, comedies which deliberately avoid social conflict and questioning of fundamental values and which dominate the popular Parisian theatres by the early 1830s. It is the rise of this public, indifferent, when not actually hostile, to traditional literary culture that makes certain the defeat of verse-drama exemplified by the resounding failure of Hugo's *Les Burgraves* (1843). Romantic drama, whatever different forms it assumes in Dumas, Hugo, Vigny, and Musset, sets itself consciously in opposition not only to imitations of the French classics, but also to Scribe's 'well-made play', the preferred theatrical form of the majority of Parisian playgoers at the time.

In this sense, Romantic drama strives to create a heroic image of human activity, as opposed to the domesticated and essentially trivial human image conveyed by the well-made play. Here, Romantic drama connects with another of the dominant theatrical modes of the period: the melodrama. For the new middle-class public of the mid thirties of the last century, the melodrama had been eclipsed by the well-made play, though it retained its hold over the working-class public. The melodrama had no rival as a popular art-form in the first twenty years of the nineteenth century. Tolerated by that great cultural conservative, Napoleon, under the First Empire, because its sensationalism was merely a theatrical convention and its morality of the edifying kind which punished subversion in all its forms, the melodrama survived under the Restoration as the popular alternative to official neo-classicism, as a popular image of heroic action.

The presiding genius of this 'tragedy of the masses', as it has been called, was Guilbert de Pixerécourt (1773-1844), nicknamed, without irony, by his admiring contemporaries 'le Corneille des boulevards'. In something like fifty-nine melodramas, written alone or in collaboration and ranging from *Victor ou l'enfant de la forêt* (1798) and *Cœlina ou l'enfant du mystère* (1800) to *Latude ou trente-cinq ans de captivité* (1834), he created a distinctive popular drama which the critic Charles Nodier felt able to describe as 'un genre nouveau; il est à la fois le tableau véritable du monde que la société nous a fait et la seule tragédie populaire qui convienne à notre époque'. By this, I think Nodier meant that with the melodrama violence emerges as a significant literary theme, connected with a period of political and social upheaval.

For Hugo, in particular, the melodrama spelt vitality and community; it was a genuinely *popular* art-form, the nearest thing to a communal rite then existing in French social life. Its impact on the public mind and sensibility was such that it was, perhaps, inevitable that Dumas, Hugo, and the Vigny of *La Maréchale d'Ancre* should call on the devices and conventions of melodrama in their attempts to create a theatrical form appropriate to their time. What Pixerécourt and his imitators offered was: rapid and episodic action; a complicated plot providing ample incident and diversion; suspense and excitement induced by arbitrary means rather than by the logic of events or feelings; mistaken identity; stock characters; physical accessories (disguises, hidden keys, 'revealing' letters) so crucial to the forwarding of the plot that they were almost raised to the status of characters; crude sensationalism and horror calculated to assault the audience's nerves, as in Pixerécourt's *Les Fossoyeurs écossais* (1829), when the 'body-snatchers' bring the medical student, Édouard, the corpse of his former mistress to dissect; and, finally, spectacle.

Increasingly, between 1800 and 1825, the Parisian boulevard theatres like the Ambigu-Comique, the Gaîté, and the Porte-Saint-Martin, experimented with striking sets and effects. Daguerre's 'Diorama' (1823), virtually coinciding with the introduction of gas lighting into the French theatre, provided startling new effects with its revolutionary system of changing lights and colour-filters.

Designers mounted increasingly lavish and spectacular sets: grottoes, crypts, catacombs; Alpine panoramas with bridges precariously spanning mountain torrents; great vistas dominated by clouds and ruins, as in Cicéri's much admired set for the melodrama *Bertram ou le pirate* (1822). Elaborately picturesque reconstructions of feudal castles or Renaissance palaces, earthquakes, volcanic eruptions, storms, pitched battles, interludes of ballet all called on every mechanical resource of the stage, and created the conception of the play as a theatrical synthesis, to which Hugo proved peculiarly susceptible. In melodrama, the 'drama' tends to be taken over by the machinery of illusion, and there is no full understanding of the impact made by Romantic drama in the hands of Dumas and Hugo unless one recognizes the elements of spectacle and vivid theatricality that they have taken from the popular melodrama.

But it is not enough to see French Romantic drama (or the melodrama from which it is so largely derived) solely in terms of theatrical convention. Both, though in stylized and indirect ways, respond to the social and political pressures of their age, and these pressures lie behind two dominant themes of Romantic drama: historical violence and the quest for identity.

Romantic drama is haunted by violence, a violence as much linked to the conflicts of specific social and political systems as it is to the disorders of individual personality. In Hugo's *Hernani* (1830) violence springs from Spanish feudal particularism; in Musset's *Lorenzaccio* (1834) from the exercise of arbitrary ducal power in an Italian city-state; in Vigny's *Chatterton* (1835) from the economic and ethical consequences of the factory system.

For the Romantic dramatists violence existed both as a fact of their recent history (the Convention, regicide, the Terror, the bloody military campaigns of the First Empire) and as myth, by which I mean the form this violence takes when recreated either in the popular mind or in the literary imagination. The generation of Romantic playwrights who came of age in the 1820s under a staid and relatively stagnant Restoration society, necessarily tended to contrast the flatness and mediocrity of their own age with the violent upheavals and changes of the period spanned by the Revolution, Directory, and First Empire, and to be concerned with the significance of this public violence since it had transformed the pattern of society. More specifically, these playwrights had available to them in the recent French past an image of life totally at variance with all settled and rational conventions. It was an image characterized by crisis, violence, chance, accident, and extreme social vicissitudes. Obscure lawyers became charismatic leaders, old families were ruined, victims saved by a hair's breadth from the guillotine, and armies commanded by men who had lately been sergeants.

What Romantic drama and its predecessor, melodrama, seem in fact to do is to invent appropriate forms and conventions for re-ordering this experience in imaginative terms, distancing it in time, so as to give it new and stylized life on the stage. The obsession with murder, assassination, and execution which runs through the plays of Dumas and Hugo, and which is also present in Vigny's *La Maréchale d'Ancre* (1831) and Musset's *Lorenzaccio*, is a reflection of this preoccupation with the violence of recent French history. It is also a convention borrowed from melodrama which, in its pattern of popular virtue triumphing over conspiracy and catastrophe, itself represents a conventional Republican image of the public violence of the Revolution of 1789-95. It is, of course, necessary to discriminate between the performance of different dramatists and to recognize, for example, that violence in Vigny's theatre is rarely unconnected with a serious moral issue: the death penalty in *La Maréchale d'Ancre*, the morality of suicide in *Chatterton*. These 'idealistic' concerns tend to make his drama distinct, in an important way, from that of Dumas and Hugo.

One other element, the problem of personal identity, seems to link the image of human life thrown up by the conflicts of revolutionary and imperial France with the preoccupations and conventions of melodrama and the Romantic theatre. A sense of personal identity is, perhaps, intimately connected with the individual's ability to place himself in relation to the moral and social schemes available to him. It follows that, in a rapidly shifting social and political scene, like that of the Revolution, the vicissitudes of life are multiplied for the individual and may have dramatic effects on his status and role in society and so make the question of his personal identity at best a matter of doubt for him and, at worst, highly problematic. It seems likely that the cases of doubtful or mistaken identity which constantly occur in melodrama and Romantic plays are not simply a device for creating surprise and suspense, but also represent an insight which transcends particular historical situations and can be applied more generally to the human predicament. It is this insight which Keats crystallized in a memorable phrase, 'the pursuit of identity in a world of circumstance'.

The world of circumstance is pre-eminently, in Romantic drama, the world of high politics, and the problem of identity arises when the individual character has to come to grips with the shifting realities of power, as these are expressed in intrigue, transfer of allegiance, and conspiracy. Hugo renders this world (or the surface of this world) with graphic power, but in such a way as to obliterate understanding of human motive and complexity through the mechanisms of gross melodrama, culminating too frequently in scenes of gothic horror: coffins waiting to be filled, hooded processions moving to the gallows, the insistent tolling of funeral bells. But within this violent context, the search for identity occupies a prominent place.

At one level, Hugo's plays represent a kind of rite of unmasking, in which impersonations and disguises are thrown aside and true identity revealed. In the play to which he gives his name, Hernani is successively brigand, wandering beggar, and grandee of Spain; Marion de Lorme, the object of the mysterious Didier's chaste passion, turns out to be one of the most celebrated courtesans of the time; Jane, in *Marie Tudor*, is finally revealed as the heiress of Lord Talbot; and Ruy Blas, the king's first minister, is unmasked before the queen as a valet in disguise.

The exact significance of this shuffling with identities is not always easy to grasp. Sometimes it seems to be connected with the idea of redeeming one's corrupt past through an act of disinterested love, as when Marion de Lorme sacrifices her body to the sinister royal agent, Laffemas, in order to save Didier from the gallows. Sometimes true identity is linked with a vaguely egalitarian ideal, though in a confused and incoherent way: *Hernani* illustrates this aptly. The most impressive rhetorical flight in the play is, arguably, don Carlos's vision of empire at the tomb of Charlemagne, and it tends to clinch the feudal and hierarchical image of society which we are offered by the play as a whole. Hernani, as brigand, seems to set himself against this hallowed and traditional framework in the name of some other, undefined order of values, which is why doña Sol is prompted to say of him:

> Que mon bandit vaut mieux cent fois! Roi, je proclame
> Que, si l'homme naissait où le place son âme,
> Si Dieu faisait le rang à la hauteur du cœur,
> Certe, il serait le roi, prince, et vous le voleur!

At first glance, this expression of egalitarian sentiment seems intended to be a significant statement in which plebeian virtue is contrasted with aristocratic vice. In fact, it is an empty verbal gesture, and its radical implications are at no time worked out in the substance of the drama, since they are quite incompatible with Hernani's true identity as the scion of an illustrious house, not above glorifying his lineage in bad verses:

> Dieu qui donne le sceptre et qui te le donna
> M'a fait duc de Segorbe et duc de Cardona,
> Marquis de Monroy, comte Albatera, vicomte
> De Gor, seigneur de lieux dont j'ignore le compte.

The truth is that Hernani is not alienated from feudal society, but only temporarily disaffected. Don Carlos's offer of a pardon for his treason enables him to return to his traditional place within the feudal hierarchy, and he celebrates this by refurbishing his ancestral estate so as to make it a worthy setting for his brilliant marriage ceremony. The fact that don Ruy Gomez's lust for revenge prevents the consummation of Hernani's marriage and provokes catastrophe in no sense affects the reality of Hernani's reconcilation with the traditional order of society. Indeed, by keeping his oath to don Ruy Gomez, Hernani actually exhibits a code of honour derived from feudalism.

The relationship between society, character, and identity is also illustrated by don Ruy Gomez. If, in *Hernani*, his loving enumeration of the portraits of his ancestors is uncertain as a purely theatrical effect (its solemn nature diminished by being placed in the mouth of a verbose and infatuated old man inadequately aware of the king's rising anger), it does succeed in establishing his nostalgia for a vanished moral and social order which contrasts both with the brigandage of the present and with the overweening claims of royal power. Thus the scene of the portraits is, at once, a trick for sustaining suspense (since we know Hernani is hidden behind one of the portraits) and the expression of a sense of historical continuity and feudal honour in a changing world. This look to the family past is also a means by which don Ruy Gomez, bewildered by the clash between the sacred claims of hospitality and the duty owed to a sovereign, can reaffirm his own identity.

The problem of character and class is restated in terms of the honest craftsman, Gilbert, in *Marie Tudor*. The sub-title of the 'première journée' (that is, the first Act) refers to him as 'L'homme du peuple', but, though he is rewarded with the hand of a peeress, he never emerges as *representative* of the common people. The virtue he displays for us as an individual drawn from the lower classes is effaced by that highly-coloured image of the 'people' as a fickle and bloodthirsty mob which we see through Mary Tudor's contemptuous eyes. In the same way, although Ruy Blas's spectacular rise to the position of first minister may serve to exemplify the virtues and abilities of the common man (while echoing the merits of the Napoleonic 'carrière ouverte aux talents'), the implications of this rise of the common man for the established order of society are nowhere explored in the play. Had they been, *Ruy Blas* might have emerged as a significant statement about the larger moral and political conflicts dividing French society at the period. In fact, such implications are short-circuited by Ruy Blas's love for the queen and by mechanical complications of plot arising from that clandestine love, as in the farcical scene where don César comes down the chimney of his own house and nearly ruins don Salluste's plot to compromise the queen. In the end, the 'lackey' is redeemed, not by affirming his lowly origins and identifying himself with the cause of the common people, but by the quality and fidelity of his private devotion to the queen, by what is most 'inward' about him. He emerges as a superior spirit in a mediocre world, but not as the exemplar of a new class.

Hugo's failure to work out, in imaginative terms, the full implications of those ambiguities, both social and moral, with which he surrounds his major characters contributes to our sense of their incoherence. It is difficult to reconcile don Ruy Gomez's nobility of stature with his credulity (as when he surprises don Carlos and Hernani in doña Sol's room) and with his readiness to exploit the ideal of feudal honour (Hernani's oath) so as to achieve a squalid personal revenge. Nor is it easier to reconcile don Carlos's princely virtues, after his election to the throne of the Holy Roman Empire, with his crude and unprincipled conduct before, as when he adduces 'reasons of state' as an alibi for removing doña Sol from the custody of don Ruy Gomez (Act III, scene VI). It is possible that Hugo intends these inconsistencies as the index to a fuller sense of life, to a dynamic conception of character in which human frailty and human capacity for growth and change are given their proper place. If this were the intention, I think it tends to be defeated by local failures of tact (the farce of don Carlos in the closet), restless proliferation of incident, and mechanical complication of plot (doña Sol's hidden dagger).

This conception of volatile and elusive main characters in search of their true identity is not felt by Hugo to be incompatible, within the framework of his drama, with the existence of a whole range of stereotypes, conventional embodiments of good and evil, loyalty and treachery, innocence and corruption. It may even be that these stereotypes, in the stability of their fixed natures, act as a theatrical device for throwing into relief the shifting ambiguities of the major characters.

As critics have noticed, the dress worn by characters serves as a schematic metaphor of their moral nature. The frivolous and corrupt are garbed in brilliant silks and velvets, the mysterious agents of misery or death in black cloaks. In a rather puzzling way, even the 'undefined' heroes have a symbolic costume—usually sober black, grey, or brown. Other conventional indices to character, borrowed from the tradition of the melodrama, are freely exploited by Hugo: white hair, standing for honourable and dignified old age; baldness for wickedness or demonic power. It is quite clear that Hugo uses these conventions deliberately, though not in a significantly different way from his predecessors. Perhaps they represent a conscious attempt on his part to retain a feature that could appeal to a large and unsophisticated public and reconcile them to the elaborate use of historical material in his plays and the richly-patterned text of his verse-dramas.

One of Hugo's central problems as a dramatist is to get us to take on trust the hero's view of himself and to accept the play's accidents, coincidences, and sensational reversals of fortune as proof that the hero is indeed one of the elect, marked out for a special doom. This, in fact, he conspicuously fails to do because he cannot persuade us that the hero's fate is linked with his character in a coherent and organic way. What happens to Hernani, or Didier in *Marion de Lorme*, or Ruy Blas cannot be said to spring, with tragic inevitability, from what they *are*, if only because what they are is so dauntingly enigmatic (in Didier's case) or so lost in impersonation (in the lives of Hernani and Ruy Blas). Where there is no subsisting and intelligible core of motive, no explored identity, except in terms of disguise, the whole notion of character tends to collapse. Characters like Hernani or Didier impress one as voids waiting to be filled, toys of the fleeting moment who respond to every change of pressure and who suggest confusion and gratuitousness rather than a full human complexity.

This is not to say that Hugo's main protagonists are not seen by the dramatist in the light of a powerful and ambiguous fate that is neither the inexorable necessity known to the Greek tragic hero confronting the riddle of a divinely sustained order of the universe, nor the determinism of the Naturalists. Hugo's fate sometimes *appears* to imply the immovable constraints of a particular order of society (don Carlos's royal autocracy in Spain or Richelieu's rule in France), but, gradually, it emerges as the expression of a particular and exceptional nature, the kind of nature that is not at home in the world. Hence, Hernani's fate does not come from his being victimized by society (he is, in fact, reconciled with it), but from his 'nature', from his alienation from the normal world of men:

> . . . Je suis une force qui va!
> Agent aveugle et sourd de mystères funèbres!
> Une âme de malheur faite avec des ténèbres!
> Où vais-je? je ne sais. Mais je me sens poussé
> D'un souffle impétueux, d'un destin insensé.
> Je descends, je descends, et jamais ne m'arrête.

The source of this alienation may lie (as the final image of a bottom-less pit suggests) in a deep sense of being radically and inexplicably different from other men, of being cut off from a meaningful role in the world.

Lorenzo's failure to act meaningfully in the great world is, in a similar way, inseparable from the problem of identity in Musset's *Lorenzaccio*. This play is, among other things, about Musset's refusal to share the values of French society under the July Monarchy. It is a drama about unemployed idealism, and its distinctive qualities and preoccupations stem from a mind and sensibility alienated from the society in which they have their being. The play's moods of doubt, intensity of feeling, covert heroic aspiration, and implied defence of the creative individual against a corrupt society all point to the dilemma of the artist living with loathing in the society of Louis Philippe and 'M. Joseph Prudhomme' but lacking conviction or ideology to change it after the fiasco of the revolution of 1830. In this sense, Florentine Lorenzo is a period figure of the 1830s in France, a superior intellect in an increasingly vulgar society. He is also an intellectual divided against himself, searching for a valid basis for action and manœuvring so as to find a point of contact with the real world of factions and institutions without being capable of full involvement in that world. Lorenzo's fury when he strikes down the duke is the fury of impotence experienced by the creative artist in the face of practical politics. For all its imperfections, this play remains a subtle and persuasive exploration of a divided mind and an illuminating study of the impotence of the liberal intellectual caught up in a period of radical change.

Impersonation is central to Lorenzo's character and his playing of roles in the drama represents a trying on of identities by a character profoundly uncertain of his true place in society. This role-playing is, of course, an eminently theatrical device. That is why the scene in which Lorenzo practises his sword-play with his servant Scoronconcolo (Act III, scene 1) is one of the most striking in the play and comes most fully alive. It is a scene in which this actor plays out his fantasy. At this point it remains fantasy, but the miming of violence soon gives way to the reality of murder. In a way impossible to the classical stage, the drama of the unconscious is fully exteriorized in movement, speech, and gesture. Aspects of Lorenzo's character are exteriorized in other characters in the play and he grasps his own identity through the intermittent glimpses he has of it in others. Hence, Catherine is the innocence he once possessed and has now lost, as Alexandre is the image of his own depravity. In killing Alexandre he perhaps hopes to destroy the corrupt part of himself or, at least, to exorcise it through a kind of blood sacrifice.

Significantly, all Lorenzo's activities take on the character of masquerade. He is an actor, not an agent, and an actor too equivocal, even in his final gesture of violence, to offer the play a persuasive moral centre. His tendency to impersonate historical or legendary characters suggests the vanity and self-regarding nature of his acts: 'Qu'ils m'appellent comme ils voudront, Brutus ou Érostrate, il ne me plait pas qu'ils m'oublient.' Lorenzo yearns, in fact, to transcend his mortal and historical limitations, and, as the reference to Herostratus confirms, he is prepared for a purely nihilistic act so long as it confers immortality on him. He is not concerned with the practical and objective consequences of his acts, but only with their effect on his 'inner life'. Congruent with this histrionic posturing is the kind of rhetoric he uses. It is conspicuously ornamental, something superadded to the action, as at the crucial moment when he has stabbed the duke (Act IV, scene XI): 'Regarde, il m'a mordu au doigt. Je garderai jusqu'à la mort cetter bague sanglante, inestimable diamant.' Here, 'inestimable diamant' is simply a piece of preciosity echoing the poetic conceit of 'bague sanglante'. Both expressions tend to diminish the horror of murder to the level of a literary exercise.

Such impersonation and such literary procedures make of *Lorenzaccio* an overwhelmingly ironical structure. A debauchee offers himself as the saviour of republican liberties, but the murder he commits in pursuit of that goal proves pointless. Tyranny survives; the republicans themselves prove impotent at the moment of decision, and the common people, in whose ultimate interest the superior intellect of the hero has worked, welcome their new tyrant and hug their chains. The claims of society and the claims of the subjective self are nowhere reconciled.

Like *Lorenzaccio*, *Chatterton* (1835) reflects intellectual tendencies of the period. It is, at once, a drama about individual lives
caught up in a painful predicament and a statement, in theatrical
terms, about the nature of the artist and his function in society. In
this latter respect, Vigny shows himself to be attuned to the ideas
about the artist as sage and prophet which are to be found in the
Utopian-socialist writings of Saint-Simon, writings especially
influential in the early thirties of the nineteenth century. Saint-
Simon offered a vision of a reorganized and regenerated society
moving toward Utopia through the co-operation of three productive
classes: the industrialists, the scientists, and the creative artists.

The artist's or poet's distinctive gift was seen as the power of
divining imaginatively fundamental truths about human kind and
so of helping man towards a condition of perfectibility. These gifts
constituted both a privilege and a kind of doom which set the artist
apart from other mortals, condemning him to loneliness and suffering. The grandiose role allotted to the artist in the Saint-Simonian
scheme implied a special sensitivity to spiritual values, as opposed
to the prevailing materialism of the age, and its humane impulse
accorded very well with Vigny's instinctive sympathy with the poor.
It is also true that the Simonians' emphasis on an élite, and the
paternalism underlying the managerial society they favoured,
appealed to Vigny's social conservatism and could be reconciled
with his cult of aristocratic obligation.

These affinities between Vigny's personal philosophy and the
ideas of the Saint-Simonians brought him into a temporary alliance
with Buchez and his dissident Saint-Simonian sect (1828-9).
Though he later moved away from their ideology, Vigny never quite
lost the vision of the poet as one of the 'unacknowledged legislators
of the world'. It is that exalted conviction which animates *Chatterton*, supplies it with its intellectual energy and direction, and gives
it what status it possesses as a drama of ideas. The barely disguised
dialogue between realism and idealism, which is the central theme
of *Stello* (1832), is revived in *Chatterton*, and Wordsworth's
'marvellous Boy' is seen both as a symbol of misunderstood genius
and as the sacrificial victim of the new Moloch of *laissez-faire*
capitalism.

Chatterton's suicide is not viewed in the drama as a tragic individual case, but as characteristic of the plight of the artist in a society dedicated to the maximizing of profits. Chatterton's fate simply echoes, in the realm of the spirit, the pitiful predicament of the dismissed worker, Tobie (Act I, scene II), in the mundane world of supply and demand. In this sense, *Chatterton* is a play about the violence done to the spirit by the machine. With the death of Chatterton and Kitty Bell, an ethic of love is seen to be defeated by an ethic of calculation, and John Bell and Lord Mayor Beckford, honoured members of an acquisitive society that is both callous and philistine, emerge as the blind and self-righteous instruments of catastrophe.

Undoubtedly, the rather schematic distribution of characters too obviously serves the didactic impulse in the work. The dichotomy which the play establishes between purity and corruption is more edifying than true to the complexity of moral life. It is not, for example, easy to accept John Bell, Beckford, and Lord Talbot (here living up to Oscar Wilde's description of the English country gentleman as 'the unspeakable in full pursuit of the uneatable') as offering an adequate image of 'society'. It is true that the presence of the Quaker appears to suggest a middle way between what Vigny calls 'martyrs' and 'executioners', though he is too much the contemplative, too firmly outside the life of society, to offer an alternative way of living in the world.

Vigny expresses in the 'Dernière nuit de travail', which serves as a preface to *Chatterton*, a large ethical conception of the function of art, and the play itself may be thought to reflect a groping towards what Matthew Arnold called the 'grand style', the style that 'arises in poetry when a noble nature, poetically gifted, treats with simplicity or with severity a serious subject'. It does not seem to me that Vigny actually achieves this style in *Chatterton*, though it is certainly the style appropriate to his subject-matter. In fact, the play exhibits, at the level of dialogue, a good deal of woodenness and sententiousness, rather in the manner of the eighteenth-century 'drame bourgeois'. It is true that Vigny makes a serious attempt to find a voice appropriate to each of the main characters and, to some extent, he succeeds. John Bell's flat and utilitarian idiom hits off his character very well, just as Talbot's coarseness is entirely suited to his nature. The Quaker's sententious and biblical style of utterance tends, however, to create too broad an effect—to be too much concerned, that is, with establishing him as a picturesque and patriarchal figure. The result is to inhibit our sympathy for him because his mode of speech effectively masks his funds of charity and goodwill.

The compassionate love of Kitty Bell for Chatterton, and his restrained and reverent devotion to her, are conveyed with rare delicacy of feeling, though Chatterton, especially in his soliloquies, slips too easily into the histrionic, as in the final words of his long soliloquy in Act III, scene 1: 'Caton n'a pas caché son épée. Reste comme tu es, Romain, et regarde en face.' Such a phrase necessarily tends to 'theatricalize' Chatterton's despair for us, and so to rob it of some part of its genuine pathos; but it also points to the poet's need to make a myth of his own life. This need implies a certain conception of his own exemplary status, and the persuasiveness of the play perhaps depends ultimately on the degree to which we are able to take Chatterton's genius on trust and to accept his life as a valid image of poetic integrity. Vigny does not seem to me quite to bring this off, and I think the reason for the failure is principally connected with tone. The general tone of the work tends to be set by the Quaker and Chatterton himself, if only because they are the most articulate on the level of ideas. It is a tone compounded of ethical fervour, lofty admonition, and righteous anger on the one hand, and disdain, self-pity, and self-dramatization on the other. Its effect is to convince us that we are being preached at rather than imaginatively involved. Such a tone brings the 'drame de la pensée' dangerously close to the problem-play.

The more equivocal aspects of such a tone are emphasized for us by the kind of language Chatterton uses to describe himself and which points to a man struggling in the net of circumstances to find his true self, his 'real' identity. He thinks of himself as 'plague-victim', 'leper', 'wild-boar at bay', 'martyr'; in a word, as an *outcast* but, significantly, an outcast like Christ, whose words he echoes: 'Il est écrit que je ne pourrai poser ma tête nulle part.' The metaphor is certainly ambitious and, most would think, excessive, and the pressure behind such a metaphor comes less from the spiritual quality revealed by Chatterton in the play than from the dramatist's own conception of the poet's status, as this is developed in 'La dernière nuit de travail'. The pathos of Chatterton's situation in Vigny's drama is very real, but it cannot validate the attempt to raise the vicissitudes of the poetic life to the level of religious myth, if only because Chatterton has not that intense awareness of the suffering of others (the Tobies, the Kitty Bells) which is itself a kind of martyrdom in the world.

The whole question of character in Romantic drama is difficult to separate from the new styles of acting which actors like Frédérick Lemaître, Bocage, and Marie Dorval learned while playing melo-drama in the boulevard theatres and which they refined through imitation of the English manner of acting, made fashionable in Paris by the spectacularly successful visit (September 1827 to July 1828) of a company which included Charles Kemble, Edmund Kean, Macready, and Harriet Smithson. Their interpretation of Shakespearian plays introduced an astonished and largely admiring French public to a range of emotional effects, a dynamic style of performance, and a technique of acting marked by a vitality, naturalness, and expressiveness remote from the monotonous and declamatory delivery and highly stylized gestures characteristic of French tragic actors on the 'official' Parisian stages.

Lemaître, Bocage, and Marie Dorval took over this style of acting, but chiefly as a vehicle for imposing their personalities on the character of plays. This was not a conscientious interpretative technique but an exhibition of sensibility, something akin to a style of life which found a sympathetic echo in the young generation of playgoers. They unified plays through a display of personality, often endowing Dumas's hectic and chaotic dramas with an illusory coherence and richness of experience. In tailoring roles to the gifts and idiosyncrasies of such actors, playwrights like Dumas, Hugo, and the Vigny of *La Maréchale d'Ancre* tend to make the colour and weight of a particular character depend overmuch on the personality of a particular actor. This intensifies the sense the modern reader or spectator of these plays experiences, that there are indeterminate zones in some of the major characters and that these zones suggest blankness rather than fruitful ambiguity. In this way, the period style of frenetic acting, together with the playwrights' temptation to prefabricate aspects of character on the basis of actors' personalities (as both Hugo and Vigny did for Marie Dorval), tend to exaggerate still further the notion of uncertain identity which was first borrowed, as a theatrical trick, from melodrama.

Perhaps only in *Lorenzaccio* do we gain a sense that Romantic drama is capable of illuminating human experience, of exploring the complex possibilities of our human nature. Hugo, like Dumas, is capable of creating sweeping, colourful, but essentially naïve entertainments; unlike Dumas, he sometimes compels us to surrender to his metaphoric vitality and the sheer physical movement of his verse. In retrospect, the historical or costume drama they favoured wears a rather gimcrack appearance. It looks increasingly irrelevant as a theatrical form for a society that was, even then, moving towards the urban, industrial, socially levelling pattern with which we are familiar. The only *historical* drama in the Romantic repertory that avoids arbitrary sensational incident and offers a significant degree of emotional and intellectual control and subtlety is Musset's *Lorenzaccio*, a play which uses historical analogy to illuminate a contemporary problem in a way that foreshadows Sartre's handling of the German Peasant Revolt in *Le Diable et le bon Dieu*.

In the end, and in spite of strained rhetoric and an over-all impression of bloodlessness, Vigny's *Chatterton* stands out as an ambitious attempt by a Romantic dramatist to create a tragic play out of the materials of modern life, and so to revitalize a form that challenged the imagination of all the Romantic playwrights.

NOTE

Editions. For Hugo, the best and most compact edition of the plays is the Pléiade *Théâtre*, ed. J.-J. Thierry and J. Mélèse (2 vols., 1963-4). Useful editions of single plays include: *Hernani*, ed. P. Richard (1951), and *Ruy Blas*, ed. F. Lafon (1966). For Dumas *père*, the most complete edition of the plays is: *Théâtre complet* (15 vols., 1863-74). *Henri III et sa cour*, ed. R. E. Palmer (1964) is a useful modern edition of one of Dumas's most celebrated plays.

The standard edition of Vigny's plays is *Théâtre*, ed. F. Baldensperger (2 vols., 1926-7). The plays can also be read in the 'Édition l'Intégrale' of his *Œuvres complètes*, ed. P. Viallaneix (1965). For *Chatterton* the best critical edition is that of L. Petroni (Bologna, 1962). There is a helpful and scholarly edition by A. H. Diverres (1967).

Musset's plays are most easily accessible in the authoritative *Comédies et proverbes*, ed. P. Gastinel (2 vols., 1934-52), or in the 'Édition l'Intégrale' of his *Œuvres complètes*, ed. P. Van Tieghem (1963). Two useful editions of *Lorenzaccio* are: ed. J. Nathan (1964) and ed. P. E. Crump (1959).

Memoirs. Informative for actors and acting are: Alexandre Dumas, *Souvenirs dramatiques* (2 vols., 1868); Edmond Got, *Journal* (1910); Ernest Legouvée, *Soixante ans de souvenirs* (1886-7); Frédérick Lemaître, *Souvenirs* (1880); Charles Séchan, *Souvenirs d'un homme de théâtre* (1883).

Criticism. Important general studies of the Romantic drama include: M. A. Allevy, *La Mise en scène en France dans la première moitié du XIXᵉ siècle* (1938); J. L. Borgerhoff, *Le Théâtre anglais à Paris* (1912); M. Descotes, *Le Drame romantique et ses grands créateurs, 1827-1839* (1955); F. W. M. Draper, *The Rise and Fall of the French Romantic Drama* (1923); D. O. Evans, *Le Drame moderne à l'époque romantique, 1827-1850* (1937); Théophile Gautier, *Histoire de l'art dramatique en France depuis vingt-cinq ans* (6 vols., 1858-9; reprint 1968); Grace P. Ihrig, *Heroines in French Drama of the Romantic Period, 1829-1848* (1950); A. Le Breton, *Le Théâtre romantique* (n.d.); J. Marsan, *La Bataille romantique* (2 vols., 1912-25); P. Nebout, *Le Drame romantique* (1895). There are also valuable chapters in: F. Brunetière, *Les Époques du théâtre français, 1636-1850* (1892); M. Descotes, *Le Public de théâtre et son histoire* (1964); M. Lioure, *Le Drame* (1963); and some suggestive pages in George Steiner, *The Death of Tragedy* (1961).

For the melodrama, the most useful studies are: P. Ginisty, *Le Mélodrame* (1910); W. G. Hartog, *Guilbert de Pixerécourt: sa vie, son mélodrame, sa technique et son influence* (1912); A. Lacey, *Pixerécourt and the French Romantic Drama* (1928).

On Hugo, useful studies include: J. Gaudon, *Victor Hugo dramaturge* (1955), a highly intelligent and suggestive essay; P. and V. Glachant, *Un Laboratoire dramaturgique: essai critique sur le théâtre de Victor Hugo* (2 vols., 1902-3); G. Lote, *En préface à Hernani. Cent ans après* (1930); H. Lyonnet, *Les Premières de Victor Hugo* (1930); W. D. Pendell, *Victor Hugo's Acted Dramas and the Contemporary Press* (1947); P. Souchon, *Autour de Ruy Blas* (1939); M. Souriau, *La Préface de Cromwell* (1897).

On Dumas *père*, the most important contributions are: H. Clouard, *Alexandre Dumas* (1955); A. Maurois, *Les Trois Dumas* (1957); and H. Parigot, *Alexandre Dumas père* (1902).

On Vigny as a playwright, there are two valuable studies: C. W. Bird, *Alfred de Vigny's Chatterton: a Contribution to the Study of its Genesis and Sources* (1941), and E. Sakellaridès, *Vigny, auteur dramatique* (1902).

Musset's theatre has been the subject of the following suggestive essays: A. Brun, *Deux Proses de théâtre* (1954); P. Dimoff, *La Genèse de Lorenzaccio de Musset* (1936; reprint 1964); H. Gochberg, *Stage of Dreams: the Dramatic Art of Alfred de Musset, 1828-1834* (1967); L. Lafoscade, *Le Théâtre d'Alfred de Musset* (1901; reprint 1966); A. Lebois, *Vues sur le théâtre de Musset* (1966); H. Lefebvre, *Alfred de Musset dramaturge* (1955); H. Lyonnet, *Les Premières de Musset* (1927); B. Masson, *Musset et le théâtre intérieur: nouvelles recherches sur 'Lorenzaccio'* (1974); J. Pommier, *Variétés sur Alfred de Musset et son théâtre* (1974; reprint 1966); F. Tonge, *L'Art du dialogue dans les comédies en prose d'Alfred de Musset: étude de stylistique dramatique* (1967).

F

9. Nerval

NERVAL'S works can be characterized, in his own phrase, as the creation of a second life: 'l'on arrive pour ainsi dire à s'incarner dans le héros de son imagination, si bien que sa vie devienne la vôtre et qu'on brûle des flammes factices de ses ambitions et de ses amours!... Inventer, au fond, c'est se ressouvenir' (preface to *Les Filles du feu*). By this method memory and imagination are indistinguishable. Any hero of fiction, history, or legend can be appropriated to represent the self and to define the outlines of Nerval's life, not as he lived it, but as he re-imagined it. For example, when Nerval was about thirty he had an unhappy love-affair with a light-opera singer, Jenny Colon—or, more accurately, with a stage-image which took its colouring from the roles she played. Many of Nerval's works are literary transpositions of this experience. Thus Brisacier, the hero of a fragment entitled 'Le Roman tragique', having joined a troupe of strolling players for love of the leading lady, is tempted to change the plays in which he takes part with her and use them to act out his fantasies of possession—to set fire to the theatre and carry off the actress through the flames.

But Nerval's fantasies, whether expressed in the third person through 'another self', as here, or through the mode of pseudo-autobiography which is the characteristic genre of later years, are never merely self-indulgent. In his creation of a second life, wish-fulfilment is limited by a rigorous honesty. Brisacier, with his blend of self-aggrandizement and self-irony, recalling Nerval's own *Lettres à Jenny Colon* (which were never posted and exist half-way between reality and fantasy), is a faithful portrait of the complex imaginative processes of his creator.

But Nerval's works, especially after his first attack of madness in 1841, contain self-projection at a deeper level than the fantasy rearrangement of reality represented by 'Le Roman tragique'. In terms of modern psychology he was a manic-depressive. His periodic and increasingly frequent attacks moved through cycles of exultant euphoria, in which he felt as omniscient and omnipotent as a god, and deep melancholy, in which a sense of doom and utter sterility was complicated by the confused fear that everyone was conspiring against him. If he sometimes spoke lightly of his madness, it was because he knew its depths and its dangers. In the interests of his reputation he was ready to conform to the image of himself, created by friends who perhaps felt guilty at not being able to help him, as a merely amusing eccentric. He accepted, and indeed sought, the role of the highbrow journalist suffering from 'un grain de folie'. But the image hardly corresponds to the exhausted, tragically mistrustful face which looks out at us from his photographs. The truth was that Nerval, when the fit was on him, could be frighteningly violent, throwing stones, terrorizing and even attacking perfect strangers, raving and tearing off his clothes in the streets of Paris, having to be forcibly restrained. His madness was the threat of total confusion.

But it was also a descent into the other world of dreams and death. It is the visionary experience, not the more superficial rearrangement of circumstance, which he himself dignifies with the title of a second life: 'Le Rêve est une seconde vie'. This is the world to which he feels he truly belongs, a world so intensely real that it invades his waking perceptions and appears as the theatre of his destiny. To work out this destiny—not to submit passively to the fragmentary illuminations of madness, but to shape them voluntarily into a continuous and meaningful pattern—this is Nerval's deepest enterprise as a writer.

At one level, he is concerned with the conflicting claims of dream and reality, and the heroes into whom he projects his experience are torn between the desire for a sweet normality, symbolized by a village girl, and the lure of visionary experience, centred in the ideal figure of his dreams. This conflict is the ostensible subject of Nerval's beautiful *nouvelle*, *Sylvie*. But at a deeper level reality is secretly shaped by the dream-destiny to which it theoretically offers an alternative, so that Sylvie, the village sweetheart, appears in the end as a facet of the identity of Adrienne, the ideal dream-love.

Nerval works the patterns of his deeper destiny into even the most apparently disengaged passages of his journalistic writing. It finds its fullest expression first in vicarious form, through the legendary heroes of the two *contes* inserted in the *Voyage en Orient*, and finally in the directly autobiographical *Aurélia*.

The salient facts of Nerval's early life must be recalled here. When he was two years old his father, Dr. Labrunie, enlisted as a medical officer in the armies of Napoleon, taking his young wife with him. She died during the retreat from Moscow, so that her son never saw her again. His early childhood was spent in the charge of his mother's uncle, Antoine Boucher, who lived at Mortefontaine, a village in the Valois region to the north of Paris. Later memories were of a place ringing with the happy voices of women and girls (his mother's sister, his maternal grandmother, his nurse Gabrielle, the village girls). When the lad was seven Dr. Labrunie came home, and in *Promenades et Souvenirs* Nerval presents his father's return as the traumatic rupture of a happy paradise.

Aurélia is a mythical transcription of Nerval's dreams and visions which involves the telescoping of events and persons. Thus Jenny Colon, after her death, is assimilated with Nerval's mother in the figure of Aurélia, at once mother, lover, and goddess, the Eternal Feminine, the one-in-many. She becomes the central figure in a dream of penetrating beauty in which the hero is welcomed into the community of his lost family, based on idealized memories of Nerval's Valois childhood. As an intruder from the land of the living he is not allowed to stay in the family paradise, but on his return to 'earth' he retains the conviction that he is immortal and will certainly be reunited with those he loves. This prospect is disturbed by the presence of the double: his other self, blessed and resplendent, may marry Aurélia and take his place in the dream-world, while he is ignored as though he did not exist. But there is a happy ending: after being cut off for a long time from felicity, he is pardoned through her intervention and finds salvation at her side. The role of the father-figure in these dreams fluctuates. He is sometimes a threatening figure who tries to exclude the hero from reunion with his true family, sometimes loving and benevolent.

The family is not only the dream-equivalent of the half-imagined, half-remembered figures of childhood: it is also the family of man. Time past, writes Nerval in the 1840 preface to his translation of Goethe's *Faust*, lies about us in a series of concentric circles, which the visionary can re-enter and re-animate. Thus history is the cyclical repetition of the same basic actions in the struggle between two warring races whose discord has destroyed the original harmony of paradise. Nerval's imagination is syncretic as well as synchronic: successive religions are facets of a single truth. Beneath her different masks, the mother-goddess is always the same and, whether in the form of the Egyptian Isis (her 'identité primitive') or of the Christian Mary, she enacts always, with the son who will be the saviour of the world, the same ritual of separation and salvation (*Isis*, 1845). Thus Nerval telescopes the mythologies of man into a single myth in which his own dream-destiny becomes that of the human race.

In *Aurélia* he therefore imposes on the successive memories of his visionary attacks a continuous unity which they never really had (we can see this by comparing the notes for the opening chapters with the final version), and which assign to certain dreams a significance which they only took on in the light of subsequent events. It is essential for Nerval's peace of mind that *Aurélia* give an account of the dream-destiny which is not only coherent and meaningful, but also leads to an ultimate salvation. The result is beautiful and moving: this must be one of the most lucid accounts of madness ever written. But no man's destiny is complete until he is dead; *Aurélia* remains an artificial and, in spite of the profound honesty of the writing, essentially a false interpretation of Nerval to himself and to the world.

Les Chimères, a series of twelve sonnets published the year before Nerval's death (though seven had appeared ten years earlier), represents the culmination of his creative effort and the most faithful reflection of his visionary experience. For the first time he is recording the illuminations of madness directly, without reference to the world of sanity and rationality. *Les Chimères* does not, as *Aurélia* did, attempt to impose a total narrative coherence. Instead, the impression it gives is of vivid but tantalizingly incomplete glimpses of the other world. The reader has the sense of a meaning, glimpsed but not grasped, alluringly numinous but too vast and too

intense to be formulated by human faculties. We are left at once
excited and frustrated, with the feeling that if only we knew how to
read the poems, their meaning would suddenly stand out clearly.

This challenge, combined with the fact that *Les Chimères* has
been adopted as a model of all the qualities expected in a certain
tradition of 'modern' poetry (obscurity, suggestiveness, incantation,
and a total effect which transcends paraphrasable meaning), has
attracted a good deal of critical attention over the last twenty years,
and the sonnets are now surrounded by a formidable tangle of
exegesis, some of which is harder to understand than the poetry
itself. Too many critics, having paid hasty lip-service to the
mysterious beauty of a poem like 'El Desdichado', go on to propose
a 'solution' as though it were a kind of riddle. Thus it has been
interpreted as a set of hermetic symbols (alchemy, tarot cards,
Nerval's horoscope), as disguised and condensed autobiography, or
in the light of the historical or legendary figures to whom it refers.
These have been identified variously, but with unvarying confidence. One critic has been led to the despairing but understandable
conclusion that all these *external* meanings have simultaneous
validity, in which case reading the poem is like biting into a multi-
layered cake. But one or two recent critics, admirably, have returned
to the bottom layer, the words, and shown that they can be appreciated on their own terms.[1] We would suggest two principles of
interpretation: firstly, it shall make use only of allusions which are
generally known, and shall never *depend* on external evidence;
secondly, the obscurity of the poem is not to be explained away—
if this were possible—but treated as an essential part of its meaning.

Ten of the sonnets—'Le Christ aux Oliviers' (1844—a sequence
of five), 'Vers dorés' (1844), 'Delfica' (1845), 'Myrtho' (1854),
'Horus' (1854), and 'Antéros' (1854)—although falling into two
chronological groups, form a loose cycle expressing what can be
called the theme of revolt. The syncretic method enables the same
basic myth to be presented through the figures of successive mythologies: an original race, belonging both to the childhood paradise
of Nerval's dreams and to the paradise of man's innocence, has been

[1] See especially the work of Gérard and Geninasca. Details are given in the Note at the
end of this chapter.

suppressed by a dynasty of sterile but powerful usurpers (identified loosely with Nerval's father). The sonnets are about the efforts of a primitive, life-bearing force to reassert itself. They embody the violence of Nerval's feelings, clearly an essential part of his inner experience, which was glossed over in the more explicit prose works.

Having been loosely adumbrated in 'Le Christ aux Oliviers', the theme is first expressed through the Pythagorean animism of 'Vers dorés': man the thinker, cut off from his original communion with things, is too arrogant to notice the secret life which lurks in plants and animals, even in stones and metals. This has two aspects: it is love, and yet it works towards a mysterious purpose of its own which constitutes a potential threat to man. In the later sonnets the theme is expressed, no longer through a known philosophical doctrine, but through Nerval's private system of mythological allusions. 'Delfica', belonging chronologically to the first group, can be seen as a transition:

> La connais-tu, DAFNE, cette ancienne romance,
> Au pied du sycomore, ou sous les lauriers blancs,
> Sous l'olivier, le myrthe ou les saules tremblants,
> Cette chanson d'amour…qui toujours recommence!
>
> Reconnais-tu le TEMPLE, au péristyle immense,
> Et les citrons amers où s'imprimaient tes dents?
> Et la grotte, fatale aux hôtes imprudents,
> Où du dragon vaincu dort l'antique semence.
>
> Ils reviendront ces dieux que tu pleures toujours!
> Le temps va ramener l'ordre des anciens jours;
> La terre a tressailli d'un souffle prophétique…
>
> Cependant la sibylle au visage latin
> Est endormie encor sous l'arc de Constantin:
> — Et rien n'a dérangé le sévère portique.

The mythological allusion of the first quatrain gives a deeper significance to the animism of 'Vers dorés'. Daphne was the priestess of Mother Earth, who changed her into a laurel-bush so that she might avoid the unwanted embraces of the god Apollo. The song which sighs in the leaves is a sign that the spirit of the former gods whom she laments is not dead, but lives on in nature. But who are the old gods? And who has vanquished them? The title gives a clue: Delfica is obviously based on Delphi, the shrine of the earth-deity Python, who was defeated by Apollo. Apollo is a usurper, harnessing the oracular powers of the vanquished spirit and building his imposing temple on the site of Python's underground lair. The power of prophecy is thus linked with the forces of revolt. The image of the earth-tremor in line eleven suggests that they are already stirring, and the 'souffle prophétique' which is breathed out refers both to the oracle and to the return of the old gods to power, which now seems imminent. The second tercet marks a change of scene but not of theme. The arch of Constantine celebrates the institution of the new cult of Christianity as the official religion of the Roman Empire, so that it appears, like the Temple of Apollo, as another grandiose monument to the usurping dynasty. The last line refers to the arch, but the severe portico also reminds us of the immense peristyle of the temple at Delphi, just as the oracular power of the Delphic priestess, and with it the spirit of revolt, is transferred to the Latin sybil.

'Myrtho', 'Horus', and 'Antéros', though the first has close affinities with 'Delfica', extend the system of unexplained allusion still further beyond the point where prose paraphrase is still possible. They represent in strongly condensed form different moments of the drama, or different attitudes to it, but if they are considered together their unity of theme is strikingly apparent:

Myrtho

Je pense à toi, Myrtho, divine enchanteresse,
Au Pausilippe altier, de mille feux brillant,
A ton front inondé des clartés d'Orient,
Aux raisins noirs mêlés avec l'or de ta tresse.

C'est dans ta coupe aussi que j'avais bu l'ivresse,
Et dans l'éclair furtif de ton œil souriant,
Quand aux pieds d'Iacchus on me voyait priant,
Car la Muse m'a fait l'un des fils de la Grèce.

Je sais pourquoi là-bas le volcan s'est rouvert...
C'est qu'hier tu l'avais touché d'un pied agile,
Et de cendres soudain l'horizon s'est couvert.

Depuis qu'un duc normand brisa tes dieux d'argile,
Toujours, sous les rameaux du laurier de Virgile,
Le pâle Hortensia s'unit au Myrthe vert!

Horus

Le dieu Kneph en tremblant ébranlait l'univers:
Isis, la mère, alors se leva sur sa couche,
Fit un geste de haine à son époux farouche,
Et l'ardeur d'autrefois brilla dans ses yeux verts.

'Le voyez-vous, dit-elle, il meurt, ce vieux pervers,
Tous les frimas du monde ont passé par sa bouche,
Attachez son pied tors, éteignez son œil louche,
C'est le dieu des volcans et le roi des hivers!

L'aigle a déjà passé, l'esprit nouveau m'appelle,
J'ai revêtu pour lui la robe de Cybèle...
C'est l'enfant bien-aimé d'Hermès et d'Osiris!'

La Déesse avait fui sur sa conque dorée,
La mer nous renvoyait son image adorée,
Et les cieux rayonnaient sous l'écharpe d'Iris.

Antéros

Tu demandes pourquoi j'ai tant de rage au cœur
Et sur un col flexible une tête indomptée;
C'est que je suis issu de la race d'Antée,
Je retourne les dards contre le dieu vainqueur.

Oui, je suis de ceux-là qu'inspire le Vengeur,
Il m'a marqué le front de sa lèvre irritée,
Sous la pâleur d'Abel, hélas! ensanglantée,
J'ai parfois de Caïn l'implacable rougeur!

Jéhovah! le dernier, vaincu par ton génie,
Qui, du fond des enfers, criait: 'O tyrannie!'
C'est mon aïeul Bélus ou mon père Dagon...

Ils m'ont plongé trois fois dans les eaux du Cocyte,
Et protégeant tout seul ma mère Amalécyte,
Je ressème à ses pieds les dents du vieux dragon.

The original race of gods, as in 'Delfica', has been vanquished and banished to an underground retreat. They have affinities with the earth from which all things spring: Daphne was priestess of Mother Earth, of whom Cybele, the identity taken on by Isis in 'Horus' (line 10), is another incarnation, as is Demeter, mother of Iacchus ('Myrtho', line 7), while Anthaeus in 'Antéros' is the son of the earth-goddess Gaia. The secondary element of revolt is fire, which breathes life into the earth. Hence the suppressed fire of the volcano which threatens to erupt ('Myrtho', 'Delfica'), the fire reflected in the proud flush of a brow glowing with the shame of defeat ('Antéros'), the fire whose joyous light either sparkles round the forehead of Myrtho as a halo of morning sun, shines with shy happiness in her eyes (line 6), or burns with the ardent hatred which flashes from those of Isis ('Horus', line 4).

As in 'Vers dorés' and 'Delfica', the forces of revolt have a dual aspect. Their revolt is sustained by rage ('Antéros', line 1) and hatred ('Horus', line 3); they are menacing and destructive in 'Antéros' and reach a paroxysm of mocking cruelty in 'Horus'. Yet at the same time, in 'Myrtho' and 'Delfica', the most joyous and serene of the sonnets, they are life-giving. The light in the eyes of Myrtho (spirit of Aphrodite's sacred plant, the myrtle, as Daphne is the spirit of the laurel) is also the fire of intoxication: her golden hair is entwined with the black grapes which inspire the devotee of Iacchus, who, Nerval tells us in *Isis*, founded the mysteries of Eleusis, so that the theme of intoxication links the brilliance of Mediterranean sunlight with the dark mysteries of the underworld.

The usurpers appear in different guises: historical in 'Myrtho', when the 'duc normand', a brutal invader from the Christian North, smashes the fragile statues of the classical gods; mythological in the case of the Egyptian god Kneph in 'Horus' or the Old Testament Jehovah in 'Antéros'. But their characteristics are stable: they are an old, dying race, severe and formal in 'Delfica', cold, deformed, and dying in 'Horus'.

The notion of renewal, symbolized in the evergreen plants, is central. What has been lost will be restored. The climax of each sonnet is the prophecy of a future which will be the past revived.

But in every case it comes just before the end, in the first tercet: the call of the spirit of the new age in 'Horus', the cry of revolt in 'Antéros', the moment which follows the prophetic rumbling in 'Myrtho'. In the second tercet each poem settles back into the latent power of a hope unaccomplished: the growth of the laurel and myrtle in the happy sonnet 'Myrtho', the sowing of the dragon's teeth, the promise of the rainbow, the sleeping sybil. The flash in Myrtho's eyes was only 'furtif', and when the volcano reopens, it releases, not a glorious rain of fire, but a cloud of ash which chokes the horizon.

These uneasy, muted climaxes combine longing with the knowledge that longing can exist only in a latent form as a pressure striving upwards towards the future. Despite his secret affinity with the signs of revolt ('Je sais pourquoi'), the poet of 'Myrtho' does not actually witness them ('là-bas'), and the final lines of 'Horus' suggest that the Golden Age will be restored in another latitude to which he apparently has no access. The poem ends with the departure of the goddess, leaving the scene pregnant with her absence. True, the rainbow, Iris's scarf, is a symbol of the reconciliation of God and man (*Genesis*), so that the final suggestion is of the resolution of conflict. But the impression of loss strongly remains. For all their strangeness, these sonnets are a soberly honest account of the tragically unresolved situation of Nerval's inner self, held helpless between longing and defeat. His profound need is for the reconciliation of these opposites. Thus the attributes of the usurping and vanquished races are sometimes interchangeable: Kneph is 'le roi des hivers' but also 'le dieu des volcans'. The interchangeability of opposites reflects Nerval's generous impulse to embrace those he loves and those he longs not to hate, in the community of human fellowship.

'Artémis' and 'El Desdichado' (which, significantly, are the only two completely irregular sonnets) belong to a more intensely private cycle of love and death. But their incorporation of the theme of revolt, as well as of certain central images, links them to the sonnets already discussed, and their denser structure resolves the conflicting tensions of a multiple meaning on a purely linguistic level.

Artémis

La Treizième revient... C'est encor la première ;
Et c'est toujours la seule, — ou c'est le seul moment :
Car es-tu reine, ô toi ! la première ou dernière ?
Es-tu roi, toi le seul ou le dernier amant ?...

Aimez qui vous aima du berceau dans la bière ;
Celle que j'aimai seul m'aime encor tendrement :
C'est la mort — ou la morte... O délice ! ô tourment !
La rose qu'elle tient, c'est la *Rose trémière*.

Sainte napolitaine aux mains pleines de feux,
Rose au cœur violet, fleur de sainte Gudule :
As-tu trouvé ta croix dans le désert des cieux ?

Roses blanches, tombez ! vous insultez nos dieux :
Tombez fantômes blancs de votre ciel qui brûle :
— La sainte de l'abîme est plus sainte à mes yeux !

As is confirmed by a manuscript footnote and the variant title, 'Le Ballet des heures', the first line refers to the thirteenth hour of the twenty-four hour clock, which is the same as the first. 'Encor' means both that the thirteenth hour is *also* the first and that it is *still* the first, so that the two are at once different and the same. But Nerval did not write 'la treizième heure': 'la Treizième' gives the superimposed suggestion of a series of feminine identities, and lines three and four make the statement about time mysteriously dependent ('car') on a question about identity. The two levels are seen as continuous or even commingling, for the word 'dernière' which rounds off the statement about the time-cycle first appears in the context of identity. So too, the fact that in line two 'le seul' is balanced by 'la seule' suggests on the purely grammatical level, and in the context of the hours, the contrast between man and woman in lines three and four. The latter contrast is again reinforced on the level of language by the appropriately placed masculine and feminine rhymes. This is not confusion, but an inextricable profusion of meanings. The questions are ambiguous: line three could either read 'oh Queen, are you the first or the last?' or 'are you, in fact, Queen—you who are the first and the last?' (similarly with line four). The multiplicity of meanings leaves the impression of a mystery which cannot be formulated but which has been intricately explored: the unity of identity and time.

The definite articles and the royal appellations point to archetypal figures rather than to individuals, indicating that Nerval is writing about a cycle in which the same love-story is enacted over and over again by a series of couples whose basic and exemplary identity is always the same. Thus we have, in time itself, a kind of eternity. But the second quatrain moves on to the idea of individual survival beyond the grave ('dans la bière'—*into* the grave). The passage from the third person mode of the opening lines to the 'je' of line six indicates that the poet, having considered the universal aspects of the lovers' destiny, is now speaking about his own experience of it. The second person imperative of line five is a way of speaking to oneself (self-exhortation), and provides a transition. The effect is to make us feel that 'je', 'vous', and 'il' are all the same.

The ellipsis (omission of 'celle'—or 'celui'...) strengthens the effect of the repetition 'aimez–aima', so that the second quatrain, like the first, has the sound of a magic spell, whilst persuasively suggesting the monotony and reciprocity of love and continuing the suggestion of cyclical recurrence already established. As before, the apparently simple language conceals a multiplicity of apparently conflicting meanings. The adverbial phrase of line five may have a passive or an active effect, depending on whether we understand it to mean 'aimez (celle) qui vous aima du berceau dans la bière' or 'aimez du berceau dans la bière (celle) qui vous aima', and there are four permutations in the reading of 'du berceau dans la bière', including the suggestions that she is his daughter, and that he is dead (if she loved him from *her* cradle to *his* grave), and that she is his mother, and is now dead herself (if the love lasted from *his* cradle to *her* grave). Furthermore, the tenses are doubly contradictory, since the imperative 'aimez' suggests that he will continue to love her, while 'j'aimai' makes his love a thing of the past. So too (though in reverse order) with 'qui vous aima' and 'm'aime encor'.

Nerval passes from simplicity to complexity and back to simplicity. At first sight the words look clear, even banal. Another reading reveals that they do not mean what we expected them to mean: 'celle que j'aimai seul', for example, arouses our expectations of the conventional compliment that she is the only one he loved, but turns out to mean the opposite, which leaves us puzzled. The more we look, the more we lose ourselves in a labyrinth of ambiguities. Yet the final meaning is surely simple: that all these *internal* meanings are true simultaneously. He and she are each dead and yet alive; their love is interrupted by death and yet continues after death; it is that of mother and son, father and daughter, man and woman. The diversity of human experience of love is gathered together in a single polyvalent statement. At the same time the statement refers to the love of an individual couple which continues beyond death.

Thus the word 'ou' in line seven (as in line two) designates an alternative which is apparent rather than real, both because of the unifying tendency which merges contradictory meanings into a single over-all meaning, and because, on the individual level, both his death ('la mort') and hers ('la morte') are necessary if their love is to be eternal. In this case the obvious reading of line seven as a balanced pair of antitheses, by which *his* death would lead to reunion and delight, while *her* death would lead to the torment of separation, will appear as superficial.

The essential meaning of 'O délice! ô tourment!' will then be that, given an eternal love not interrupted by the accident of death, a deeper doubt arises as to the *nature* of the beloved. This doubt is pursued through the strongly dualistic structure of the tercets, which pick up the theme of revolt. Lines eight to ten ascribe to the beloved the attribute of the red rose, the flower of flame, which is contrasted to the pale roses and the empty desert of heaven. Having stated the couple's affiliation to the old gods whom Christianity has insulted, the poet ends with the triumphant choice of the Infernal Saint whose place is in the underworld of exile and revolt.

Yet the movement from unity in diversity (quatrains) to duality (tercets) is underpinned by a series of strong impulses towards a final coherence. On the formal level, the tercets are continuous from the quatrains because the new element of rose imagery is introduced in line eight, not line nine. And the pair of words which introduces the theme of dualism ('O délice! ô tourment!') has close structural and semantic correspondence with the pair whose

apparent contradiction tends to be absorbed in the unity-in-
diversity of the first eight lines: 'C'est la mort—ou la morte'.
Furthermore the polarity of the tercets is not between two identities
(there is no 'sainte du ciel' to balance the 'sainte de l'abîme'), but
between two sets of attributes, red rose and white, and two spiritual
environments, heaven and hell. Despite the resounding final line,
the over-all impression is of an Eternal Feminine whose nature is
alternately infernal and celestial. The fact that 'votre ciel qui brûle'
suggests hell and that, conversely, we should normally expect to
find the '*sainte* de l'abîme' in heaven, is a reversal of traditional
values typical at once of Romantic Satanism and of Nervalian
revolt. But it also indicates Nerval's search, among the complexities of his syncretic and synchronic vision, for an enduring
understructure of unity. For the logic of the Romantic idea of hell
as the inverted image of heaven is that the two are one.

El Desdichado

Je suis le ténébreux, — le veuf, — l'inconsolé,
Le prince d'Aquitaine à la tour abolie:
Ma seule *étoile* est morte, — et mon luth constellé
Porte le *Soleil noir* de la *Mélancolie*.

Dans la nuit du tombeau, toi qui m'as consolé,
Rends-moi le Pausilippe et la mer d'Italie,
La *fleur* qui plaisait tant à mon cœur désolé,
Et la treille où le pampre à la rose s'allie.

Suis-je Amour ou Phébus?... Lusignan ou Biron?
Mon front est rouge encor du baiser de la reine;
J'ai rêvé dans la grotte où nage la syrène...

Et j'ai deux fois vainqueur traversé l'Achéron:
Modulant tour à tour sur la lyre d'Orphée
Les soupirs de la sainte et les cris de la fée.

The first two lines are the statement of a permanent and static
destiny: I am the man of shadows, the one who is bereaved and
disconsolate, whose castle is in ruins. Once again the definite article
confers on the poet an archetypal status. 'Le prince d'Aquitaine
à la tour abolie' suggests too that the demolished tower is the

emblem of the prince's family, not an accident in his career. Line two is at once mysterious and crystal-clear: we do not know who the prince is, but the manner of his presentation implies that everyone will recognize in him *the* outstanding exemplar of misfortune. His significance is thus created in the poem, and research in the annals of early French history is irrelevant. He is a universal, not a historical image, except in the general sense that the sonorous title, together with the lute in the following line, gives a cultural colouring to the first quatrain. The sense of solemnity is heightened by the choice of the rare word 'abolie' (which rhymes so magnificently with 'mélancolie'), suggesting total and irremediable destruction as though by the decree of some higher power, yet almost abstract, and held in a satisfying balance of sound and rhythm with the three preceding syllables.

Line three, following the suggestion of 'veuf', gives the reason for his distress: the beloved is dead. The image of the beloved as a star lighting and guiding the poet's life is traditional, and we understand it without any additional exploration of the multiple resonance it undoubtedly held for Nerval. Similarly, a reading of Nerval's correspondence, *Le Voyage en Orient*, and *Aurélia* would reveal a series of associated suggestions (depression, doomsday, the fallen angel) which enrich the meaning of line four, but would not explain its function in the poem. The image of the star-studded lute indicates the transition from man to poet, from personal experience to its creative expression. Formerly the poet's lute had been resplendent with his star. Now it carries, like the emblem of his mood, the black sun of melancholy. The dark splendour of the visual image marvellously conveys the poet's brooding silence.

The second quatrain prepares for his liberation from the apparently immutable identity of despair. Without the aid of a reference to light which would make explicit the contrast with the darkness of the first quatrain, it evokes a luminous impression of happiness which could offer consolation to the disconsolate. The Bay of Naples, as in 'Myrtho', is a scene of life, warmth, and colour, in which the couple's union was symbolized by the marriage of rose and vine. The opposition between Mediterranean clarity and Nordic gloom provides a further contrast on the cultural level.

The way in which 'dans la nuit du tombeau' echoes the darkness of the opening lines suggests, as 'Artémis' did, an ambiguous assessment of death. The dark realm of death can be infused with the light of happiness if the moment of their union can be re-enacted by the poet's following the beloved into the underworld. Conversely, if she is dead, the whole world is as dark and dreary as the tomb, but if the poet were to rescue her from death the pair might return to happiness and light. Lines twelve and thirteen can be read as supporting either of these meanings, depending on whether we interpret 'deux fois' literally—indicating that the poet had gone down into the underworld and back, like Orpheus, but had, unlike Orpheus, returned successfully with his beloved—or loosely, referring to two successive visits to the realm of death where she remains a prisoner, from which he emerges victorious only in respect of his own conquest of death. The latter would mean that the light of happiness could only be restored intermittently, during his 'visits' to the other world.

Like 'Artémis' the poem points in the direction of a total meaning in which its separate meanings are subsumed. If the poet's destiny is exemplary and eternal, each of the different ways of envisaging his situation will be true at once. And like 'Artémis' the poem passes from an ambiguous assessment of death to a consideration of the dual aspects of love. The opening statement which had fixed him in the identity of despair ('je suis') gives way, now that fixity has been dispersed by hope, to a new, anxious questioning about identity: 'Suis-je Amour ou Phébus?... Lusignan ou Biron?' For Nerval, as we have seen, self-identification with historical or legendary figures is a means of self-definition, so the line asks the question: 'What type of man, or lover, am I?' Without embarking on a detailed discussion about who these figures might be and what they stand for, we can note the obvious suggestion that 'Amour' (in the story of Cupid and Psyche) could be associated with dark-ness, and therefore with the mood of the first quatrain, while 'Phébus' (Apollo, the sun-god) would represent day and therefore the mood of the second. But both this and the second pair of names are susceptible of a wide variety of interpretations, while there is the added possibility of attaching the first pair to the Mediterranean culture of the second quatrain, and the second pair to the French-historical culture of the first. Further permutations are possible in deciding which male identity corresponds to which of the successive pairs of female identities, 'reine' and 'sirène', 'sainte' and 'fée'.

Since the sonnet itself leaves all this open, any interpretation which depends on the imposition of a rigid pattern (for example: 'amant du Pausilippe'/'Phébus'/'Biron'—'reine'/'sainte' in contrast to 'prince d'Aquitaine'/'Amour'/'Lusignan'—'syrène'/'fée') will be insufficient. The second quatrain suggests that the passage from despair to consolation, from darkness to light, is a recurrent cycle, and the lyre of the closing lines (animating the silent lute of the opening) transposes the sighs of the saint and the cries of the fairy alternately and continuously. Sighs of passion and cries of pain can be indistinguishable. The poem's structure corresponds to the alternating phases of Nerval's cyclical temperament: the periods of elation and euphoria, followed by a monotonous despair which can be broken only by the prospect of renewal. He is alternately the Prince of Aquitania and the victorious Orpheus, damned and saved, abandoned and loved, consigned to darkness and dwelling in light. The poem is a movingly honest and marvellously condensed statement of this unresolved inner destiny.

Perhaps the main reason for Nerval's appeal to the mid-twentieth-century reader is that we have come to understand the importance of the irrational in man. It is no longer possible, after Freud and Hitler, to hold the eighteenth- and nineteenth-century view that we are primarily rational beings capable of submitting our behaviour to the control of enlightened common sense. We realize that our actions may be determined by profound and primitive impulses which we do not fully understand. The discovery of the irrational had two sides. It has been exploited, more consciously since the Surrealists, but already by writers like Baudelaire or Rimbaud, Lautréamont or Apollinaire, as well as Nerval, as a source of strange, rich beauties. At the same time we are fascinated and appalled by its dangerous violence. If Nerval seems so much a writer of our time that his work 'n'existe pas pour lui et les témoins de sa vie de la même manière qu'elle existe pour nous' (R. Jean), it is because, so far from ignoring the irrational undercurrents of experience, he takes them as the material for literary creation, shaping a mythic representation of his inner tensions which embodies both beauty and violence. *Les Chimères* ritualizes the irrational by giving it a compelling artistic form. In recognizing this, we have recognized Nerval as a major writer.

NOTE

GÉRARD DE NERVAL was the pen-name of Gérard Labrunie, 1808–55, who wrote partly to prove his responsibility and respectability in the face of the condescension of friends, who saw him as a harmless eccentric, and of the disapproval of a father who wished him to take up a safe professional career. After 1836 a permanent burden of debt forced him to meet the ephemeral but pressing commitments of intellectual journalism, and virtually all his work was published in the form of articles before being collected, towards the end of his life, in the books which he hoped would stand as more permanent monuments to his name. Travel articles went into *Lorély* (1852) and the *Voyage en Orient* (1851); his *nouvelles*, some semi-autobiographical like *Sylvie*, into *Les Filles du feu* (1854). All his life he strove for a popular success in the theatre, but even his admirable political melodrama, *Léo Burckart* (1838–9), was not appreciated, and most of his plays were mediocre. His deeper, visionary concerns, though never entirely absent from his work, are increasingly apparent in the arranged autobiography of *Petits Châteaux de Bohême* (1853), *Les Nuits d'octobre* (1852), *Promenades et Souvenirs* (1854–5), and above all *Aurélia* (1855), a direct account and interpretation of his visionary experience, of which the sonnets of *Les Chimères* (1854) are a more brilliant, more disturbing, and more fragmentary reflection. He was found hanged in January 1855, having apparently committed suicide.

Editions. The best modern editions are in the 'Classiques Garnier' and Pléiade series (2 volumes each), while articles and unpublished or inaccessible works are currently appearing in the eight-volume *Œuvres complémentaires*. The many cheaper editions include the 'Classiques Larousse', 'Livre de Poche', and 'Poètes d'aujourd'hui' collections.

Criticism. A useful *instrument de travail* is J. Villas, *Gérard de Nerval: a Critical Bibliography, 1900–1967* (1968). There are three excellent general studies: L. Cellier, *Nerval, l'homme et l'œuvre* (1956); R. Jean, *Nerval par lui-même* (1964); Norma Rinsler, *Gérard de Nerval* (1973). Much of the recent criticism is specialized and even abstruse, but the controversial 'psychocritique' of C. Mauron, *Des métaphores obsédantes au mythe personnel* (1963), has many valuable insights. The most useful articles on *Les Chimères* are: Alison Fairlie, 'An Approach to Nerval', in *Studies presented to P. Mansell Jones* (1961); A. Gérard, 'Images, structures et thèmes dans El Desdichado', in *Modern Language Review* (October 1963); J. Geninasca, 'Une lecture de El Desdichado', *Archives des lettres modernes* (1965); J. Dhaenens, *Le Destin d'Orphée: études sur 'El Desdichado' de Nerval* (1972).

10. The Novel of Self-disclosure

THE value of introspection as a means to knowledge has always had its advocates. The famous injunction, 'Know thyself', inscribed in the temple at Delphi, is simply one early and well-known example in a long tradition of exhortation. At the same time the study of what is other than the self, and (allegedly) clearly distinct from it, is the source of a strong counter-tradition. Behind this latter attitude, and apart from its assumptions concerning the nature of 'objective' reality, lies a conviction neatly summed up in Jacques Rivière's phrase: 'On cesse d'être sincère au moment où l'on intervient en soi.' The marked contrast between these two approaches to truth is a long-standing one and we may well be tempted to see the whole history of European speculative thought as alternating between acceptance and rejection of the unique value of self-knowledge and the individual standpoint.

The idea of introspection, however stoutly defended as an answer to truth or pursued as a temperamental need, raises a variety of psychological and philosophical problems. On the psychological level, apart from the difficulty of seeing how the self can be both the object and the instrument of one and the same inquiry, we are continually reminded that unconscious psychical processes and complex censoring mechanisms intervene to undermine self-awareness and, therefore, direct self-knowledge. In the sphere of philosophy, a statement such as Descartes's 'je pense, donc je suis' has been the subject of much logical sport—because this assertion assumes the existence of the self ('je pense') which it goes on to demonstrate, or because the pronoun 'je' is used as a grammatical subject only and does not necessarily stand for any actually existing entity. This is not the place, however, to examine these problems further. Indeed—no doubt happily both from their point of view and from ours—the writers to be discussed in this chapter do not seem to have been seriously troubled by them. Senancour, Constant, Sainte-Beuve, and Fromentin all took the 'common sense' view that self-examination is a psychological possibility. They also seem to have shared the conviction that self-disclosure in imaginative writing is an activity worth pursuing.

Nevertheless, in the field of so-called 'confessional' literature, difficulties still arise. For example, how far does an author reveal himself by what he confesses and how far by what he passes over in silence? To what extent does he reveal himself by the manner, as well as by the matter, of his writings? Again, can we be sure that the centre of gravity, as it were, of the writing self corresponds to that of the fictional self-portrait? Not least of all, is it possible for a writer, without loss or distortion, to transform his relatively unstructured private experience into a self-conscious work of literature? These are some of the problems underlying any discussion of the four novelists mentioned above. Whatever the answers we arrive at—and they will vary with each individual novelist—the further fact remains that all writing, whether intentionally personal or not, reveals something of its author. There is an element of self-disclosure in all writing, however objective its aims and posture.

Stendhal's well-known phrase—'tout ouvrage d'art est un *beau mensonge*'—has particular relevance for the autobiographically-inclined novelist. The author who elects to write about himself is tempted by at least two forms of distortion, one moral and the other aesthetic. Firstly, there is the temptation to make his self-portrait more flattering or more coherent than direct scrutiny of the original biographical facts would justify. Secondly, a fully aesthetic realization of these same facts may well require him, as an artist, to make significant alterations to his material. This is not to deny the point made above that all writing is in some measure self-revelatory. Nor is it to deny that the way in which a writer alters the details of his own life may itself tell us a good deal about him. It does mean, however, that the novelist who embarks on self-disclosure is obliged to hold a delicate balance between autobiography and art, between the demands of sincerity and those of literary technique. Indeed, it is possible to characterize the four novels which concern us here precisely in terms of 'truth' and 'fiction'. *Oberman* (1804)[1] is a truthful portrait of Senancour and, as a novel, carries immense human conviction; *Adolphe* (1816) is not always a truthful picture of Constant, but artistically it compels our belief and admiration; *Volupté* (1834) is untruthful as a portrait of Sainte-Beuve and carries limited artistic conviction; *Dominique* (1863) is a partially truthful account of a particular incident in Fromentin's life and perhaps convinces most by its qualities of detachment. Obviously, all these statements require qualification and expansion. In the end, they may not amount to saying much more than that, in my opinion, *Adolphe* is the finest of these novels and *Oberman* the most impressive human document. I think they also suggest that the term 'novel of self-disclosure' may be more appropriate and less paradoxical than the term 'fictional autobiography'.

Senancour's inward-turning temperament, together with his melancholy view of the world, makes him a typical *mal du siècle* figure. He shows all the traits of apathy, disenchantment, and thwarted imagination associated with Romantic *ennui*. His biography, in some respects reminiscent of that of Vigny, is a story of frustration in various forms: he grew up an aristocrat in a revolutionary age; the Revolution reduced him to relative poverty; he made a very unhappy marriage; his literary ambitions remained unrealized. While growing up in a strictly religious home, he read the eighteenth-century *philosophes* in secret and also dreamt of high adventure in exotic lands. Like Oberman, he found himself at odds with his surroundings:

J'interrogeai mon être, je considérai rapidement tout ce qui m'entourait; je demandai aux hommes s'ils sentaient comme moi; je demandai aux choses si elles étaient selon mes penchans, et je vis qu'il n'y avait pas d'accord entre moi et la société, ni entre mes besoins et les choses qu'elle a faites. . . . J'offris successivement à mon cœur ce que les hommes cherchent dans les divers états qu'ils embrassent. Je voulus même embellir, par le prestige de l'imagination, ces objets multipliés qu'ils proposent à leurs passions, et la fin chimérique à laquelle ils consacrent leurs années. Je le voulais, je ne le pus pas. (*Oberman*, I)[2]

[1] Throughout I have used the spelling 'Oberman' rather than 'Obermann' in conformity with the first edition of 1804—preferable in several ways to those of 1833 and 1840.

[2] Roman numerals refer to the 91 letters of which *Oberman* is composed.

At the same time, Senancour respected the parents against whom he had also rebelled (see XLV), and this was one fact among several which made him divided against himself. He refers frequently to his own contradictions—contradictions which drew his attention in upon himself, yet which he could not satisfactorily resolve. In one letter Oberman writes: 'Je ne vois pas du tout pourquoi partir, comme je ne vois pas bien pourquoi rester. . . . La vie m'ennuie et m'amuse' (LXXVIII). Later he observes: 'Il n'est pas si facile de concilier les divers principes de notre conduite' (LXXXVI). This divided self quickly became for Senancour both a source of suffering and an object of fascination—and he came to regard the suffering and the fascination as the surest ways to truth. On the subject of unhappiness he writes in *Oberman*, in the 'Premier Fragment' following letter XXXV:

C'est un avantage pour la vie entière d'avoir été malheureux dans l'âge où la tête et le cœur commencent à vivre. C'est la leçon du sort: elle forme les hommes bons; elle étend les idées, et mûrit les cœurs avant que la vieillesse les ait affaiblis; elle fait l'homme assez tôt pour qu'il soit entièrement homme. Si elle ôte la joie et les plaisirs, elle inspire le sentiment de l'ordre et le goût des biens domestiques: elle donne le plus grand bonheur que nous devions attendre, celui de n'en attendre d'autre que de végéter utiles et paisibles.

As regards his self-absorption, Oberman proclaims: '. . . la vie réelle de l'homme est en lui-même' (I), recalling Saint Augustine's famous phrase in *De vera religione*: 'Truth dwells in the inner man.'

Although he places the source of truth within the individual, Senancour does not make the mistake of assuming that this truth is readily and directly accessible. His aim in *Oberman*—'je déterminerai ce que je suis'—is clear enough, but it is not suggested that such an aim is easily realized. On the contrary, Oberman speaks quite unambiguously of self-scrutiny as the 'triste faculté de penser à ce qui n'est point présent' and drives a wedge between the observing self and the self observed. In a later letter (LXIII) we read: 'Un être isolé n'est jamais parfait; son existence est incomplète. . . . Le complément de chaque chose fut placé hors d'elle, mais il est réciproque.' Here we have a hint of the conditions, arising from the nature of our situation in the world, which make self-knowledge—but self-knowledge arrived at indirectly—possible. We develop our ideas and values, we 'make' ourselves, in large measure through contact with others.[1] We identify and define much of what we admire or dislike, and thus identify and define ourselves as persons, by this dialectical relationship with the world outside the self. We turn outwards in order to equip ourselves to look inwards. We materialize our identity in things outside us which thus become starting-points for self-knowledge. Of course it is true that we are 'inside' our own experiences in a way in which we can never be 'inside' the experiences of others. But this 'insideness' is *subjectivity*, not *knowledge*. It is Senancour's awareness of this distinction which was an important contributory factor to his remarkable achievement as an introspective writer.

If subjectivity and self-knowledge are distinct, they also stand in an intimate relationship to one another. While in a general sense we look to the world of the non-self for certain forms of self-recognition, what we see there partly depends on our subjectivity and partly reveals it. In *Oberman* Senancour carries on a twofold enterprise which mirrors this fact: he describes his innermost feelings and his ideas while also analysing his response to the ideas and experiences of others (he discusses such subjects as suicide, capital punishment, feminism, marriage, religion, and the disturbing prospect of a wholly secular society in which, as he puts it, 'l'homme est livré à la providence de l'homme'). He realizes, in particular, that the path to self-knowledge is tortuous and long—and his novel gives ample evidence of the fact. Where Constant, for example, adopts a reductive method of self-disclosure, Senancour seeks a cumulative one. While Constant's Adolphe gives himself a precise identity which we are meant to see continually at work throughout the various vicissitudes of his story, Oberman emphasizes the plurality of the self, stresses the element of self-deception lurking within subjectivity, and therefore travels through many contradictory emotions and conflicting viewpoints before concluding his self-portrait. Indeed, whereas both Constant and Sainte-Beuve equate personal identity with a reductive consistency, Senancour characterizes it by antithesis and polarity.

[1] Cf. Sartre: 'Autrui détient un secret: le secret de ce que je suis' (*L'Être et le Néant*).

While a slowly cumulative method is one notable feature of *Oberman*, its rarefied atmosphere—in keeping with the Alpine heights among which so many of the letters are written—is another. Significantly, Oberman finds self-absorption, self-recognition, and deep consolation in fundamentally inhuman and grandiose landscapes. These offer 'la paisible harmonie des choses' (the word *choses* is important), and writing of landscape elsewhere, in his *Rêveries*, Senancour suggests why his favourite landscapes are without human figures: '. . . les chants d'une voix lointaine nous accablent d'un sentiment indéfinissable de nos pertes.' At the same time, the extent to which he withdraws into thought and feeling, spurning active life, prompts Senancour to deny that *Oberman* is a novel at all. In the preliminary 'Observations' he writes:

> Ces lettres ne sont pas un *roman*. Il n'y a point de mouvement dramatique, d'événemens préparés et conduits, point de dénouement; rien de ce qu'on appelle l'intérêt d'un ouvrage, de cette série progressive, de ces incidens, de cet aliment de la curiosité, magie de plusieurs bons écrits, et charlatanisme de plusieurs mauvais.

These objections seem relatively unimportant in an age when the 'well-made' novel is under something of a cloud. What *Oberman* does offer, and to an exceptional degree, is a strongly personal disclosure of a man's inner life. The very intensity of the work enables the author to dispense with elaborate formal structures. *Oberman* is lyrical, expansive, pessimistic, contradictory, and finally shapeless—and all these features contribute to an impression of directness and truth. It was Matthew Arnold who rightly called Senancour 'the least attitudinizing' of writers.

A final word should be added on the nature of Senancour's pessimism. The unhappiness experienced by Oberman is essentially metaphysical; 'on végète dans un lieu d'exil', and this is the common fate of all men. In contrast, Adolphe, Amaury, and Dominique are all unhappy for more immediate and specific reasons and are in any case, unlike Oberman, primarily unhappy in love. In fact, Oberman distinguishes between two forms of unhappiness when he writes: '. . . souffrir ou être malheureux, ce n'est pas la même chose' (XVIII). On the basis of this distinction, we must say that Oberman is 'malheureux'—and his unhappiness has a universal quality inseparable from general human existence. By the same token, Adolphe, Amaury, and Dominique 'souffrent'—and their suffering has an individual quality inseparable from the particular circumstances of their lives. Significantly enough, it is metaphysical suffering that most readily allows of energetic rebellion. It is Oberman—not Adolphe, Amaury, or Dominique—who writes: 'L'homme est périssable. — Il se peut, mais périssons en résistant, et, si le néant nous est réservé, ne faisons pas que ce soit une justice' (XC).

In the case of Constant, warmth and sincerity are two of his reiterated ideals, and they are obviously important in a writer given to self-disclosure. He began life with rather different aims, possibly at variance with his true nature, but in 1794 (at the age of 26) he wrote a famous letter to his aunt, the Comtesse de Nassau, which contains the following passage suggesting that he is emerging from a form of personal crisis:

J'ai trop senti qu'on a beau se piquer de se mettre au-dessus des côtés touchants pour ne voir que les côtés ridicules, on ne sonde pas les profondeurs; le plaisir d'amour-propre que cette manie donne n'équivaut pas à une minute où l'on sent. Je suis fatigué de mon propre persiflage, je suis fatigué d'entourer mon cœur d'une triste atmosphère d'indifférence qui me prive des sensations les plus douces. Puisque ce faste de dédain ne m'a pas rendu heureux, au diable la gloire d'être supérieur à ceux qui sentent; j'aime mieux la folie de l'enthousiasme, si ce qui rend heureux est folie, que cette funeste sagesse, et quand ce ne serait que par égoïsme et par calcul, je veux cesser d'être calculateur et égoïste.

Inevitably, this passage has given rise to a good deal of comment and speculation. Some readers have seen in it a particularly clear expression of Constant's dual nature—the so-called 'dédoublement constantien'. Others have pointed out that in some ways these lines suggest the moral development of Adolphe in Constant's novel. Adolphe sets about winning Ellénore's affection in a calculating manner that suggests the libertine approach, yet he goes on to experience later promptings of conscience and moments of regret that prevent him from carrying out the logical consequences of his initial *démarche*. Critics ready to risk bolder generalizations have suggested that the letter indicates the meeting-point of two centuries and reveals late eighteenth-century rationalism and cynicism giving way to the emotion and sensibility that were to characterize Romanticism. Whatever the value of these various interpretations, the point of immediate relevance to the study of *Adolphe* is that in the first and second chapters respectively we find statements consistent with the last phrase quoted above: 'Je ne veux pas ici me justifier' and 'Presque toujours, pour vivre en repos avec nous-mêmes, nous travestissons en calculs et en systèmes nos impuissances et nos faiblesses'. In a word, Constant is aware of—and apparently determined to resist—what Senancour called 'cette manie des beaux dehors'.

When we look at *Adolphe* more closely, however, we may doubt the hero's disclaimer of any attempt at self-justification. Adolphe's analytical account of his adolescence (which closely resembles Constant's own youth) is in fact an elaborate way of saying that he was bound to behave less than well towards Ellénore because of an eccentric upbringing and the effect of corrupting social influences. What we are offered is certainly not unvarnished self-disclosure but a subtly ordered self-analysis which comes close to self-excuse as it alternates between blaming the individual and blaming society. Despite protests to the contrary, Adolphe tells his story in a manner that frequently confuses explanation with justification. This is why, in the second of the two brief letters which follow the *anecdote* proper, Constant writes (in the person of the *éditeur*, thus putting a distinct distance between himself and Adolphe):

La grande question dans la vie, c'est la douleur que l'on cause, et la métaphysique la plus ingénieuse ne justifie pas l'homme qui a déchiré le cœur qui l'aimait. Je hais d'ailleurs cette fatuité d'un esprit qui croit excuser ce qu'il explique; je hais cette vanité qui s'occupe d'elle-même en racontant le mal qu'elle a fait. . . .

With characteristically acute perception Constant is aware of the morally disturbing relationship established in the novel between necessity and responsibility, between 'I was unable to help it' and 'I ought not to have done it'. If we add to this the evidence of a strongly autobiographical element in the book (the circumstantial similarities to Constant's own life; his phrase in his *Journaux intimes*: 'Commencé un roman qui sera notre histoire'; the evidence of such witnesses as Sismondi and Charles de Constant) we can see that he is exploring the possibilities, and encountering the difficulties, of an *apologia pro vita sua*.

The element of moral ambiguity just referred to takes on a much more positive role, however—and indeed becomes a moving and central theme—once we read *Adolphe* primarily as a novel about human nature generally, rather than as an essay in self-disclosure by Constant. For example, the prefaces which Constant wrote to the second and third editions of the book make it clear that he wished to emphasize, *en connaissance de cause*, the dangers inherent in certain human relationships—relationships entered upon too casually or irresponsibly. These dangers, leading to intense human unhappiness, are particularly associated with the break-up of a liaison based on insecure foundations and formed within a certain kind of social context. The obvious sufferings of the deserted woman are set out by Constant in his preface to the second edition. The sufferings of the man involved, perhaps less obvious but equally deep, are also described with typical insight:

Pour les hommes mêmes, il n'est pas indifférent de faire ce mal. Presque tous se croient bien plus mauvais, plus légers qu'ils ne sont. Ils pensent pouvoir rompre avec facilité le lien qu'ils contractent avec insouciance. . . . Mais lorsque ces larmes coulent, la nature revient en eux, malgré l'atmosphère factice dont ils s'étaient environnés. Ils sentent qu'un être qui souffre par ce qu'il aime est sacré. Ils sentent que dans leur cœur même qu'ils ne croyaient pas avoir mis de la partie, se sont enfoncées les racines du sentiment qu'ils ont inspiré, et s'ils veulent dompter ce que par habitude ils nomment faiblesse, il faut qu'ils descendent dans ce cœur misérable, qu'ils y froissent ce qu'il y a de généreux, qu'ils y brisent ce qu'il y a de fidèle, qu'ils y tuent ce qu'il y a de bon. Ils réussissent, mais en frappant de mort une portion de leur âme, et ils sortent de ce travail ayant trompé la confiance, bravé la sympathie, abusé de la faiblesse, insulté la morale en la rendant l'excuse de la dureté, profané toutes les expressions et foulé aux pieds tous les sentiments. Ils survivent ainsi à leur meilleure nature, pervertis par leur victoire, ou honteux de cette victoire, si elle ne les a pas pervertis.

Up to this point Constant largely confines himself to the viewpoint of the stern moralist. In the last paragraph of this same preface, however, he takes the argument further and shows the full tragic dilemma facing Adolphe who can, at best, only choose between two evils. He writes:

Quelques personnes m'ont demandé ce qu'aurait dû faire Adolphe, pour éprouver et causer moins de peine? Sa position et celle d'Ellénore étaient sans ressource, et c'est précisément ce que j'ai voulu. Je l'ai montré tourmenté, parce qu'il n'aimait que faiblement Ellénore; mais il n'eût pas été moins tourmenté, s'il l'eût aimée davantage. Il souffrait par elle, faute de sentiments: avec un sentiment plus passionné, il eût souffert pour elle. La société, désapprobatrice et dédaigneuse, aurait versé tous ses venins sur l'affection que son aveu n'eût pas sanctionnée.

In this novel, then, we see a young man caught in a trap of his own (largely thoughtless) devising. He cannot feel love for a woman towards whom he has nevertheless assumed considerable obligations. Although he does not love her, Adolphe pities and admires Ellénore to such an extent that to desert her appears both unthinkable and also the only possible solution to his problem. He has an equally ambivalent attitude towards the society in which he lives and which disapproves of his persistence in this liaison. He scorns the fundamental hypocrisy of this particular society, yet also wishes to obtain its fruits, to rise within its system of hierarchies. His conflict is one between personal integrity and social advancement. Whichever alternative he chooses will bring him moral damage, cause suffering to others, and reduce radically his own evaluation of himself. Furthermore, as regards his particular relationship with Ellénore, there is the cruel fact that his best qualities—pity, the promptings of his 'better self', and genuine concern for Ellénore's plight—add to and heighten the tragedy. His very virtues prolong the agony experienced both by Ellénore and by himself. Indeed, one of the most moving aspects of this novel is its demonstration of the way in which sensitivity to the sufferings of others may simply intensify those sufferings. *Adolphe* presents us with a situation, in fact, in which normal moral distinctions threaten to become either finally irrelevant, or positively damaging, or both.

Passages such as those quoted above give some idea of Constant's ability to dissect human experience. This same analytical intelligence continually informs the *anecdote* itself. Within the fictional framework, and through the characters of Adolphe and Ellénore, Constant lays bare the complex interactions of egotism and pity, weakness and the workings of conscience, social conformity and self-deceit. A brief example, which also conveys the characteristic tone of the novel, is provided by part of the early account of Ellénore's reaction to her situation as the Comte de P***'s mistress:

Ellénore n'avait qu'un esprit ordinaire; mais ses idées étaient justes, et ses expressions, toujours simples, étaient quelquefois frappantes par la noblesse et l'élévation de ses sentiments. Elle avait beaucoup de préjugés; mais tous ses préjugés étaient en sens inverse de son intérêt. Elle attachait le plus grand prix à la régularité de la conduite, précisément parce que la sienne n'était pas régulière suivant les notions reçues. Elle était très religieuse, parce que la religion condamnait rigoureusement son genre de vie. Elle repoussait sévèrement dans la conversation tout ce qui n'aurait paru à d'autres femmes que des plaisanteries innocentes, parce qu'elle craignait toujours qu'on ne se crût autorisé par son état à lui en adresser de déplacées. Elle aurait désiré ne recevoir chez elle que des hommes du rang le plus élevé et de mœurs irréprochables, parce que les femmes, à qui elle frémissait d'être comparée, se forment d'ordinaire une société mélangée, et, se résignant à la perte de la considération, ne cherchent dans leurs relations que l'amusement. Ellénore, en un mot, était en lutte constante avec sa destinée.

It is worth pointing out, incidentally, that Constant moves repeatedly from individual notations of this type to generalized assertions about human beings. The human relevance of Adolphe's and Ellénore's dilemma is broadened to such a degree that Adolphe himself becomes a paradigm of human weakness at large. Constant regularly moves from the individuality of Adolphe's character and situation to such universal statements as: 'Nous sommes des créatures tellement mobiles que les sentiments que nous feignons, nous finissons par les éprouver.'

At the technical level *Adolphe* is a stylish and closely structured novel. Constant skilfully ensures that the various parts interlock tightly. The whole unhappy story of Adolphe's failure to love Ellénore—and also of his inability not to pity her profoundly—

takes on the quality of tragic inevitability. Words, echoes of words, and images all contribute to the closely knit unity of the book. Again, the analyses of Adolphe's character and of Ellénore's social situation, backed up by suggestions of premonition on Ellénore's part, point to the fatal growth of a liaison, already sapped by social disapproval, from its birth and development to its deterioration and death. At times, too, the connecting links are formed by means of ironic counterpointing. For example, the ecstatic address to love which opens chapter iv ('Charme de l'amour, qui pourrait vous peindre...') contains a series of theoretical statements which Adolphe's subsequent experiences prove to be entirely false—at least where he himself is concerned. The six chapters which follow this passage deny at every point Adolphe's initial conviction that love can be accurately characterized as 'tant de plaisir dans la présence, et dans l'absence tant d'espoir, ce détachement de tous les soins vulgaires, cette supériorité sur tout ce qui nous entoure, cette certitude que désormais le monde ne peut nous atteindre où nous vivons, cette intelligence mutuelle qui devine chaque pensée et qui répond à chaque émotion . . .'. Ultimately the whole story is tautly drawn together, focused, and unified in the complex personality of the hero himself. It is the moral complexity within unity of Adolphe's character, and the moral subtlety of his situation, which make this one of the finest examples of psychological fiction.

Such high claims can hardly be made for Sainte-Beuve's *Volupté*. It has something of the slow pace of *Oberman* and lacks the concision and stylistic *éclat* of *Adolphe*; it is not nearly as humanly convincing as the former, just as it is technically inferior to the latter. Once again this is a novel with distinct autobiographical elements. There are various similarities between the fictional relationship of Amaury and Mme de Couaën and the real-life relationship of Sainte-Beuve and Mme Hugo. Sainte-Beuve himself lays claim to authenticity and sincerity. He speaks of 'le personnage non fictif' who is the main character of *Volupté* and adds: '. . . j'y ai mis le plus que j'ai pu de mon observation et de mon expérience . . . sous une forme presque directe, et avec peu d'arrangements.' More frequently and intrusively than Adolphe, Amaury speaks of destiny and fate in such phrases as 'j'aurais dû lire l'intention de la Providence sur ma destinée' or 'l'enchaînement plus ou moins fatal des motifs'. In contrast with Constant, however, Sainte-Beuve does not work a tragic destiny into the very texture and structure of his novel. He refers to destiny, he apostrophizes fate, but he hardly uncovers the springs of inevitability in the nature and situation of his characters.

Again, unlike either Senancour or Constant, Sainte-Beuve allows himself a great deal of moralizing and not a little humbug. The following few lines are typical of a recurring didacticism throughout the novel:

Il y a en ce monde la beauté selon les sens, il y a la beauté selon l'âme: la première, charnelle, opaque, immédiatement discernable; la seconde, qui ne frappe pas moins peut-être à la simple vue, mais qui demande qu'on s'y élève davantage, qu'on en pénètre la transparente substance et qu'on en saisisse les symboles voilés. Idole et symbole, révélation et piège, voilà le double aspect de l'humaine beauté depuis Ève.

As regards what I call humbug, examples abound. The following passage, self-conscious and wordy, is merely the beginning of Amaury's account of how, frustrated by Mme de Couaën's inaccessibility, he looked for and found a prostitute:

Un jour enfin . . . je sortis du logis dans une résolution violente. Ce jour-là, rien de particulier ne m'était arrivé; en la voyant le matin (faut-il hélas! que je mêle ce saint nom par aucun rapprochement en de tels récits!), le matin, dis-je, elle n'avait été pour moi ni trop distraite ni trop attentive; elle ne m'avait ni troublé les sens ni froissé l'âme. Je n'avais eu non plus, si je m'en souviens, ni spectacle ulcérant pour mon ambition, ni querelle avec personne, ni accès de colère, aucun de ces petits torts ou désappointements qui, nous mettant mal avec nous-mêmes, nous rabaissent à l'ivresse, à la satisfaction brutale, comme dédommagement et oubli. Rien donc ne me poussait, ce jour-là, que ma seule démence: mais je voulais en finir, et je m'étais dit cela en me levant.

Both these passages contain that element of attitudinizing which lies in wait for the 'confessional' novelist and from which only Senancour is triumphantly free. Sainte-Beuve indulges in the kind of posturing which we think of as one of the most common personal and literary vices of Romanticism. As a result, despite the use of the fictional first person singular, we are uncomfortably aware of a

gap between Sainte-Beuve and Amaury—a gap largely filled with
complacent rhetoric and the assumption of morally unconvincing
attitudes. A different gap—that between the Romantic sensibility
and our own—is perhaps suggested by the fact that the Amaury
whom Sainte-Beuve offered to our sympathetic understanding is
half-brother to the Clamence whom Camus invited us to condemn.

What has been said above suggests that *Volupté* is a very 'literary'
novel in the sense of rather self-conscious posturing. It is also
'literary' in its author's consciousness of other novels of a similar
type and in its reminiscences of *Adolphe*. Some of the more penetrating psychological analyses recall *Adolphe* quite directly, as
when Amaury confesses: '. . . l'imagination en ce genre est si
mobile, le cœur si bizarre et si aisément mensonger, qu'à mesure
que je prodiguais ces expansions d'un jeune Werther, je me les
persuadais suffisamment.'

Finally, apart from posturing and a tendency (natural, perhaps,
in a major literary critic such as Sainte-Beuve) to lean on other
novelists, a further fault in *Volupté* is the unconvincing quality of the
dialogue. There are many examples of dialogue that is purely literary
and fails completely to catch the rhythm of the spoken word. The
following exchange between Amaury and Mme de Couaën is typical:

'Ainsi, disais-je, ainsi sans doute dans la vie, quand tout est dépouillé
en nous, quand nous descendons les avenues sans feuillage, il est de ces
jours où les cœurs rajeunis étincellent comme au printemps: les premiers
tintements de l'âge glacé nous arrivent dans un angélus presque joyeux.
Est-ce illusion décevante; un écho perdu de la jeunesse sur cette pente
qui mène à la mort? Est-ce annonce et promesse d'un séjour d'au-delà?'
— 'C'est promesse assurément', disait-elle. — 'Oui, reprenais-je, c'est
quelque appel lointain, une excitation affectueuse de se hâter et d'avoir
confiance à l'entrée des jours ténébreux, de ces jours dont il est dit *non
placent*.'

If *Volupté* is a typical product of the Romantic sensibility in its
less admirable manifestations, Fromentin's *Dominique* has rightly
been described as 'a farewell to Romanticism'. It is true that
Fromentin wrote his novel out of a close familiarity with his predecessors in the genre, including *Oberman*, *Adolphe*, and *Volupté*
(which he claimed to have read close on twenty times). The fact

G

remains, however, that *Dominique* is very different from these other novels despite the presence of several stock scenes from the Romantic *roman personnel* and other reminiscences of Fromentin's reading. The novel possesses, for instance, a very significant structure. The main story of the youthful and now distant love of Dominique for Madeleine, balanced by Julie's passion for Dominique's friend Olivier, is preceded and followed by sections relating to Dominique's present life. In these he appears as a gentleman farmer now living a peaceful and contented life with his wife and children. It is his memory of an adolescent love-affair, seen from the vantage-point of his present calm existence, which gives rise to the central section of the book. The extent to which Dominique has now distanced himself from Romantic attitudes is suggested by some phrases attributed to him on the very first page: 'Certainement je n'ai pas à me plaindre. . . . J'ai trouvé la certitude et le repos, ce qui vaut mieux que toutes les hypothèses. Je me suis mis d'accord avec moi-même. . . .' Self-knowledge, maturity, and the conquest of inner conflicts represent the nature of Dominique's triumph over Romanticism in the form of self-dramatization and a striving after impossible goals. A searching self-scrutiny has made this triumph possible. On the last page of the novel Dominique is described as 'un esprit dont la plus réelle originalité était d'avoir strictement suivi la maxime ancienne de se connaître soi-même!' There is a sense, then, in which *Dominique* is a novel of comfort for middle age rather than of stimulation for youth. It possesses autumnal charm and a certain wistful beauty as it reiterates the view (also expressed in Oberman's ideal of becoming 'sans état comme sans passions') that happiness can only be experienced once we have related our aims and ambitions to a realistic assessment of our own limitations. Fromentin regards self-knowledge as a means to both happiness and truth once it has revealed those personal facts which prompt renunciation rather than aspiration.

Like the other authors discussed in this chapter, Fromentin underwent various forms of frustration and estrangement which induced a distinct strain of melancholy in him and turned him in upon himself. With considerable justification he wrote in a letter of 1842: 'Je suis né pour une activité tout intérieure.' It is not surprising that his hopeless love for Jenny Chessé (who married in 1834 and died ten years later) encouraged both self-absorption and self-disclosure. He wrote at the time of her death: 'Amie, ma divine et sainte amie, je veux et vais écrire notre histoire commune, depuis le premier jour jusqu'au dernier.' The result of this resolve was *Dominique*, though he did not begin the composition of the novel until fifteen years later. The lapse of time is significant. Time, as well as the demands of art, brought about various changes in the real-life characters and situations forming the material of his novel. One should add, however, that as a description of his own temperament *Dominique* seems to have remained very accurate. What is mainly important about the time-lag between experience and writing is that Fromentin, by recollecting his own past 'in tranquillity', allowed memory both to filter and to intensify the experience. Much more than the other three novels already discussed, *Dominique* depends on the joint mechanism of absence and recollection, a mechanism described in chapter ii:

L'absence unit et désunit, elle rapproche aussi bien qu'elle divise, elle fait se souvenir, elle fait oublier; elle relâche certains liens très-solides, elle les tend et les éprouve au point de les briser; il y a des liaisons soi-disant indestructibles dans lesquelles elle fait d'irrémédiables avaries; elle accumule des mondes d'indifférence sur des promesses de souvenirs éternels. Et puis d'un germe imperceptible, d'un lien inaperçu, d'un *adieu, monsieur*, qui ne devait pas avoir de lendemain, elle compose, avec des riens, en les tissant je ne sais comment, une de ces trames vigoureuses sur lesquelles deux amitiés viriles peuvent très-bien se reposer pour le reste de leur vie, car ces attaches-là sont de toute durée. Les chaînes composées de la sorte à notre insu, avec la substance la plus pure et la plus vivace de nos sentiments, par cette mystérieuse ouvrière, sont comme un insaisissable rayon qui va de l'un à l'autre, et ne craignent plus rien, ni des distances ni du temps. Le temps les fortifie, la distance peut les prolonger indéfiniment sans les rompre.

Dominique closely resembles Fromentin when he describes himself as possessing 'je ne sais quelle mémoire spéciale assez peu sensible aux faits, mais d'une aptitude singulière à se pénétrer des impressions'.

If this 'affective' and impressionistic memory has much to do with the formal shaping of *Dominique*, it also contributes significantly to the tonality of the novel. Furthermore, the fact that Fromentin was a painter and art critic, as well as a man of letters, is especially noticeable in the descriptions of the landscape around La Rochelle which contribute to the moral tone as well as the physical setting of the book. They are carefully composed, they show a penetrating eye for detail, and they abound in acute perceptions of colour, taste, and smell. But they also possess a moral dimension built up, in particular, by attaching epithets with primarily human associations to natural phenomena: 'une ombre sévère', 'un silence hargneux', etc. Fromentin arranges these details in such a way that landscape and individual mood reinforce one another without the customary Romantic invocations of the pathetic fallacy. The provinces of Saintonge and Aunis, with their desolate plains and lonely farms, materialize the moral elements in a story which Fromentin puts in artistic rather than didactic terms.

The novel of self-disclosure has not always been well regarded by critics. Thibaudet, for example (in *Réflexions sur le roman*), looked to purely imaginative works for evidence of the authentic novelist: '. . . le romancier authentique crée ses personnages avec les directions infinies de sa vie possible, le romancier factice les crée avec la ligne unique de sa vie réelle.' The misunderstanding inherent in this statement arises from Thibaudet's assumption that the line between the writing self and the fictional self can be direct and undeviating. The novels examined in this chapter make it clear, in fact (Senancour is perhaps a unique exception), that deliberate and successful self-disclosure in fiction requires imagination and artistry of a high order. The novelist's objectivity as an artist is in continual conflict with his subjectivity as the material of his own novel. This difficulty, which Proust was later to overcome in such a brilliant manner, lies behind his distinction, reversing that of Thibaudet, between 'la pente facile de l'imagination' and 'la pente abrupte de l'introspection'.

NOTE

ÉTIENNE PIVERT DE SENANCOUR, 1770–1846, lived a life marked by financial straits, disillusionment in marriage, and general lack of social adaptability. On returning to his native Paris from Switzerland in 1794 he lived mainly by his pen. In 1795 he published *Aldomen ou le bonheur dans l'obscurité*, an embryonic version of *Oberman* (1804). Other works include *Rêveries sur la nature primitive de l'homme* (1799), *De l'amour considéré dans les lois réelles et dans les formes sociales de l'union des sexes* (1806), *Observations critiques sur l'ouvrage intitulé 'Génie du Christianisme'* (1816), *Libres Méditations d'un solitaire inconnu* (1819), and an unsuccessful novel *Isabelle* (1833).

HENRI-BENJAMIN CONSTANT DE REBECQUE, 1767–1830, was born in Lausanne of Swiss Protestant stock. He had a colourful career as man-of-letters, lover (to Mme de Staël, Mme Récamier, and others), liberal politician, journalist, and religious thinker. Constant wrote two novels, *Adolphe* (1816) and *Cécile* (posth. publ. 1951). Other major publications in his lifetime include: *Cours de politique constitutionnelle* (4 vols., 1818–19); *De la religion considérée dans sa source, ses formes et ses développements* (5 vols., 1824–31); *Mélanges de littérature et de politique* (1829). Also of major importance are the posthumously published *Journal intime* (1895)—a more reliable version is *Journaux intimes*, ed. A. Roulin and C. Roth, 1952—and *Le Cahier rouge* (1907).

CHARLES-AUGUSTIN SAINTE-BEUVE, 1804–69, is the most famous of French literary critics. Some of his best critical writing is to be found in *Critiques et portraits littéraires* (5 vols., 1836–9), *Port-Royal* (6 vols., 1840–59), *Causeries du lundi* (15 vols., 1851–62), and *Nouveaux lundis* (13 vols., 1863–70). In addition to the novel *Volupté* (1834) he also published volumes of poetry: *Vie, Poésies et Pensées de Joseph Delorme* (1829), *Les Consolations* (1830), and the privately circulated *Livre d'amour* containing poems addressed to Hugo's wife.

EUGÈNE FROMENTIN, 1820–76, was a painter and art critic as well as a writer and traveller. His main travel-writings are *Un Été dans le Sahara* (1857) and *Une Année dans le Sahel* (1859). In addition to his one novel, *Dominique* (1862), he published a well-known study of Dutch and Flemish painting, *Les Maîtres d'autrefois* (1876).

Editions. The best editions of the four novels discussed in the preceding chapter are: *Oberman* (introd. G. Borgeaud, 1965); *Adolphe* (ed. J. H. Bornecque, 1963); *Volupté* (ed. M. P. Poux, 2 vols., 1927); *Dominique* (ed. Barbara Wright, 1965).

Criticism. Oberman: see J. Merlant, *Senancour, sa vie, son œuvre, son influence* (1907); G. Michaut, *Senancour, ses amis et ses ennemis* (1910); A. Monglond, *Le Journal intime d'Oberman* (1947); M. Raymond, *Senancour: sensations et révélations* (1965); and Béatrice Le Gall, *L'Imaginaire chez Senancour* (2 vols., 1966).

Adolphe: see G. Rudler, *'Adolphe' de Benjamin Constant* (1935); H. Nicolson, *Benjamin Constant* (1949), pp. 168–86; M. Turnell, *The Novel in France* (1950), pp. 79-122; J. Cruickshank, *Benjamin Constant* (1974). Three indispensable articles by Alison Fairlie are: 'The Art of Constant's *Adolphe*: Structure and Style', *French Studies*, 20 (1966); 'The Art of Constant's *Adolphe*: Creation of Character', *Forum for Modern Language Studies*, 2 (1966); 'The Art of Constant's *Adolphe*: the Stylization of Experience', *Modern Language Review*, 12 (1967).

Volupté: see M. Allem, *Sainte-Beuve et 'Volupté'* (1935); Y. le Hir, *L'Originalité littéraire de Sainte-Beuve dans 'Volupté'* (1953); H. Nicolson, *Sainte-Beuve* (1957), pp. 80-99; and R. Grimsley, 'Romantic Melancholy in Sainte-Beuve's *Volupté*', in *Studies in Modern French Literature presented to P. Mansell Jones* (1961).

Dominique: see C. Reynaud, *La Genèse de 'Dominique'* (1937); A. Lagrange, *L'Art de Fromentin* (1952); J. Vier, *Pour l'étude du 'Dominique' de Fromentin* (1958); and C. J. Greshoff, *Seven Studies in the French Novel* (1964), pp. 53-70.

General studies. The problems of self-knowledge are discussed from various psychological and philosophical angles in such books as J. Laird, *Problems of the Self* (1917), J. Rivière, *De la sincérité envers soi-même* (1925), G. Gusdorf, *La Découverte de soi* (1948), and S. Shoemaker, *Self-knowledge and Self-identity* (1963). The best book on the literary implications of self-disclosure remains P. Mansell Jones, *French Introspectives from Montaigne to Gide* (1937). Other useful works include J. Merlant, *Le Roman personnel de Rousseau à Fromentin* (1905), J. Hytier, *Les Romans de l'individu* (1928), R. Pascal, *Design and Truth in Autobiography* (1960), H. Peyre, *Literature and Sincerity* (1963), and L. Trilling, *Sincerity and Authenticity* (1972).

11. Baudelaire

IN *Le Spleen de Paris*, Baudelaire's posthumous collection of prose-poems, there is a piece called 'Assommons les pauvres!' Probably the title alone is enough to explain why it was never published; it was rejected by one magazine in 1865. It is a simple anecdote describing the right way to deal with the poor. The poet tells how he was approached by a beggar 'avec un de ces regards inoubliables qui culbuteraient les trônes, si l'esprit remuait la matière'; and how, at the same time, his good Demon whispered in his ear: 'Celui-là, seul, est l'égal d'un autre, qui le prouve, et celui-là, seul, est digne de la liberté, qui sait la conquérir.' It was clear what he ought to do: 'Immédiatement, je sautai sur mon mendiant.' The fight that follows is worthy of Hemingway, brutal in details and terse in description. The poet breaks a nail, the beggar a couple of teeth. And then — 'tout à coup, — ô miracle! ô puissance du philosophe qui vérifie l'excellence de sa théorie! — je vis cette antique carcasse se retourner, se redresser avec une énergie que je n'aurais jamais soupçonnée', and the poet loses four teeth. The beggar 'me battit dru comme plâtre'. And so there is a happy ending; the poet congratulates his conqueror—'Monsieur, vous êtes mon égal!'—and shares his money with him.

What was the 'theory' that the poet verified, and that the beggar, to his delight, understood? It was that aggression should not be bottled up, but released; that humanitarianism is degrading, for it does not treat men as equals; that if you 'insist on loving humanity, . . . sure as fate you'll come to hate everybody'; that 'wise speech and good intentions' are 'invariably maggotty, . . . something foul'. It was a rejection of the liberal, humanist, optimist beliefs so central to the nineteenth century, the doctrines of the progressive bourgeoisie—of John Stuart Mill in England, say, or of Proudhon in France. And the first version of 'Assommons les pauvres' had a final sentence which Baudelaire later removed, 'Qu'en dis-tu, citoyen Proudhon?'

Baudelaire's hostility to liberalism and the bourgeoisie pervades all his work. 'Pourquoi les démocrates n'aiment pas les chats', he wrote in *Fusées*, his private diaries, 'il est facile de deviner. Le chat est beau.' In his essay on the Exposition Universelle of 1855 he denounced progress as 'ce fanal perfide . . . qui a déchargé chacun de son devoir, délivré toute âme de sa responsabilité, dégagé la volonté de tous les biens que lui imposait l'amour du beau'. He regards poetry and progress as 'deux ambitieux qui se haïssent d'une haine instinctive' ('Salon de 1859'); and elsewhere in *Fusées* he describes the enmity between the poet and the bourgeois with a characteristic note, in which irony trembles on the edge of direct malice: 'Si un poète demandait à l'État le droit d'avoir quelques bourgeois dans son écuelle, on serait fort étonné, tandis que si un bourgeois demandait du poète rôti, on le trouverait tout naturel.'

By this hostility, Baudelaire places himself in a long line of writers (too long, we may sadly feel) who since his day have rejected liberalism because its view of man is too rational, or too superficial, and have rejected too the social benefits of the liberal attitude. In England, the most famous of these is D. H. Lawrence; and with a little stylistic doctoring, 'Assommons les pauvres' could easily pass for Lawrence, the Lawrence who wrote 'in my opinion, there are worse insults than floggings. I would rather be flogged than have most people "like" me', and whose contempt for 'loving humanity' and for 'wise speech and good intentions' has already been quoted on the previous page.

It is not merely the respectable bourgeoisie, the stuffed shirts, the *bons pères de familles*, the small-town mayors, M. de Rênal and M. Valenod, whom Baudelaire rejects; he is equally contemptuous of the radicals, those who reject respectability in the name of a society that will be better suited to man's best aspirations. In both art and literature Baudelaire rejected realism, the aesthetic creed of radicalism; he soon repented of his support for the revolutionaries of 1848; he despised the Utopians 'qui veulent, par un décret, rendre tous les Français riches et vertueux d'un seul coup' ('Projet de préface pour *Les Fleurs du mal*'). The human heart, as Baudelaire

sees it, offers little or no ground for faith in man. It is 'un abîme
béant', 'un volcan', 'un monstre gémissant'. The very first lines of
Les Fleurs du mal announce his view of man:

> La sottise, l'erreur, le péché, la lésine,
> Occupent nos esprits et travaillent nos corps...

The result of this attitude is that Baudelaire's poetry is continually concerned with extreme, even with perverted experiences,
and that these are set against the normal, the healthy, the everyday
—the bourgeois. As a framework, therefore, for a discussion of his
poems, let us draw up a rough list of the forms which such extreme
experience can take: drugs, art, necrophilia, satanism, sex, spleen,
travel. It is a list of the subjects of *Les Fleurs du mal*.

First, drugs: their attraction is that they heighten sensibility,
enable us to be more receptive, and open up areas of experience that
the daily round excludes. The two drugs that interested Baudelaire
were alcohol and hashish. The poems grouped under the general
title, *Le Vin*, are studies of various kinds of frenetic experience, such
as that of the drunken rag-and-bone man who sees himself as a
conqueror:

> Il prête des serments, dicte des lois sublimes,
> Terrasse les méchants, relève les victimes,
> Et sous le firmament comme un dais suspendu
> S'enivre des splendeurs de sa propre vertu.

To narcotics Baudelaire devoted a fascinating book called *Les
Paradis artificiels*: his own essay on hashish, followed by his translation of de Quincey's *Confessions of an English Opium Eater*. The
modern reader will naturally compare this with the work of Michaux
and Huxley, both of whom have written of drugs as a way of en-
larging experience. Yet though experience is, in one sense, enlarged,
the word is misleading: most of those who have taken the milder
drugs report that they have not *escaped* from the self but *explored* it.
Thus Baudelaire reports that your dream under hashish will retain
'la tonalité particulière de l'individu'. It offers nothing but an
exaggeration of what is yours, anyway: it is 'un miroir grossissant,
mais un pur miroir'.

This might seem to us an attraction, but in the last section of his essay Baudelaire uses it as a ground for condemning the drug: 'le haschisch ne révèle à l'individu rien que l'individu lui-même.' After some of the almost ecstatic descriptions he has given us, it comes as a surprise to find how completely, in the last section, Baudelaire condemns hashish. The Egyptian government is right to ban it if it makes neither warriors nor citizens. But his real reason for the rejection is not so social or sensible, it is that 'tout homme qui n'accepte pas les conditions de la vie, vend son âme'. We sell our souls if we try to escape from 'la liberté humaine et l'indispensable douleur'. It is a characteristic argument: the human condition is precious, above all for its pain. There is to be no easy way out.

Nothing could be more firmly moral than this: and even the wild poems about wine are, in their way, surprisingly moral. The best of them is probably 'Le Vin des chiffonniers', and in the stanza already quoted we can see where it gets its stiffening. The stanza is written with great gusto, but it is a self-conscious gusto. At each chopped phrase—'Il prête des serments—dicte des lois sublimes' —we can see the drunkard making another and wilder gesture, until he almost topples down at 'terrasse les méchants', and staggers up on 'relève les victimes'. The poem enjoys the inebriation, but at the same time shows us how exaggerated, how precarious the joy is. And the stanza ends on a line—'S'enivre des splendeurs de sa propre vertu'—that could be either the happy thought passing through the poor devil's own mind or the cool comment of a bystander. For all the careful distinction that Baudelaire draws in his essay between wine and hashish, we can see that the wine too is a way of selling one's soul.

'L'homme n'est pas si abandonné, si privé de moyens honnêtes pour gagner le ciel, qu'il soit obligé d'invoquer la pharmacie et la sorcellerie.' Such is the final scathing assertion of the *Paradis artificiels*. What are the 'moyens honnêtes'? The most obvious is art: and it is clear that Baudelaire valued art for much the same qualities as he would have valued drug-taking, if he had not despised it. This is quite explicit in his most memorable piece of art criticism, the essay on Constantin Guys, called 'Le Peintre de la vie moderne'. Here Baudelaire compares the artist to the child and to the convalescent, because they are not bored by the everyday.

'L'enfant voit tout en *nouveauté*; il est toujours *ivre*.' It is a doctrine similar to that of great English Romantics, trying with their poetry to lift the film of familiarity from common things, to 'throw over them a certain colouring of imagination, whereby ordinary things be presented to the mind in an unusual aspect'. The difference is that the everyday subject-matter, both of Guys and of the *Tableaux parisiens* of Baudelaire, is not rocks and stones and trees but city life, and that Baudelaire stresses, as Wordsworth does not, the physical intensity of the reaction of child, artist, and convalescent: 'j'affirme que l'inspiration a quelque rapport avec la *congestion*, et que toute pensée sublime est accompagnée d'une secousse nerveuse, plus ou moins forte, qui retentit jusque dans le cervelet.' Baudelaire's conception of sensibility thus looks not only back to the Romantics, but forward to Proust and Virginia Woolf. This is a point we shall return to shortly.

Let us turn now to perhaps the most scandalous form of extreme emotion that Baudelaire throws at us, the necrophilia or love of death that runs through many of the poems on other subjects, and dominates a few of the sonnets. It is not simply the melancholy death-wish of Keats or Lamartine, the longing to find shelter from the complexities of living in an infantile, erotic, and often very moving self-surrender. Baudelaire has that too, but his really shocking poems on death are those that linger floatingly on physical decay, that tell us, with something like triumph, of rotting corpses and damp graves—poems like 'Une Charogne', 'Un Voyage à Cythère', and 'Remords posthume':

> Lorsque tu dormiras, ma belle ténébreuse,
> Au fond d'un monument construit en marbre noir,
> Et lorsque tu n'auras pour alcôve et manoir,
> Qu'un caveau pluvieux et qu'une fosse creuse,
>
> Quand la pierre, opprimant ta poitrine peureuse
> Et tes flancs qu'assouplit un charmant nonchaloir,
> Empêchera ton cœur de battre et de vouloir,
> Et tes pieds de courir leur course aventureuse,
>
> Le tombeau, confident de mon rêve infini
> (Car le tombeau toujours comprendra le poète),
> Durant ces grandes nuits d'où le somme est banni,

Te dira: 'Que vous sert, courtisane imparfaite,
De n'avoir pas connu ce que pleurent les morts?'
— Et le ver rongera ta peau comme un remords.

Extreme experience does not in itself guarantee poetic power. The truth might even be nearer the opposite. Shocking the bourgeoisie is not likely to call forth a poet's full powers, since the desire to shock is a thin frenetic desire, unlikely to engage the whole personality in the way a great poem must. It is therefore a central problem with Baudelaire's poetry, to ask what stiffens the otherwise shrill and crude impulse, and turns a mere flout or sneer into a true poem. Partly, the answer lies in the form itself. Baudelaire's poems wear impeccable uniform, and the fact has more than a merely mechanical importance: the perfection with which a sonnet is turned or a rhyme-scheme maintained implies a control over even the shrillest emotion, and can turn it from a snigger to a poem. This point must not be underrated, but it is not enough in itself: for of the finest poems we demand not merely formal control, but an element of mastery in the emotional content too; and this sonnet, powerful and moving, though not one of Baudelaire's masterpieces, will help to show how that is present. It is present because of *ma belle ténébreuse*. The revolting facts of death are thrown not directly at the reader, but at her. We are to feel that this is the home truth that she, in her pride and beauty, most needs. That is why the tomb is the friend of the poet: they both know what to say; they are both (the metaphor is a traditional one) eloquent, one in words, one with the macabre eloquence of decay. The result is not a merely shocking poem, but an ironically inverted act of homage.

I have spoken of 'Remords posthume' as a necrophilic poem: it might equally have been called a perverted love poem. Necrophilia and sex are never far apart in Baudelaire; and sex is the most prominent theme in *Les Fleurs du mal*: almost half the poems are to or about women. At a first glance, there would seem to be a strong contrast between the true love poems, some very beautiful and very complimentary, and the often disgusting anatomizing of cruelty and decay. On reflection they are not so far apart.

No doubt it is a charming compliment to have it said of one:

> Son haleine fait la musique,
> Comme sa voix fait le parfum!

—charming if conventional. The poem ('Tout entière') is a slight one and not worth deep analysis—all the more so since it says that analysis is vain, and that the poet cannot tell his Demon what he most prefers about his mistress. There we have Baudelaire's characteristic attitude: he can compliment, he can confess his infatuation, but he cannot pause to think about the woman as a person. Sometimes he says this. In 'Semper eadem', for instance, his mistress begins by asking about his feelings:

> D'où vous vient, disiez-vous, cette tristesse étrange,
> Montant comme la mer sur le roc noir et nu?

It is a touching beginning, as a typical Baudelairean image (the sea for him is always sad, puzzling, an echo of something in oneself) seems to be leading us into the exploration of a human relationship. And then the poem turns round and refuses to explore:

> Cessez donc de chercher, ô belle curieuse!
> Et, bien que votre voix soit douce, taisez-vous!

It is a common note: 'sois charmante et tais-toi'; or 'Qu'importe ta bêtise ou ton indifférence?' These are poems of infatuation, telling us of the poet's urgent need for a haven from his own inner torments. Two things are startlingly real: the woman's beauty, and the emotional needs of the poet. The verse can become very eloquent over the former (nowhere more so than in the marvellous 'La Chevelure'), and very moving over the latter. The one thing that is not real at all is the woman as a person.

The same could be said of most of the great love poetry of the Renaissance; but for a nineteenth-century poet who is not following a main tradition, such poetry may have a curious hollowness at the centre—a hollowness that hardly matters as long as we pay no attention to it, but that can be filled up with something really alarming. We happen to know, from the details of Baudelaire's life, who most of the women were; and even without going outside the poetry, we can begin to see that its central image of woman is of a prostitute one falls in love with. A shift of emphasis—from the love to the dark thoughts it is a reaction from, or from the woman's beauty to her character—and we have the perverted love poems, the cruelty that gurgles over death and decay, that sees woman as a 'vil animal' out of whom nature, 'grande en ses desseins cachés', forms a genius—who is, of course, male.

As an example of this 'negative' love poetry we may choose 'Une Charogne', perhaps the most openly disgusting poem Baudelaire ever wrote. It begins—as is proper for a poem of disgust—with an almost excessive politeness, a poised diction, a peaceful atmosphere:

> Rappelez-vous l'objet que nous vîmes, mon âme,
> Ce beau matin d'été si doux...

The 'objet' (though that smiling *passé simple* hardly announces it!) was a rotting carcass, covered with flies and grubs, on which a dog was feeding. The lady was, not surprisingly, overcome:

> La puanteur était si forte, que sur l'herbe
> Vous crûtes vous évanouir.

The poet's reaction was less direct: he found a strange music in the noise of the flies, and the decomposing body haunted him:

> Les formes s'effaçaient et n'étaient plus qu'un rêve,
> Une ébauche lente à venir,
> Sur la toile oubliée, et que l'artiste achève
> Seulement par le souvenir.

The stanza, we notice, though it tells us that the music of decomposition has obliterated forms, hints at a way of reconstructing them, through artistic creation, and hints too that decay itself is a stimulus to the imagination. The poet then turns to the woman, and with careful cruelty reminds her, for two stanzas:

> Oui! telle vous serez, ô la reine des grâces,
> Après les derniers sacrements.

Finally comes a stanza of—dare we call it?—consolation. There is at any rate one thing he can do for her:

> Alors, ô ma beauté! dites à la vermine
> Qui vous mangera de baisers,
> Que j'ai gardé la forme et l'essence divine
> De mes amours décomposés!

He uses, we notice, the very word, 'forme', that he had used earlier. It was a true hint, evidently: the artist can complete what nature destroys. 'Les formes s'effaçaient'; but the poet can keep, in memory or in art, 'la forme divine'. 'Forme', we may remember, is Plato's word for the essences that exist in a perfect world of the Mind of which this natural world is a mere copy.

Of a poem like this we naturally want to ask whether it expresses trust in the spirit or a disgust with the flesh. The answer is that not only are these two sentiments compatible, but that one flows naturally from the other. Sexual revulsion has always been a common starting-point for a religious *contemptus mundi*. We can see this very clearly if we turn for a moment to another poem, 'Les Métamorphoses du vampire', one of the six pieces Baudelaire was forced by his trial to remove from the volume. The first half of this is a monologue by a woman, glorifying her sexual powers and the fact that on her bed even 'les anges impuissants se donneraient pour moi'. The second half relates how the poet, turning towards her to return her kiss, found she had begun to decompose, and before long had become a mere skeleton, creaking in the wind. It would be interesting to know for which half this poem was censored. The bourgeoisie were most likely to be shocked by the second part, which is obviously disgusting; yet it is this very disgust and rejection that removes the different kind of shock in the first, replacing a poem in wild praise of sex by a potentially very orthodox rejection of the flesh.

But in the end, to say that disgust with the flesh is complementary to praise of the spirit does not tell us what we want to know about 'Une Charogne'. They may be complementary, but they are not the same: by leaning one way or another on a compound doctrine you can, through a change of emphasis, produce a very different poem. In this case, we can pivot the difference on a single phrase:

> Oui! telle vous serez, ô la reine des grâces,
>   Après les derniers sacrements,
> Quand vous irez, sous l'herbe et les floraisons grasses,
>   Moisir parmi les ossements.

'Telle vous serez.' It can be said sadly, or with a chortle of delight. Only the context can tell us which is correct and, poetically, the difference is crucial. There is nothing in the context to make the line a sad one, and a good deal to suggest that it is a chortle. The reason is simple, and has already been mentioned: it is that the woman is not present in the poem. Nothing is imaginatively realized except the rotting flesh and the beauty of the spirit. The spirit belongs to the poet, the flesh to the woman. 'Telle vous serez' is a chortle, and prepares the poem's triumph. Out of physical hideousness Baudelaire has made a poem of great beauty and, in the end, of moral hideousness.

There remain for discussion two other forms which Baudelaire's longing takes, two other contrasts with the ordinariness of bourgeois life: spleen and travel. In writing of these, Baudelaire is at his greatest; and there is perhaps no finer way into his poetry than the group of four poems, all called 'Spleen', and all expressing the same strange emotion.

It is odd that we should need to look for a translation for the word 'spleen', since it is after all an English word, borrowed by Baudelaire. But so marked is the individuality of these poems that they can be said first to identify, then to describe, an emotion never before so well understood. The nearest word in Baudelaire's vocabulary is *ennui*, but we cannot translate *spleen* by 'boredom'; there is an intensity of self-contemplation in these poems that is the very opposite of bored. Their method is simple: a procession of images unrolls before us, identifying, with the aid of a sombre rhythm and occasional explicit comments, a state of being. Some of the images describe the world outside:

> Quand la pluie étalant ses immenses traînées
> D'une vaste prison imite les barreaux

and some the world inside:

> Je suis un vieux boudoir plein de roses fanées

but the difference is unimportant, so perfectly do these poems match feeling to setting.

There are no other poems of Baudelaire so purely lyric as these. There is no dramatic content, no story, no argument: they simply evoke an emotion. I have called this purely lyric, though some would call it purely poetic—examples of *poésie pure*. It is these poems that raise, better than any others, the question of Baudelaire's relationship to modern poetry.

Within a generation of Baudelaire's death, French poetry, and after it all European poetry, was transformed by symbolism. The modern movement, which has produced a poetry so different from anything that went before as to appear new in kind, is the result of Mallarmé's careful destruction of syntax, Rimbaud's whirl of imagery, and the theories of Valéry. The symbolists themselves often claimed Baudelaire as their father: 'ni Verlaine, ni Mallarmé, ni Rimbaud', claimed Valéry in 'Situation de Baudelaire', 'n'eussent été ce qu'ils furent sans la lecture qu'ils firent des *Fleurs du mal* à l'âge décisif.' He sees Baudelaire as the man who freed French poetry from the prosaic and opened to it the 'état pur', the unsullied poetic state. So behind the haunting, unreal images of Mallarmé, it is claimed, lie the haunting, unreal images of Baudelaire—such, for instance, as the filthy pack of cards in which

> Le beau valet de cœur et la dame de pique
> Causent sinistrement de leurs amours défunts.

Now it is because this line of descent can so easily lead to a mis-reading of Baudelaire that it is worth asserting that he was not the founder but the ancestor of symbolism. The essence of symbolism is the belief that poetry is discontinuous with prose: that a poem should do what only poetry can do—evoke an emotion by the associative power of imagery, sound, and form—and should do nothing else. Narrative and argument are the functions of prose, and should be left to prose. Abandoning them can lead to the abandoning of syntax, since no logical structure is needed when the aim is simply evocation:

> Le sens trop précis rature
> Ta vague littérature.

Pure evocation will shake free of 'la voix publique, cette collection de termes et de règles traditionnels et irrationnels', the language of every day, within which the symbolist poet tries to construct another and purer language. It will shake free, too, of its origin in the poet's own life. A symbolist poem is an objective construct, not a personal statement: it may even be reluctant to use the pronoun 'I'.

If we turn to Baudelaire with these prescriptions in mind, we shall see that he is not a Symbolist but a Romantic. His poems do without hesitation all that symbolism forbids a poem to do. They tell stories; they have a paraphrasable content; they name the emotion they are describing. There is even a rhetorical declamatory streak in Baudelaire that to the English reader must seem pre-Romantic. It consists in a lavish use of abstractions, of melodramatic invocations ('O cité!') or exclamations ('Un éclair...puis la nuit!') or solemn threats ('Meurs, vieux lâche! il est trop tard!'). It is something that went out of the best English poetry in the nineteenth century, though it is common enough in Lamartine and Hugo. Though this style produced one of his greatest poems, the sombre, tragic, Racinian 'Femmes damnées', it is the side of Baudelaire that is least acceptable to us today.

But Baudelaire is neither a neo-classic nor a symbolist: he is a poet of his age, who looks both before and after. The symbolists were not altogether wrong to see him as their ancestor. The 'roi d'un pays pluvieux' of the third 'Spleen' poem is just what we now understand by a symbol. He has no existence outside his poem; his whole identity consists of the string of images that fit him to the shape of the emotion he represents; he is not an allegoric figure, corresponding to some external reality that could be independently perceived, but he embodies what cannot be fully stated without him.

But though this makes Baudelaire an ancestor of modern poetry, it is not peculiar to him. In this sense Gautier too is an ancestor, or Hugo—or Keats, or Blake, or Shakespeare. Such symbolism is perhaps a feature of all poetry, and very markedly of Romantic poetry. Looking through English poems for parallels to Baudelaire, we shall probably not do much better than this:

> From the sad eaves the drip-drop of the rain;
> The water washing at the latched door . . .
> The clicking of an embered hearth and cold
> The rainy Robin tic-tac at the pane.

The lines were written by Sidney Dobell in 1850. When Baudelaire sat indoors during rainy weather and heard

> L'âme d'un vieux poète erre dans la gouttière
> Avec la triste voix d'un fantôme frileux,

it could as easily have been a dead English as an unborn French poet.

To underline this historical point, and apply it to a complete poem, we can look at 'Les Sept Vieillards', a poem in which *ennui* is replaced by something like nightmare. On a misty morning in Paris, the 'fourmillante cité', the poet saw a hideous old man

> dont les guenilles jaunes
> Imitaient la couleur de ce ciel pluvieux

(in true romantic vein Baudelaire matches setting and emotion). The ugliness and evil of the figure occupy four stanzas; then a second identical creature appears, 'du même enfer venu', and eventually seven have filed past. Then come two stanzas of direct commentary: 'Aurais-je, sans mourir, contemplé le huitième. . . .' And then he returns home, terrified, and the last stanza leaves us with his terror.

'Les Sept Vieillards' is a vision of evil. The spectral nature of the old men, the fact that we learn nothing of who they are or whence they came, make it clear that this is metaphysical, not empirical evil: a principle in the universe, not any actual wicked acts. Yet the power of the poem comes from the cloak of realism that it throws over the nightmare. Though Paris is described as a 'cité pleine de rêves', it really is Paris and the poem is quite rightly one of the *Tableaux parisiens*. The streets are real streets, the 'brouillard sale et jaune' is real enough, and we are perhaps not meant to be sure, at first, whether it was a real old man or a spectre. In this city 'le spectre en plein jour raccroche le passant'.

The natural comparison for the English reader to make is with T. S. Eliot. It is not only that Eliot borrowed the phrase 'fourmillante cité' when speaking of the London of 'The Waste Land'. Eliot too describes a real and frightening city where man and ghost mingle; and in 'Rhapsody on a Windy Night' he returns after nightmare wanderings in the street to shut his door and feel 'the last twist of the knife'. The comparison is just, since Eliot as a poet of city life is enormously indebted to Baudelaire; and it will show us immediately that Eliot is a modern poet, and Baudelaire not. 'The Waste Land' is a kaleidoscopic series of broken images and dramatic fragments; 'Rhapsody on a Windy Night' is written in the first person, but the speaker seems a mere camera who records the bewilderment of the night itself. In contrast, 'Les Sept Vieillards' is held together by the constant presence of the author. The episode described is something that happened to the speaker, and he describes it as it happened. In the stanzas of direct commentary his presence may even seem to us excessive, especially when he urges us not to laugh at his distress. But it is also the source of some of the most vivid effects:

> Il n'était pas voûté, mais cassé . . .
> . . . et ces spectres baroques
> Marchaient du même pas vers un but inconnu.

Comments like these imply the silent presence of the narrator, correcting his impressions, not sure what is going on:

> Car je comptai sept fois, de minute en minute,
> Ce sinistre vieillard qui se multipliait!

The terror is rendered through our being shown what terrified the poet, and how he reacted. This is a bewildering but not a bewildered poem.

In the last and finest stanza the first person is indispensable:

> Vainement ma raison voulait prendre la barre;
> La tempête en jouant déroutait mes efforts,
> Et mon âme dansait, dansait, vieille gabarre
> Sans mâts, sur une mer monstrueuse et sans bords!

Of course this must recall the *Bateau ivre* of Rimbaud, that wild journey through tormented imagery on to just such a sea. Yet we are not quite in that symbolist world, but in a poem that informs us what the image represents, that begins, in fact, with statement before it proceeds to imagery. We have not wholly left the world of 'Past cure I am now reason is past care'. And it is at least arguable that the marvellous last line, with its feeling of total distress, gains enormously by the way it emerges wildly from the explicit and clear-sighted lines that precede it.

This poem has, as it happens, ended on an image of voyaging, and has shown us how perfectly this image can represent the terror of extreme experience. Its usual function in Baudelaire, however, is to represent its beauty. All Baudelaire's poetry is shot through with the fascination of the exotic, of the vast ocean far from 'l'immonde cité'. The most moving moment in 'Le Cygne', a sad poem about the dry reality of Paris, is that in which a negress hunts in mud and fog for 'Les cocotiers absents de la superbe Afrique'. The voyage, one of the central romantic symbols for an escape from the ordinary, is central to Baudelaire too; and with him, as with so many of his contemporaries, we can ask whether this makes him a poet of escape, and if so, whether that is a limitation.

The wish to escape to warm strange lands has this in common with the wish to shock the bourgeoisie, that it is a very simple impulse—too simple for great poetry. Such clear, crude impulses can produce marvellous moments in a poem, when they emerge with striking force from a complicated setting: such perhaps is the negress's longing in 'Le Cygne'. But as a basis for a whole poem they provide only something thin, something that does not engage the whole personality. Baudelaire's love of the exotic is better used as an image when the poem has another subject, than as a full subject in itself. This is done most triumphantly in 'La Chevelure', in which voyage and sex mingle in a haunting, sustained metaphor:

> J'irai là-bas où l'arbre et l'homme, pleins de sève,
> Se pâment longuement sous l'ardeur des climats;
> Fortes tresses, soyez la houle qui m'enlève!
> Tu contiens, mer d'ébène, un éblouissant rêve
> De voiles, de rameurs, de flammes et de mâts.

Here the longing to escape, without losing any of its own power, becomes a perfect symbol for sexual surrender. The images so lovingly particularized in the last line carry us away, yet also leave us aware of the lover imagining these strange joys as he strokes or twists the 'cheveux bleus, pavillon de ténèbres tendues'.

Baudelaire seldom makes such profound use of the symbol of the voyage; and he must himself have realized how limiting it might become for his poetry. For in 'Le Voyage', the longest of all his poems, placed at the very end of the volume, he treats his own love of the exotic with a new and brilliant irony.

Of the eight parts of 'Le Voyage' it is perhaps best to regard I and II as introductory poems, and the rest (which forms a continuous argument) as an almost complete entity. The first section announces the subject: not only the travels of those who voyage through unhappy love, politics, or maladjustment, but the travels of the 'vrais voyageurs': those 'qui partent pour partir'. The longing to escape is too fundamental to be explained by particular causes. The second section (the weakest, on the whole) describes an imaginary voyage of escape. Then, in the third, we move to a particular situation: that in which the stay-at-homes question the travellers. 'Nous voulons voyager sans vapeur et sans voile!' The answer is, at first, bored:

Nous avons vu des astres
Et des flots; nous avons vu des sables aussi . . .

As they continue, some of the fascination of the voyage creeps in; but the lands and landscapes they travel to fascinate only to disappoint. The most beautiful cities were always those 'que le hasard fait avec les nuages'. Here we have one of the poem's complex ironies. The stay-at-homes are showing their naïvety, the travellers answer them with kindly contempt: yet here they confess that they are none the better for their travels, that no voyage is as wonderful as that of the man who never sets off.

Another stanza or two and the travellers are really launched. They describe real marvels, idols, thrones, palaces, strange women, and they cannot resist a dig at the bourgeois standards of the stay-at-homes:

Des palais ouvragés dont la féerique pompe
Serait pour vos banquiers un rêve ruineux.

But even with the dig, the listeners are carried away. The strange women and the magicians are too much for them and they interrupt breathlessly: 'Et puis, et puis encore?' These words form the whole of the fifth section. By singling out this trivial touch of dialogue, Baudelaire puts the dramatic situation vividly in front of us and, beyond that, the point of the poem. There is, after all, nothing magical about the exotic; the over-eager interruption is the last straw and the travellers now turn on their listeners in contempt.

The most important thing they saw on their travels was 'Le spectacle ennuyeux de l'immortel péché'. Then they give a ruthless account of what they really saw, which was the human condition; and a furious and cynical realism completely destroys all longing to escape. We see from this scathing sixth section that, as well as the contrast between real and imaginary voyages, there is another contrast that informs the poem: that between the voyage as escape and the voyage as an exploration of the self, of the here and now. The true voyage, taken with open eyes, brings only the latter experience.

What then is left? The longing for something new and strange is as strong as ever, but now is accompanied by the knowledge that if we are honest we shall never get it. So there is only one voyage left, and by a supreme act of imagination we can persuade ourselves that that one will satisfy us at last:

> O Mort, vieux capitaine, il est temps! levons l'ancre!
> Ce pays nous ennuie, ô Mort! Appareillons!

Les Fleurs du mal ends with a death-wish in the central Romantic tradition: death for once is not physical and disgusting, but the longed-for solution to a situation too hard for us to endure. The lines are as tired as the feeling they mime, and they bring this complex and ironic poem to rest on a surprisingly traditional note. Baudelaire's last word is not, after all, 'Tel est du globe entier l'éternel bulletin'—the despairing admission that in a way the bourgeoisie were right: the world you have is your only world. The bourgeoisie were wrong when they thought that world worth while. 'Amer savoir, celui qu'on tire du voyage!' After this clear-eyed despair, Baudelaire turns into his last self-deception, and ends on a less characteristic but more beautiful note. Was this the final refuge of his escapism, or his poetic salvation?

NOTE

CHARLES BAUDELAIRE was born in 1821. His father died in 1827 and his mother, to whom he was deeply attached, married the very respectable General Aupick in 1828. Critics with a taste for psycho-analysis have seen in this family situation the explanation of his irregular life, his debts, his sexual licence, and his contempt for the bourgeoisie. We do know that when he joined in the 1848 revolution he shouted on the barricades that he was going to 'fusiller le général Aupick'. His worried family sent him on a voyage to India in 1841: he appears to have got as far as Mauritius, and was back in France the next year. The trip produced a few poems directly, and no doubt contributed material to the exotic settings so frequent in his work. Thereafter he hardly left Paris. He soon ran through the fortune that his family had tried to keep from him, and his last years were a time of debt and bad health. He never married, but his passion for his mulatto mistress Jeanne Duval, whom he met in 1842, lasted all his life, and many of his love poems were addressed to her. He died in 1867, in his mother's arms.

Works. Baudelaire's collection of poems was originally called *Les Limbes*; the title *Les Fleurs du mal* was not his own, though he accepted it. The book was published in 1857, and Baudelaire was almost immediately accused of obscenity (only a few months earlier, similar charges had been brought against Flaubert with the publication of *Madame Bovary*). The book was tried and condemned; Baudelaire and his publisher were fined, and ordered to suppress six poems.

Baudelaire's most important prose works are his art criticism: reviews of the Salons of 1845, 1846, 1855, and 1859, an essay on Delacroix (1863), and the superb 'Le Peintre de la vie moderne' (1863) on Constantin Guys; the *Paradis artificiels* (1860) (a translation of de Quincey's *Confessions of an English Opium Eater*, preceded by his own essay, 'Le Poème du haschisch'); the *Journaux intimes*, published posthumously; and above all, the 'petits poèmes en prose', also called *Le Spleen de Paris*, some of which appeared in periodicals during his life but were not collected until the complete works of Baudelaire were published in 1868-70.

Editions and criticism. Baudelaire's complete works are splendidly available in the Pléiade edition edited by Y.-G. Dantec and Claude Pichois. Pichois has also published *Baudelaire: études et témoignages* (1967). *Les Fleur du mal*, *Le Spleen de Paris*, and some of the art criticism are published in the 'Classiques Garnier', in what is perhaps the most useful edition. There is a sumptuous two-volume edition of the art criticism in English, with illustrations, published by the Phaidon Press. The little book by Pascal Pia, *Baudelaire par lui-même* (1956), in the series 'Écrivains de toujours', quotes at length many of the most interesting passages from his prose. On the general question of secondary material it is worth consulting both A. E. Carter, *Baudelaire et la critique française, 1848-1917* (1963) and R. T. Cargo, *Baudelaire Criticism, 1900-1967: a Bibliography with Critical Commentary* (1968). An early work by an English scholar, which still repays study, is G. T. Clapton, *Baudelaire et De Quincey* (1931). More recent important studies are: G. Blin, *Le Sadisme de Baudelaire* (1947); B. Fondane, *Baudelaire et l'expérience du gouffre* (1947); J. Prévost, *Baudelaire: essai sur l'inspiration et la création poétiques* (1953); M. A. Ruff, *Baudelaire, l'homme et l'œuvre* (1955); L. J. Austin, *L'Univers poétique de Baudelaire: symbolisme et symbolique* (1956); and Satre's psycho-analytical essay, *Baudelaire* (1947).

By far the best article on Baudelaire available in English is that by Eric Auerbach, 'The Aesthetic Dignity of the *Fleurs du mal*', in his book, *Scenes from the Drama of European Literature* (1959). The article can also be found in *Baudelaire: a Collection of Critical Essays* (1962), edited by Henri Peyre, in the series 'Twentieth Century Views'. Amid a good deal that is indifferent, this latter volume also contains a translation of Valéry's famous 'Situation de Baudelaire', an intelligent study by Middleton Murry, and an enthusiastic appreciation by Proust (Proust's essay on Baudelaire in *Contre Sainte-Beuve* (1954) is even more interesting). Enid Starkie's *Baudelaire* (1957) is a very full life; D. J. Mossop, *Baudelaire's Tragic Hero* (1961), outlines the 'architecture' of *Les Fleurs du mal*; Alison Fairlie's short study of *Les Fleurs du mal* (1960) in the Arnold 'Studies in French Literature' is useful, while F. W. Leakey, *Baudelaire and Nature* (1969) is a work of impeccable scholarship.

CHRONOLOGY

History	French literature	English literature
Bonaparte defeats Austrians at Marengo, 1800	Pixerécourt, *Cœlina ou l'enfant du mystère* (1800)	Wordsworth, *The Prelude* (written 1798–1805)
		Edgeworth, *Castle Rackrent* (1800)
Treaty of Lunéville ends Second Coalition, 1801	Chateaubriand, *Atala* (1801)	
French evacuate Egypt, 1801		
Concordat signed by Bonaparte and the Pope, 1801		
Treaty of Amiens between England and France, 1802		
Bonaparte elected First Consul for life, 1802		
England again declares war on France, 1803	Mme de Staël, *Delphine* (1803)	
Execution of Duc d'Enghien, 1804	Senancour, *Oberman* (1804)	
Bonaparte crowned Emperor Napoleon I, 1804		
Battle of Trafalgar, 1805	Chateaubriand, *Atala* and *René* (1805)	Scott, *The Lay of the Last Minstrel* (1805)
Napoleon defeats Austrians and Russians at Austerlitz, 1805	Raynouard, *Les Templiers* (1805)	
Napoleon defeats Prussians and Saxons at Jena and Auerstadt, 1806	Delille, *L'Imagination* (1806)	

Painting and music	Criticism and aesthetic theory	Ideas and philosophy
Goya, 1746–1828	Villers, *Considérations sur l'état actuel de la littérature allemande* (1800)	Cuvier, *Leçons d'anatomie comparée* (1800–5)
David, 1748–1825	Mme de Staël, *De la littérature considérée dans ses rapports avec les institutions sociales* (1800)	
	Wordsworth, preface to second edition of the *Lyrical Ballads* (1800)	
Mme Vigée-Lebrun, 1755–1842	A. W. Schlegel, *Über schöne Litteratur und Kunst* (1801–4)	Bichat, *Anatomie générale* (1801)
	Edinburgh Review founded (1802)	Bonald, *La Législation primitive* (1802)
Raeburn, 1756–1823		Chateaubriand, *Le Génie du christianisme* (1802)
		Lamarck, *Recherches sur l'organisation des êtres vivants* (1802)
		Maine de Biran, *L'Influence de l'habitude sur la faculté de penser* (1803)
Lesueur, 1760–1837		
Méhul, 1763–1817		Maine de Biran, *Mémoire sur la décomposition de la pensée* (1805)
Crome, 1768–1821	Villers, *Essai d'érotique comparée* (1806)	

History	French literature	English literature
Abolition of the slave trade in the British Empire, 1807	Mme de Staël, *Corinne* (1807)	Crabbe, *The Parish Register* (1807)
Napoleon defeats Russians at Eylau and Friedland, 1807		Lamb, *Tales from Shakespeare* (1807)
Treaty of Tilsit, 1807		Moore, *Irish Melodies* (1807-35)
Joseph Bonaparte King of Spain, 1808		Scott, *Marmion* (1808)
Murat King of Naples, 1808		
Peninsular War, 1808-14 (Battle of Corunna, 1809; Battle of Vittoria, 1813)		
Napoleon defeats Austrians at Wagram, 1809	Lemercier, *Christophe Colomb* (1809)	
Napoleon divorces Josephine, 1809, and marries Marie Louise, 1810		
		Crabbe, *The Borough* (1810)
	Millevoye, *Élégies* (1811)	Austen, *Sense and Sensibility* (1811)
Battle of Borodino, 1812		Edgeworth, *The Absentee* (1812)
French retreat from Moscow, 1812		Byron, *Childe Harold's Pilgrimage* (1812)
Battle of Dresden, 1813		Shelley, *Queen Mab* (written 1813)
Napoleon loses battle of Leipzig, 1813		Austen, *Pride and Prejudice* (1813)

...ting and music	Criticism and aesthetic theory	Ideas and philosophy
...vrence, 1769–1830		Hegel, *Die Phaenomenologie des Geistes* (1807)
...thoven, 1770–1827 (*Fidelio*, ...5; *Fifth Symphony*, 1805–7; ...*lin Concerto*, 1806; *Missa ...emnis*, 1818–23; *Ninth ...aphony*, 1825)		
	M.-J. Chénier, *Tableau de la littérature française* (1808)	Fichte, *Reden an die deutsche Nation* (1808)
		Fourier, *Théorie des quatre mouvements* (1808)
...ontini, 1774–1851	Constant's preface to his *Wallstein* (1809)	Chateaubriand, *Les Martyrs* (1809)
	A. W. Schlegel, *Über dramatische Kunst und Litteratur* (1809–11)	Lamarck, *Philosophie zoologique* (1809)
	Mme de Staël, *De l'Allemagne* (written 1810)	
...uard, 1775–1818		Maine de Biran, *Considérations sur les rapports du physique et du moral* (1811)
...eldieu, 1775–1834 (*Le ...life de Bagdad*, 1800)		Hegel, *Wissenschaft der Logik* (1812–16)
...rner, 1775–1851	Sismondi, *Histoire des littératures du Midi de l'Europe* (1813)	Constant, *De l'esprit de conquête et de l'usurpation* (1813)
		Owen, *A New View of Society* (1813)

History	French literature	English literature
Napoleon abdicates, 1814	Pixerécourt, *Le Chien de Montargis* (1814)	Byron, *The Corsair* (1814)
Accession of Louis XVIII, 1814		Austen, *Mansfield Park* (1814)
First Treaty of Paris negotiated by Talleyrand in name of Louis XVIII, 1814		Scott, *Waverley* (1814)
		Wordsworth, *The Excursion* (1814)
Congress of Vienna, 1814-15		
Landing of Napoleon in France, flight of Louis XVIII and the 'Hundred Days', 1815		Austen, *Emma* (1815)
Napoleon banished to St. Helena after defeat by Wellington and Blücher, 1815		Scott, *Guy Mannering* (1815)
Second Treaty of Paris, 1815		
Marshal Ney shot, 1815		
Ultra-Royalist Chamber dissolved by Louis XVIII, 1816	Constant, *Adolphe* (1816)	Peacock, *Headlong Hall* (1816)
	Béranger, *Chansons morales et autres* (1816)	Coleridge, *Christabel and Kubla Khan* (1816)
	Stendhal, *Rome, Naples et Florence* (1817)	Scott, *Rob Roy* (1817)
		Keats, *Poems* (1817)
		Moore, *Lalla Rookh* (1817)
		Byron, *Manfred* (1817)
Army of occupation withdrawn from France, 1818	Nodier, *Jean Sbogar* (1818)	Mary Shelley, *Frankenstein* (1818)
		Peacock, *Nightmare Abbey* (1818)
		Scott, *The Heart of Midlothian* (1818)
		Austen, *Persuasion* (1818)
		Keats, *Endymion* (1818)

Painting and music	Criticism and aesthetic theory	Ideas and philosophy
Hoffmann, 1776–1822 (*Undine*, 1816)	Mme Necker de Saussure's translation of A. W. Schlegel's Vienna lectures: *Cours de littérature dramatique* (1814)	Chateaubriand, *De Buonaparte et des Bourbons* (1814) Saint-Simon, *Réorganisation de la societé européenne* (1814)
Constable, 1776–1837	Villemain, *Discours sur les avantages et les inconvénients de la critique* (1814)	
Hummel, 1778–1837		Lamarck, *Histoire naturelle des animaux sans vertèbres* (1815–22)
Cotman, 1782–1842		
		Cuvier, *Le Règne animal distribué d'après son organisation* (1816)
Auber, 1782–1871 (*La Muette de Portici*, 1828; *Le Cheval de bronze*, 1835)		
	Lemercier, *Cours analytique de littérature générale* (1817)	Hegel, *Encyclopaedie der philosophischen Wissenschaften im Grundrisse* (1817)
	Coleridge, *Biographia Literaria* (1817)	Ricardo, *Principles of Political Economy and Taxation* (1817)
Geddes, 1783–1844	Hazlitt, *The Characters of Shakespeare's Plays* (1817)	
	Hazlitt, *Lectures on the English Poets* (1818)	Geoffroy Saint-Hilaire, *Philosophie anatomique* (1818–22)
Spohr, 1784–1859		

H

History	French literature	English literature
		Austen, *Northanger Abbey* (1818)
		Keats, *Hyperion* (written 1818-19)
Birth of Queen Victoria, 1819	Delavigne, *Les Vêpres siciliennes* (1819)	Shelley, *Prometheus Unbound* (1819)
	Desbordes-Valmore, *Élégies, Marie, et Romances* (1819)	Keats, *The Eve of St. Agnes* (written 1819)
	Chénier, *Œuvres complètes* (ed. Latouche, 1819)	Scott, *Ivanhoe* (1819)
		Shelley, *The Cenci* (1819)
		Byron, *Don Juan* (1819-24)
Assassination of Duc de Berry, 1820	Lamartine, *Méditations poétiques* (1820)	Clare, *Poems* (1820)
		Washington Irving, *The Sketch-Book* (1820)
Death of Napoleon, 1821	Nodier, *Smarra* (1821)	Scott, *Kenilworth* (1821)
		De Quincey, *The Confessions of an English Opium Eater* (1821)
		Shelley, *Adonais* (1821)
Declaration of Greek Independence, 1822	Hugo, *Odes et Poésies diverses* (1822)	
	Nodier, *Trilby* (1822)	
	Stendhal, *De l'Amour* (1822)	
	Vigny, *Poèmes* (1822 and 1829)	
France forcibly restores Ferdinand VII of Spain, 1823	Lamartine, *Nouvelles Méditations* (1823)	Lamb, *The Essays of Elia* (first series, 1823)
Monroe Doctrine excludes Europe 'from all interference in the political affairs of the American Republics', 1823	Hugo, *Han d'Islande* (1823)	Scott, *Quentin Durward* (1823)

Painting and music	Criticism and aesthetic theory	Ideas and philosophy
Wilkie, 1785-1841	Geoffroy, *Cours de littérature dramatique* (1819-20)	Schopenhauer, *Die Welt als Wille und Vorstellung* (1819)
Weber, 1786-1826 (*Der Freischütz*, 1821)	Nodier, *Mélanges de littérature et de critique* (1820)	Malthus, *Principles of Political Economy* (1820) Hegel, *Grundlinien der Philosophie des Rechts* (1820)
	Shelley, *Defence of Poetry* (1821) Guizot, *Essai sur la vie et les œuvres de Shakespeare* (1821)	Saint-Simon, *Le Système industriel* (1821) Cuvier, *Recherches sur les ossements fossiles* (1821-4)
Géricault, 1791-1824		Fourier, *Traité de l'association domestique et agricole* (1822)
Hérold, 1791-1833 (*La Fille mal gardée*, 1828)		
	Senancour, *Considérations sur la littérature romantique* (1823); *La Muse française* (1823) Stendhal, *Racine et Shakespeare* (1823)	Las Cases, *Mémorial de Sainte-Hélène* (1823)

History	French literature	English literature
Death of Louis XVIII and accession of Charles X, 1824		Hogg, *The Confessions of a Justified Sinner* (1824)
		Scott, *Redgauntlet* (1824)
		Landor, *Imaginary Conversations* (1824–9)
Law to indemnify *émigrés*, 1825	Mérimée, *Le Théâtre de Clara Gazul* (incl. *Le Carrosse du Saint-Sacrement*, 1825)	
	Hugo, *Odes et Ballades* (1826)	Fenimore Cooper, *The Last of the Mohicans* (1826)
	Chateaubriand, *Les Natchez* (1826)	
	Vigny, *Cinq-Mars* (1826)	
	Vigny, *Poèmes antiques et modernes* (1826 and 1837)	
Rigorous press censorship under Charles X, 1827	Stendhal, *Armance* (1827)	Fenimore Cooper, *The Prairie* (1827)
Citizen army disbanded, 1827	Scribe, *Le Mariage d'argent* (1827)	
	Nerval, *Faust* (1828)	

Painting and music	Criticism and aesthetic theory	Ideas and philosophy
Meyerbeer, 1791–1864 (*Les Huguenots*, 1836)	*Le Globe* (1824–31)	Guizot, *Essais sur l'histoire de France* (1824)
		Ranke, *Geschichten der romanischen und germanischen Völker, 1494–1535* (1824)
Rossini, 1792–1868 (*L'Italiana in Algeri*, 1813; *La Cenerentola*, 1817; *Guillaume Tell*, 1829)		Constant, *De la religion considérée dans sa source, ses formes et ses développements* (1824–31)
		Saint-Simon, *Le Nouveau Christianisme* (1825)
		Thierry, *Histoire de la conquête de l'Angleterre par les Normands* (1825)
		Brillat-Savarin, *La Physiologie du goût* (1825)
Barye, 1796–1875	Chateaubriand, *Mélanges littéraires* (1826)	
Corot, 1796–1875	Vigny's preface to *Cinq-Mars* (1827)	Hallam, *A Constitutional History of England* (1827)
	Hugo's preface to *Cromwell* (1827)	Ampère, *Sur la théorie mathématique des phénomènes électro-dynamiques* (1827)
	Sainte-Beuve, *Tableau historique et critique de la poésie et du théâtre français au XVIe siècle* (1827–8)	
Schubert, 1797–1828 (*Unfinished Symphony*, 1822; *Die schöne Müllerin*, 1823; *Symphony in C Major*, 1828)	Villemain, *Cours de littérature française* (1828–9)	Guizot, *Histoire de la civilisation en Europe* (1828)

History	French literature	English literature
	Mérimée, *La Chronique du règne de Charles IX* (1829)	
	Hugo, *Le dernier jour d'un condamné* (1829)	
	Pixerécourt, *Les Fossoyeurs écossais* (1829)	
	Sainte-Beuve, *Vie, poésies et pensées de Joseph Delorme* (1829)	
	Balzac, *Les Chouans* (1829)	
	Stendhal, *Promenades dans Rome* (1829)	
	Hugo, *Les Orientales* (1829)	
French conquest and occupation of Algeria begun, 1830	Sainte-Beuve, *Les Consolations* (1830)	Tennyson, *Poems chiefly Lyrical* (1830)
Charles X's Ordonnances de Saint-Cloud, 1830	Hugo, *Hernani* (1830)	
July Revolution ('Les Trois Glorieuses', 27–9 July), 1830	Musset, *Contes d'Espagne et d'Italie* (1830)	
Abdication of Charles X and accession of Louis-Philippe, 1830		
Following revolution in Belgium (1830), Britain and France agree on separation of Belgium from Holland, 1831	Vigny, *La Maréchale d'Ancre* (1831)	Peacock, *Crochet Castle* (1831)
Revolt of silk weavers in Lyon, 1831	Barbier, *Iambes* (1831)	
	Stendhal, *Le Rouge et le Noir* (1831)	
	Hugo, *Les Feuilles d'automne* (1831)	
	Hugo, *Notre-Dame de Paris* (1831)	
	Hugo, *Marion de Lorme* (1831)	

Painting and music	Criticism and aesthetic theory	Ideas and philosophy
	Hugo's preface to *Les Orientales* (1829)	Fourier, *Le Nouveau Monde industriel* (1829-30)
	Constant, *Mélanges de littérature et de politique* (1829)	
Donizetti, 1797-1848 (*L'Elisir d'amore*, 1832; *Lucia di Lammermoor*, 1835; *Don Pasquale*, 1843)		
Delacroix, 1798-1863		
		Cobbett, *Rural Rides* (1830)
		Lyell, *Principles of Geology* (1830-3)
		Comte, *Cours de philosophie positive* (1830-42)
Halévy, 1799-1862 (*La Juive*, 1835)		Michelet, *Histoire romaine* (1831)
Bellini, 1801-35 (*Norma*, 1831; *I Puritani*, 1835)		

History	French literature	English literature
French invasion of Belgium, 1832	Gautier, *Poésies* (1832)	
	Vigny, *Stello* (1832)	
	Balzac, *La Peau de chagrin* (1832)	
	Balzac, *Louis Lambert* (1832)	
	Dumas, *La Tour de Nesles* (1832)	
	Sand, *Indiana* (1832)	
Outbreak of Carlist Wars in Spain, 1833	Balzac, *Eugénie Grandet* (1833)	Tennyson, *Poems* (1833)
	Musset, *Les Caprices de Marianne* (1833)	Lamb, *The Essays of Elia* (second series, 1833)
	Sand, *Lélia* (1833)	
	Musset, *Fantasio* (1833)	
	Balzac, *Le Médecin de campagne* (1833)	
	Hugo, *Marie Tudor* (1833)	
	Scribe, *Bertrand et Raton* (1833)	
Britain, France, Spain and Portugal form Quadruple Alliance in favour of liberal governments in Spain and Portugal, 1834 Second revolt of silk-weavers in Lyon, 1834	Sainte-Beuve, *Volupté* (1834)	Bulwer-Lytton, *The Last Days of Pompeii* (1834)
	Musset, *Lorenzaccio* (1834)	Marryat, *Peter Simple* (1834)
	Musset, *On ne badine pas avec l'amour* (1834)	
	Gautier, *Mademoiselle de Maupin* (1834)	
Repressive government measures follow attempt on life of Louis-Philippe, 1835	Vigny, *Servitude et grandeur militaires* (1835)	Browning, *Paracelsus* (1835)
	Vigny, *Chatterton* (1835)	Marryat, *Midshipman Easy* (1835)
	Balzac, *Le Père Goriot* (1835)	
	Balzac, *Le Lys dans la vallée* (1835)	
	Musset, *Nuits* (1835–7)	

Painting and music	Criticism and aesthetic theory	Ideas and philosophy
Adam, 1803-56 (*Giselle*, 1841)	Nodier, *Du fantastique en littérature* (1832) Sainte-Beuve, *Critiques et portraits littéraires* (1832)	
Berlioz, 1803-69 (*Symphonie fantastique* 1830; *Benvenuto Cellini* 1834-8; *Messe des morts*, 1837; *Roméo et Juliette*, 1839)	Nisard, *Manifeste contre la littérature facile* (1833)	Thierry, *Récits des temps mérovingiens* (1833-40) Michelet, *Histoire de France* (1833-67) Carlyle, *Sartor Resartus* (1833)
Glinka, 1804-57 (*Russlan and Ludmilla*, 1842)	Nisard, *Étude de mœurs et de critique sur les poètes latins de la décadence* (1834)	Considérant, *La Destinée sociale* (1834-8) Owen, *The Book of the New Moral World* (1834) Lamennais, *Paroles d'un croyant* (1834)
	Gautier's preface to *Mademoiselle de Maupin* (1835)	Strauss, *Das Leben Jesu* (1835) De Tocqueville, *La Démocratie en Amérique* (1835-40)

History	French literature	English literature
Following his failure to seize Strasbourg, Louis-Napoleon exiled to America, 1836	Lamartine, *Jocelyn* (1836) Musset, *La Confession d'un enfant du siècle* (1836)	Dickens, *The Pickwick Papers* (1836-7)
Accession of Queen Victoria, 1837	Mérimée, *La Vénus d'Ille* (1837) Hugo, *Les Chants du crépuscule* (1837) Balzac, *Histoire de la grandeur et de la décadence de César Birotteau* (1837) Balzac, *Les Illusions perdues* (1837-43)	Browning, *Strafford* (1837) Dickens, *Oliver Twist* (1837-8)
France declares war on Mexico, 1838	Hugo, *Ruy Blas* (1838) Lamartine, *La Chute d'un ange* (1838)	Surtees, *Jorrocks's Jaunts and Jollities* (1838) Dickens, *Nicholas Nickleby* (1838-9)
Treaty of London establishes international status of Belgium, 1839	Stendhal, *La Chartreuse de Parme* (1839) Balzac, *Le Curé de village* (1839) Stendhal, *Chroniques italiennes* (1839) Lamartine, *Recueillements poétiques* (1839) Borel, *Madame Putiphar* (1839)	
Britain and France and Carlist Wars in Spain, 1840 Napoleon I buried in the Invalides, 1840	Hugo, *Les Rayons et les Ombres* (1840) Sand, *Le Compagnon du tour de France* (1840)	Browning, *Sordello* (1840) Dickens, *The Old Curiosity Shop* (1840) Ainsworth, *The Tower of London* (1840) Fenimore Cooper, *The Pathfinder* (1840) Dickens, *Barnaby Rudge* (1840) Barham, *Ingoldsby Legends* (1840)

Painting and music	Criticism and aesthetic theory	Ideas and philosophy
Palmer, 1805-81	Musset, *Lettres de Dupuis et Cotonet* (1836)	Cousin, *Cours de philosophie* (1836)
	G. Planche, *Portraits littéraires* (1836)	
	Eckermann, *Gespräche mit Goethe* (1836-48)	
Daumier, 1808-79		Carlyle, *The French Revolution* (1837)
Mendelssohn, 1809-47 (*Italian Symphony*, 1833; *Violin Concerto*, 1844)		
		Blanc, *L'Organisation du travail* (1839)
		Darwin, *The Voyage of the Beagle* (1839)
Préault, 1809-79		
Nicolai, 1810-49 (*Die lustigen Weiber von Windsor*, 1849)	Sainte-Beuve, *Port-Royal* (1840-59)	Proudhon, *Qu'est-ce que la propriété?* (1840)
		Carlyle, *Heroes and Hero-Worship* (1840)
Chopin, 1810-49		

History	French literature	English literature
Guizot Ministry, 1840–8	Balzac, *Ursule Mirouet* (1841)	Ainsworth, *Old St. Paul's* (1841)
	Laprade, *Psyché* (1841)	Fenimore Cooper, *The Deerslayer* (1841)
	Mérimée, *Colomba* (1841)	Browning, *Pippa Passes* (1841)
	Scribe, *Une Chaîne* (1841)	Marryat, *Masterman Ready* (1841)
	Banville, *Les Cariatides* (1842)	Tennyson, *Poems* (1842)
	Musset, *L'Histoire d'un merle blanc* (1842)	Macaulay, *Lays of Ancient Rome* (1842)
	Sand, *Consuelo* (1842)	
	Bertrand, *Gaspard de la nuit* (1842)	
	Süe, *Les Mystères de Paris* (1842–3)	
Queen Victoria and Prince Consort visit France, 1843	Tillier, *Mon Oncle Benjamin* (1843)	Borrow, *The Bible in Spain* (1843)
	Ponsard, *Lucrèce* (1843)	Dickens, *Martin Chuzzlewit* (1843–4)
	Hugo, *Les Burgraves* (1843)	
Treaty of Tangiers ends French war in Morocco, 1844	Dumas, *Les Trois Mousquetaires* (1844)	Disraeli, *Coningsby* (1844)
	Augier, *La Ciguë* (1844)	
	Süe, *Le Juif errant* (1844–5)	
	Balzac, *Les Paysans* (1844–55)	
Louis-Philippe visits England, 1845	Mérimée, *Carmen* (1845)	Disraeli, *Sybil* (1845)
	Dumas, *La Reine Margot* (1845)	
	Sand, *Le Meunier d'Angibault* (1845)	

Painting and music	Criticism and aesthetic theory	Ideas and philosophy
Schumann, 1810–56 (*Frauenliebe und -leben* and *Dichterliebe*, 1840; *Piano Concerto* 1845; *Second Symphony*, 1846)	Emerson, *Essays* (1841 and 1844)	Feuerbach, *Das Wesen des Christenthums* (1841)
		Joubert, *Pensées, maximes, essais et correspondance* (1842)
Théodore Rousseau, 1812–67		
Wagner, 1813–83 (*Der fliegende Holländer*, 1843; *Tannhäuser*, 1845; *Lohengrin*, 1850)	Saint-Marc Girardin, *Cours de littérature dramatique* (1843) Ruskin, *Modern Painters* (1843–60)	Macaulay, *Critical and Historical Essays* (1843) Kierkegaard, *Either/Or* (1843) Kierkegaard, *Fear and Trembling* (1843)
Millet, 1814–75	Sainte-Beuve, *Portraits de femmes* (1844) Nisard, *Histoire de la littéra- ture française* (1844–61)	Kierkegaard, *Philosophical Fragments* (1844) Kierkegaard, *The Concept of Dread* (1844)
Franz, 1815–92		

History	French literature	English literature
Drought and economic crisis in France, 1846	Balzac, *La Cousine Bette* (1846) Banville, *Les Stalactites* (1846) Sand, *La Mare au diable* (1846)	
Reform Banquets, 1847	Balzac, *Le Cousin Pons* (1847) Musset, *Un Caprice* (1847) Lamartine, *Raphaël* (1847)	Charlotte Brontë, *Jane Eyre* (1847) Emily Brontë, *Wuthering Heights* (1847) Thackeray, *Vanity Fair* (1847)
Abdication of Louis-Philippe, 1848 Proclamation of Second French Republic (1848–51) Louis-Napoleon elected President of France under new constitution, 1848	Dumas *fils*, *La Dame aux camélias* (1848) Augier, *L'Aventurière* (1848) Dumas, *Le Vicomte de Bragelonne* (1848–50)	Longfellow, *Evangeline* (1848) Mrs. Gaskell, *Mary Barton* (1848)
	Sand, *La Petite Fadette* (1849) Scribe, *Adrienne Lecouvreur* (1849) Lamartine, *Graziella* (1849) Chateaubriand, *Mémoires d'outre-tombe* (incomplete, 1849)	Dickens, *David Copperfield* (1849–50)
Loi Falloux allows religious orders to reopen schools, 1850 Universal suffrage abolished and press freedom restricted, 1850	Sand, *François le Champi* (1850)	Tennyson, *In Memoriam* (1850) Kingsley, *Alton Locke* (1850) Elizabeth Barrett Browning, *Sonnets from the Portuguese* (1850) Emerson, *Representative Men* (1850) Hawthorne, *The Scarlet Letter* (1850)
Coup d'État of Louis-Napoleon, 1851		

Painting and music	Criticism and aesthetic theory	Ideas and philosophy
Alfred Stevens, 1817–75	Sainte-Beuve, *Portraits contemporains* (1846) Poe, *The Philosophy of Composition* (1846)	Michelet, *Le Peuple* (1846) Proudhon, *Philosophie de la misère* (1846) Kierkegaard, *Concluding Un-scientific Postscript* (1846) Kierkegaard, *The Present Age* (1846) Grote, *History of Greece* (1846–56)
Daubigny, 1817–78		Marx, *The Poverty of Philosophy* (1847) Michelet, *La Révolution française* (1847–53)
Chassériau, 1819–56	Vinet, *Études sur Blaise Pascal* (1848)	Marx and Engels, *The Communist Manifesto* (1848) Renan, *L'Avenir de la science* (written 1848, publ. 1890) Mill, *Principles of Political Economy* (1848)
Courbet, 1819–77	Ruskin, *The Seven Lamps of Architecture* (1849) Vinet, *Études sur la littérature française au XIXe siècle* (1849–51) Sainte-Beuve, *Lundis* (1849–69)	Kierkegaard, *The Sickness unto Death* (1849) Proudhon, *Confessions d'un révolutionnaire* (1849) Macaulay, *History of England* (1849–61)
Harpignies, 1819–1916	P. Chasles, *Études sur la littérature et les mœurs de l'Angleterre au XIXe siècle* (1850) Poe, *The Poetic Principle* (1850)	Kierkegaard, *Training in Christianity* (1850)

Index

Académie Française, L', 101.

Ancien régime, its literary heritage, 5, 39.

Ancients and Moderns, quarrel between, 21.

Anquetil, L. P., 107, 113.

Antiquity, 3; Romantic idea of, 5, 34.

Apollinaire, Guillaume (1880–1918), 168.

Aristocrats, return of, 100; and the past, 100–1; and the theatre, 132.

Arnold, Matthew (1822–88), his 'grand style', 146; on Senancour, 175.

Art, in opposition to reality, 6; Hugo and its truth, 9 n.; theory of its autonomy, 35; its two concerns, 35–6; Baudelaire and, 192–3.

Artist, the, place as leader of society, 67; Utopian Socialism and, 145; self-disclosure through writings, 171, 186, 188.

Auerbach, E., *Mimesis*, 88, 95.

Aupick, General, 206.

Autobiography, two forms of distortion, 171–2.

Ballad poetry, 3, 5, 58.

Ballanche, Pierre-Simon (1776–1847), 13, 123.

Balzac, Honoré de (1799–1850), 59, 64, 68; character of Vautrin, 64, 120–1, 126; social doctrine, 70–1, 73, 76, 125; and the middle classes, 74, 117, 123–4; use of detail, 81, 94, 116, 128; *roman-feuilleton*, 82; use of first-hand documents, 112; a social novelist, 114–15, 116; debt to Scott, 115; and the Restoration, 115–16; ability to link fictional and real worlds, 115–16; use of historical retrospect, 116; use of collective issues, 117–18, 119; and the peasantry, 118–19; theories of power and evil, 119; and money in modern society, 119–20, 123; notion of the 'vol décent', 120–1; and struggle between good and evil, 121, 125; moral ambiguity in the novels, 121; use of melodramatic conventions, 121–2, 124, 125, 127; and the supernatural, 122–3, 124, 125, 126–7;

indictment of the aristocracy, 123; portrayal of competitive greed, 124; Manicheanism, 124–5, 126; religious values in his novels, 125; stylistic technique, 126, 128; confusion of sacred and profane, 126–7; allies environment and character, 128; rich imaginative world, 128–9; sympathy with his characters, 129; prodigious output, 130; biography, 130.

Works: *Albert Savarus*, 122; *Eugénie Grandet*, 115, 119, 126, 127, 128, 130; *Histoire de la grandeur et de la décadence de César Birotteau*, 119, 123–4; *La Comédie humaine*, 116, 121, 123, 124, 130; *avant-propos*, 112; *La Cousine Bette*, 122; *La Dernière Incarnation de Vautrin*, 121, 125; *La Fille aux yeux d'or*, 120, 128; *La Rabouilleuse*, 125, 130; *Le Cabinet des antiques*, 123; *Le Code des gens honnêtes*, 120; *Le Cousin Pons*, 120, 121, 127; *Le Curé de Tours*, 127; *Le Curé de village*, 71, 76; *Le Lys dans la vallée*, 130; *Le Médecin de campagne*, 70, 76, 115; *Le Père Goriot*, 16, 120–1, 126, 128, 130; *Les Chouans*, 112, 113, 130; *Les Illusions perdues*, 71, 76, 117–19, 130; *Les Paysans*, 71, 76, 117–19, 130; *Mémoires de deux jeunes mariées*, 122; 'Scènes de la vie de campagne', 70; *Splendeurs et misères des courtisanes*, 130; *Ursule Mirouet*, 121–2.

Barante, Guillaume-Prosper Brugière, Baron de (1782–1866), on his historical purpose, 11; lectures by, 98; on the historical novel, 108; use of old chronicles, 108; *Histoire des ducs de Bourgogne*, 104, 108, 113.

Baudelaire, Charles (1821–47), 41, 168; and opposition between art and reality, 6; his authentic *frisson nouveau*, 26; and the École mélancolico-farceuse', 33; use of things to objectify emotions, 34; rhetorical structure of his poems, 35; similarity to English Romantics, 35; on Hugo's poetry, 45–6, 52–3; rejection of humanism, 189–90; hostility to liberalism, 190–1;